**On
Taking
God Out
of the
Dictionary**

On Taking God Out of the Dictionary

WILLIAM HAMILTON

McGraw-Hill Book Company

*New York   St. Louis   San Francisco
Düsseldorf   London   Mexico   Sydney   Toronto*

Library of Congress Cataloging in Publication Data
Hamilton, William, date
  On taking God out of the dictionary.
    1. Theology—20th century. 2. Christianity—
20th century. I. Title.
BR481.H26   230   73-19691
ISBN 0-07-025802-3

Grateful acknowledgment is made to the following for permission to reprint sections from copyrighted material:
THE AMERICAN SCHOLAR, for Earl Rovit, "On the Contemporary Apocalyptic Imagination," Volume 37, Number 3, Summer, 1968, copyright © 1968 by the United Chapters of Phi Beta Kappa. CITY LIGHTS, for Allen Ginsberg, *Howl and Other Poems*, copyright © 1956, 1959 by Allen Ginsberg. DOUBLEDAY AND COMPANY, INC., for Theodore Roszak, *The Making of a Counter Culture*, copyright © 1968, 1969 by Theodore Roszak. E. P. DUTTON AND COMPANY, INC., for Benjamin DeMott, *Essays and Reports on Imagination in America*, copyright © 1969, 1968, 1967, 1966 by Benjamin DeMott. ENCOUNTER, for George Steiner, "The Thinking Eye," *Encounter*, May, 1967. HARCOURT, BRACE, JOVANOVICH, INC., for excerpts from Irving Howe, "The New York Intellectuals," in *Decline of*

the New by Irving Howe, copyright © 1968 by Irving Howe. ALFRED A. KNOPF, INC., for D. H. Lawrence, *Assorted Articles*, copyright 1929 by Alfred A. Knopf, Inc.; and for Wallace Stevens, *Opus Posthumous*, copyright © 1957 by Elsie Stevens and Holly Stevens. LITTLE, BROWN AND COMPANY, for Norman Mailer, *Existential Errands*, copyright © 1963, 1966, 1967, 1968, 1969, 1971, 1972 by Norman Mailer. MACMILLAN PUBLISHING CO., for William Butler Yeats, "The Second Coming," in *Collected Poems*, copyright 1924 by Macmillan Publishing Co., Inc., renewed 1952 by Bertha Georgie Yeats. THE NATIONAL CATHOLIC REPORTER, for Jonathan Eisen, "The Rock Rebellion: Anarchy as Life Style," *NCR*, Sept. 24, 1969. NEW AMERICAN LIBRARY, for Norman Mailer, *St. George and the Godfather*. NEW DIRECTIONS, for Henry Miller, *Sunday After the War*. copyright 1944 by Henry Miller. THE NEW YORK TIMES, for a news story of August 29, 1969, copyright © 1969 by The New York Times Company. OXFORD UNIVERSITY PRESS, Canadian Branch, for Northrup Frye, *The Modern Century*. PANTHEON BOOKS, a division of Random House, Inc., for Alan Watts, *Beyond Theology*, copyright © 1964 by Alan Watts. PARTISAN REVIEW and Leslie Fiedler, for Leslie Fiedler, "The New Mutants," copyright © 1965 by *Partisan Review*. PENGUIN BOOKS, LTD., for R. D. Laing, *The Politics of Experience*, copyright © 1967 by R. D. Laing. RANDOM HOUSE, INC., for Norman O. Brown, *Love's Body*, copyright © 1966 by Norman O. Brown; for Paul Goodman, *New Reformation: Notes of a Neolithic Conservative*, copyright © 1969, 1970 by Paul Goodman; for Robert Jay Lifton, *Boundaries*, copyright © 1967, 1968, 1969 by Robert Jay Lifton; and for Robert Jay Lifton, *Death in Life*, copyright © 1967 by Robert Jay Lifton. SCOTT MEREDITH LITERARY AGENCY, INC., and Norman Mailer, for Norman Mailer, *Cannibals and Christians*, copyright © 1966, by Norman Mailer. Reprinted by permission of the author and the author's agents, Scott Meredith Literary Agency, Inc., 580 Fifth Avenue, New York, New York 10036. SIMON AND SCHUSTER, INC., for Joseph Heller, *Catch 22*, copyright © 1955 by Joseph Heller. VIKING PRESS, INC., for Lionel Trilling, *Beyond Culture*, copyright © 1965 by Lionel Trilling. WESLEYAN UNIVERSITY PRESS, INC., for Norman O. Brown, *Life Against Death*, copyright © 1959 by Wesleyan University.

The author also wishes to thank his friend, Dr. Edward Hobbs of Berkeley, California, for some help in the formulation of parts of Chapter I, and to express gratitude to two former students for their contribution to the short story in Chapter VII, so that the solecisms there remain wholly his. They will recognize their contributions.

To my father,
and
in memory of my mother

Contents

I

Interview

Take God out of the dictionary, and you would have
Him in the street.
—Melville, in a letter to Hawthorne, April 16, 1851

Do you really want the word out of the dictionary?
Of course not. That is the point of Melville's irony.
Dictionaries don't decide usage, they report it. God is
really a lexicographical problem now. Does the word, in its
Christian usage, really work? In some areas, in some
sections, in some cultures, the answer is "yes." Perhaps the
entry should specify that the word in current usage has
become "regional." Its theological use might be labeled
"archaic," suggesting that it once had a proper usage, but
no longer.
What does Melville mean by "in the street"?
I'm not sure, though I recall a sentence from his
White-Jacket: "Our hearts are our best prayer-rooms, and
the chaplains who can most help us are ourselves." I take
"out of the dictionary and into the street" to mean a
process not of redefining the old word so it can still be
used, but an attempt to see what the old word covered, and
the search for other ways of saying the same thing.

Let's move on from the title. You are clearly still working on the death of God. I thought that the death of God had died. Everybody says so. As a matter of fact, the "death of the death of God" literature now appears to be nearly as voluminous as the death of God material itself. You and your friends were once called headline-grabbers, faddists, journalists. . . .

I suspect if we really were all that, we would have been easily exorcised long ago. That is an understandable reaction, but it is just as meretricious as it would be for us to refer to those proclaimers of the death of the death of God as establishment whores.

Well, has the death of God died?

In one sense, yes, if by "the death of God" you mean the event created by the media in late 1965. Any event the media create they can uncreate. But the answer is no if you really mean "What has happened to the death of God movement since the media event of 1965?"

All right, what has happened?

That isn't hard to answer on a descriptive level. A good many teachers and scholars, young and otherwise, are seriously affirming the death of God, assuming that "death of God" means, in one of Nietzsche's definitions, that the Christian God is no longer worthy of belief. Two directions are apparent. One continues the exploration of the idea of the death of God, its history, its meaning. A second is moving on from that; after the death of God, assuming it, what needs to be thought and said. What is Christology, what is the meaning of religion, what can the church be—after the death of God? My inclination is not to leave the first kind of problem; the younger scholars, and the college students, want to move on to the second. Increasingly I find that the students who have any interest at all in the movement assume the death of God and want to get on with the problem of implications.

It hasn't quite become a clearly defined theological movement, like liberalism or neo-orthodoxy.

No, and I think there is a good reason. The experience of the death of God in our day has been such a varied one, has come from such a wide variety of contexts, that one does not have the same sense of belonging together, of working with the same issues, that one has in other theological schools. Paul Van Buren belongs, or belonged, because he had an interest in a certain kind of theological verification. John Wren-Lewis, the British lay theologian, proceeds from an analysis of the significance of the seventeenth-century scientific revolution, and a positive appropriation of Freud's critique of religion as paranoia. Richard Rubenstein's experience is historical: the death of the six million Jews, the meaning of Auschwitz. Others start from the impact of technology on our thought and language. This variety of context, plus the fact that Jews and Catholics, as well as Protestants, continue to show an interest in the idea of the death of God, and will keep the movement itself quite loosely organized and amorphous.

What do you mean by the impact of technology on our thought and language?

I mean something more than the obvious fact that the space program, and the moon landing in particular, have destroyed the power of the ancient symbols of "heaven" and "height" to point to the unknown and unknowable. I mean that the whole pattern of contemporary technological development is so changing our experience of being in the world, of being related to nature—our very imaginations—that the traditional language about God is no longer adequate for that new experience.

Hans Jonas has made this point very well. Why is it, Jonas asks, that the idea of the death of God has moved from the edges to the center of our experience? Why didn't the seventeenth-century scientific revolution bring this about; or the political revolutions of the eighteenth, or the industrial revolution of the nineteenth? Each of these movements contributed something, but Jonas argues that it took our contemporary technological revolution to bring it about. The death of God does not follow necessarily from the de-divinized cosmology, or from the alienation of man from nature, from industrialization, urbanization, or even regicide. It follows from our contemporary experience of man as the true lord of things, improving on creation. When the three astronauts of *Apollo 10* quoted the first verses of *Genesis* from their space capsule as they flew close to the moon, something more significant than conventional Texas piety was going on. They were saying, perhaps inadvertently, that this is what God must have felt like at the dawn of creation. They had become gods. Even President Nixon, after *Apollo 11*, imperfectly programed by Dr. Peale and Dr. Graham, expressed the same sense when he told the three men on the moon that this was the greatest day in the history of man since creation. In a sense, you see, he was theologically right, for he was saying that what we had needed the idea of the Creator to express before we can now express ourselves. Mystery remains, and perhaps even the sacred. But technology makes a decisive attack on our basic sense of dependence and awe before the world of nature. Arthur C. Clarke took this as far as it can go. "For in the long run," he writes, "it may turn out that the theologians have made a slight but understandable error—which, among other things, makes totally irrelevant the recent debates about the death of God. It may be that our role on this planet is not to worship God—but to create him. And then our work will be done. It will be time to play." (*Playboy*, December 1968.)

Apart from the note of euphoria, Clarke may be right. The debates about the death of God will become irrelevant, because the issue is closed, the death has been witnessed and can be assumed. The new problem (which will entail both work and play) is the making of the new gods after the death of God. And the new question: in what sense can one continue to be Christian, Jewish, religious?

Do you kill God, or do you just find him dead?

This raises a number of questions about how radical theology sees itself, and how others see it. Many have connected the death of God theology to the climate of violence and general rebellion against authority today.

Camus's remark is worth recalling: "Contrary to the opinion of his Christian critics, Nietzsche did not form a project to kill God. He found Him dead in the soul of his contemporaries." (*The Rebel*, p. 68.) I think this is correct, though it should be remembered that it was Christianity that really killed God for Nietzsche, and that he reserved his greatest contempt for those who, like some Christian radicals today, thought they could have Jesus and Christianity after the death of God. But today, one could say, there is both a "murderer" strain and a "detective" strain in radical theology. The first sees that God must be killed, because He is evil, the killer-God, delighting in repression and death: at one time the death of animals, and now the death of men. Such a God must be killed, if men are to be liberated. Norman Mailer has a streak of this, especially in his novel, *Why Are We in Vietnam?* I feel closer to the detectives than to the murderers. The detective is one who arrives on the scene later. He is interested in finding the culprit. He is inclined to say with Wallace Stevens, "To see the gods dispelled in mid-air and dissolve like clouds is one of the great human experiences. . . . It is simply that they came to nothing." ("Two or Three Ideas," in *Opus Posthumous*, ed. by S. F. Morse, Alfred A. Knopf, 1957, p. 206.) So the detective's mood is neither defiance nor euphoria, neither Ahab nor gaudy celebration.

Are "the death of God theology" and "radical theology" the same thing?

Not really. "Death of God" is not the content of radical theology, but merely its origin, its door, its enabling act. Radical theology refers to the work that must be done by those who have decided that they must define themselves as living in the time of the death of God. "Death of God" is merely the start, the guardian of the door to the still partly unexplored room. As an idea it is doing what it has always done in the two hundred–odd years of its life: it blurs the difference between having and not-having, between belief and unbelief, between saying yes and saying no. It describes in part an experience of living within a particular

system of transcendence that has become impossible. It
tries to suggest that having had and losing is a specific sort
of religious experience; it is not "loss of faith," and it
differs from never having had, or from always having had.
And some, but not all, of us are committed to the idea that
the experience may be a Christian one.

*You say "may be." I take it that part of what you see in the
death of God theology is that it has an experimental character.*

Yes; one tries to see if it is possible to make it as a
Christian without the Christian God.

*How would such an experiment be validated? How would it be
proved or disproved?*

I'm not at all sure how to answer such a question, but it is
important and it tests the sincerity of our claims to be a
theological experiment. How are any theological positions
"validated," apart from reference to scripture or tradition?
I suppose that one might suggest certain cultural forms of
validation. The theology of Reinhold Niebuhr was "validated," became true and useful, for a number of reasons:
it enabled us to perform a whole range of important
critical tasks in the area of theology and society. It enabled
us to "understand" ourselves, and to understand the world
and the church at a particular time in our national life.
And it drew a large number of creative and gifted young
men and women to the theological enterprise just before,
during, and after the second World War. Likewise, the
theology of Paul Tillich was "validated" because it enabled
us to work, in new and fruitful ways, with a number of
problems of theology and culture: the relations between
theology and literature and between theology and psychoanalysis received a decisive and fruitful kind of clarification by virtue of Tillich's work. Barth's theology was
validated, to follow the same line, when it proved to be the
only effective instrument by which a theological "no" could
be said to the German-Christian synthesis of Christianity
and Naziism in the thirties.

Along these lines, the "death of God theology" might
claim some form of validation when we look at the collapse

of the ecumenical movement, and its concern for church unity; or at the collapse of the doctrine of God that was decisive to the secularizing theologies of more recent years; indeed, at the whole loss of morale in institutional Protestantism itself. The death of God, I feel sure, lies behind both the new conservatism and the flight from theology in much of contemporary Protestantism, with its current temptation to live from issue to issue in the social sphere. The death of God is a theological position, and it is profoundly opposed to the antitheological climate today. It is theological precisely because it is persuaded that the problem of God is still the most demanding, important, and interesting one to which the religious mind in the West can address itself.

Just what kind of a statement is "the death of God"?

It remains to be seen whether there is one correct answer to that question. There appear now to be perhaps three different answers to it. For some, *event* is the best answer. For all of his skill as a great maker of myths, I think that Professor Altizer would insist on the event character of the death of God, largely because the death of Jesus is such a central part of what he means by the death of God. God's death, for Altizer, was a kind of compassionate suicide, the last act of his great love for men, in which he withdrew his repressive presence and transcendence, that man might be truly without him, and thus truly liberated. To call the death of God an event does have the effect of calling attention to the fact that it has a history. We begin to see the idea emerge, at about the time of the French Revolution, in Jean Paul, in Hegel, and in William Blake, and it is closely related to regicide and the movements of political revolution. To call the death of God an event, then, points out that it is an idea with a history; that it is something real and not just a powerful way to talk about a personal experience.

But the word "event" is so amorphous that it may not be sufficient. So many prefer to call the death of God a metaphor. It is an adequate metaphor for the reason that any metaphor is deemed adequate: because it illuminates an actual experience more satisfactorily than any other metaphor could. "Death" of God is closely related to other metaphors, like the silence of God, the eclipse of God, the disappearance of God. These latter metaphors have always been central ones in traditional theological and mystical language, and they have always been used with the assumption that every believer lives in the dialectic between possession and nonpossession. There will be, in every religious life, a silence, but some form of speech from God can be expected. There will be an eclipse, but it will come to an end, and we will be able to experience the end of the eclipse as surely as we experienced the eclipse itself. Disappearance is short range, and he will again appear, if we will but wait patiently with proper contrition and openness.

"Death" of God is clearly in this family, but it says a little more than the more traditional metaphors say. It says that there has been a presence, but that something has happened to cause that presence to be withdrawn, and that we cannot expect a speedy or predictable return. When Bonhoeffer declared that before God, we live without him, he was simply stating the traditional experience. But the death of God theologian suspects that Bonhoeffer is simply misusing language, that this juggling with two different ideas of God will no longer satisfy, and that we must get on with our work without any expectations.

You mean no return of God is possible?

No, I don't mean that. It's more complex. Biblical and historical theology still are bound to examine the meaning of the event of God before his death: what was being offered, what was received, when language about God occurred seriously? This is more than a matter of how men conceived of God. That is a question of conceptual structures, a part of the history of ideas. When we have tried to state what was going on when language about God was received seriously, we have to go on from there. "What is going on today, in our language, that is analogous?" My answer to that is "nothing, yet." But men and women are exploring this all the time: artists, poets, playwrights, and theologians. Out of their work may come some other event that we can call the resurrection of God in language. Like the other resurrection, it may be the appearance of something that is not recognized as the return of that which really died. This appearance, if it comes, may or may not be named "God." And it may or may not be the Christian God, if it is to be named God. It may be a Christian, and it may be a post-Christian appearance. After all, one of the metaphorical meanings of "death of God" is the end of all absolutes in the spiritual life, so not even the death of God can be treated as an absolute.

You mentioned event, and metaphor. What is the third possible meaning?

More and more I am interested in the idea of the death of God as a *language event.* I am interested primarily because it is a way of facing the old question about whether the death of God is something that really happened, ontologically, as people say, or whether it is a "mere" psychological experience. It is important to question the necessity of this distinction between ontological-real and psychological-personal. Many before the radicals—Tillich and Buber among them—have noted that the subjective-objective distinction will not work to explain the character of God. I am trying to claim that it will not work to explain the character of the death of God.

What do you mean by language event?

It assumes a particular conception of the origin of language. I take it as possible, for example, that the birth of the gods was a language event. Men give the name of God to some overmastering reality in their lives when certain corporate experiences become so overwhelming and real that they can only be mastered by the act of naming the gods. It is not that there is something there, cold and unnamed, which is subsequently named. It is that man's essential humanity is his capacity to speak, to name. Thus, to name the gods is to give them their reality. And, conversely, to refuse to name them, to unname them, is to take their reality away. The gods were necessary and real when they grew naturally out of certain experiences of being in the world. When those experiences alter sufficiently, the same name can no longer be uttered. But the same point can be made if you assume the traditional distinction between word and reality. Some would say that the word is gone because the reality behind the word is gone; others would say that the word can be kept, but redefined, for the reality behind the word is still intact. Others, and here are the radicals, say that the word must go for the reality behind the word is so altered that the old word cannot honestly be used for the new reality.

"Language event" thus stands somewhere between event and metaphor, as a way of understanding the phrase "death of God."

When you look at the ways in which the death of God theology has been received, has there been anything in the reception or response that has surprised you?

One curious and interesting thing. I have come to see just how conservative the radical theology is. In politics we have always known that the radical and the conservative are closer to each other than either is to the liberal, and this seems to be the case in theology.

How do you mean, "conservative"?

I have seen this in relation to my students. From their perspective, I am asking a traditional, conservative question: is it possible to be a Christian in the modern world? Radical theology says the answer is yes, if you will do this and that. But this is simply not the religious question many of the young are asking. Increasingly, those coming to college are not defining themselves as "Jews" or "Christians." Their religious task is not to clarify "their" tradition so they can better affirm or reject. Their suspicion is that it is no longer important or necessary to proceed out of one of the major religious traditions of the West. They assume—and I suspect they will prove to be right—that these traditions, in both their theological and institutional forms, are terminally ill, and that the problem is, if you like, how to be religious after the death of God. I am seen, by them, to be the conservative, hanging back, hung up on the problem of God. And I am sure they are right, both about radical theology and about themselves. Radical theology is a bridge theology, and marginal movement in the transition between the Christian and the post-Christian eras. Instead of "Can one be a Christian without God"? they ask, "Where are the gods to be found after the death of the God of the Jewish–Christian tradition?" The most formidable theological enemy for Christians and Jews may prove to be polytheism, rather than unbelief. If so, we would really be approaching the boundary between the Christian and the post-Christian eras. This emerging polytheism is the real religious revolution of our time, more of a revolution than anything the original death of God theologies proposed. I am convinced that radical theology will need to articulate, very clearly, its own assent and dissent to this revolution. Theologically, we seem to be back at the point of the Gnostic challenge.

What are some other effects of the death of God movement?

It is easier to discern the secondary effects than the primary ones. One of the interesting secondary effects is this. I think the death of God controversy, and the continuing modest life of the death of God theology, has had the effect of changing, or at least clarifying, the way in which people in fact talk about God. It has, if you like, democratized the way God gets talked about. For the most part, in the Western religious tradition, talk about God has been primarily the prerogative of a particular class: the ordained priest in the Catholic tradition, the professor in the Protestant world. This has always imparted a special problem for theological communication, for theology— unlike many university disciplines—has a nontechnical lay constituency to which it is ultimately responsible. This combination of a special class of technicians and a lay constituency means that theological communication has always needed special bridges to span the gulf. The

cathedral, the stained-glass window, the Mass itself, have
served this function in Catholic contexts, while preaching,
adult education, Bible study, have been some of the
Protestant solutions.

But the old death of God controversy seems partly to
have broken this pattern, and we should not be surprised
to find that the traditional Protestant bridges, at least, are
weakening. Talk about God is no longer the possession of
the expert alone. We have come to a quite nontechnical
definition of what talking about God entails. It is ordinary
men and women sharing their common experiences of life
in our time—love, hate, sexuality, peace, forgiveness,
tragedy—and learning to speak to each other about what
each of these ordinary moments of life means with God,
and what each means without God. It is in this mundane
context that the radical or death of God theology will
receive its decisive validation or invalidation.

*What has been the effect of the death of God theology on the
current theologians that don't agree with you?*

Someone remarked that eccentric ideas become introduced into traditional patterns in three stages: first,
outright rejection; second, patronized as a useful correc-
tive; and third, the affirmation that "we have been saying
this all the time." Radical theology as received by its critics
has passed through the first phase, when sometimes we
were identified with sin itself. Now, it is taken more often
as mildly useful, something like an emetic, all right if taken
in small doses. But not the whole diet. We will never enter
the third stage. A number of American theologians, not
themselves "radicals," share many of the critical concerns
of the radical movement, and they are suggesting new
directions for the doctrine of God and the problem of
transcendence. The radicals owe a great deal to the work
of men like Langdon Gilkey, John Cobb, and Gregory
Baum. I expect the theological concerns of the Women's
Movement to be increasingly important.

There is another way of approaching the question.
Protestant liberalism identified God with the super-ego,

and against this a decisive attack was mounted, both from secular–Freudian sources, and from the Biblical and theological side. But the doctrine of God of the Biblical and theological revival proved unstable and we have seen a broad protest against it, not only by radical theology but by secular and philosophical theologies as well. Today, one might suggest, the revisionists are working along two lines. When God as super-ego goes, you can always experiment with reconnecting Him to the id. This is partly what Altizer does. It is done classically by Norman O. Brown, and by Sam Keen in another way. Or, on the other hand, God can be seen as performing the function of the ego. The ego is "the name for the unifying drive toward meaning and the specific forms and outcomes of that drive." (Herbert Fingarette, *The Self in Transformation*, p. 27.) Paul Tillich, on his existentialist side, begins this identification, and it is a clear theme in Schubert Ogden, John A. T. Robinson, and much of the theology of hope.

How would you compare radical theology with traditional forms of atheism? In some ways, the similarities appear quite close, in others there appear to be differences. Isn't it possible that the movement is simply another example of "the loss of faith," purely negative, but decked out in pretentious theological clothing?

There is, of course, an experience of loss in the first generation radical theologians, and this connects us with earlier versions of the same experience: Matthew Arnold in Victorian England, Feuerbach against Hegel, Melville against the Puritans and the transcendentalists. So, in a literal and limited sense, "atheism" may be accepted, though the protest of radical theology is against a specific conception of God—the classical, mainstream conception of God in the Jewish–Christian tradition. We also share with the modern atheist the view that men, in their communities and in their individuality, must be empowered to do for themselves what once they asked God to do, or did only in response to God.

Such as?

Facing death, forgiveness, concern for justice and freedom. In the Christian tradition these human realities are based—to take them in order—in the power of God, the love of God, the righteousness of God. Now these *are* realities, and they do not lose their reality when we say they must receive their justification today in human terms.

You would not repudiate your comments of some years ago about a "new optimism"?

That article reflects the strength and weakness of mood-theology. There was a period in our national life, between the death of John Kennedy and the escalation of the war in Vietnam, when there was a rising hope and confidence in our ability to take on our gravest social problems and come to terms with them. Some important domestic legislation came out of that period, and there was a greatness in Lyndon Johnson's leadership at that time that cannot be taken from him. This was also the period of the impact of John XXIII on the Catholic community. Of course, the escalation in Vietnam intervened between then and now, and the old words about optimism look either dated or insensitive or both. But I still feel that my criticism of some of the social uses to which the Christian doctrine of sin has been put is valid, and the affirmation of confidence in what man in community can achieve can still stand.

But there may be something fundamentally unsatisfactory about the very distinction between optimism and pessimism. This is a polarity out of the old world of the Christian debate between liberalism and neo-orthodoxy, and perhaps between Christianity and Marxism. That polarity doesn't go deeply enough. Today the issue has been clarified by what the journalists used to call the generation gap and by the counterculture. Today the tension seems to exist between the young, who really do not seem to believe in the future, and those of us who do, partly because we are well into whatever future we have left. I am a child of the old culture; I believe we will have a future, and that it may well be awful. This is why I am interested in exploring the category of survival as a central ethical value, and in seeing if it can be rescued from its conservative history. Ethics as survival. My optimism has become a confidence, not that we can be merry, but that we can survive.

Very well. You have spoken of the affinities between radical theology and atheism. How would you locate and define the differences?

If some of what we can call the God-work is to be taken over by the human community, I would not claim that it can be taken over without remainder. There is still mystery, transcendence, the sacred.

But these experiences cannot be taken as pointers to God, arguments for the need of God.

No. We need to distinguish between the ways in which these areas of life have been cut off from us by our contemporary experience, and the ways in which they are still real. If real, we must seek to develop non-theistic explanations.

But atheists, or at least sensitive religious humanists, might say the same.

Correct. So radical theology is not Christian because it can say good things about transcendence or the sacred. It is Christian because it has its center in an allegiance to Jesus.

But not to Jesus's God. Will this really work?

Perhaps not. But while we find out, we can point out that Jesus's message can be separated—it always has been throughout the last 200 years—from the thought-forms in which it is expressed.

You identify Jesus's words about filial dependence on God as Father with the other conditioned elements in his message?

Yes; demon possession, cosmology, apocalypticism. We've sought for contemporary equivalents for these motifs in Jesus's teaching and life; what I'm saying is that his words about God need to find the same sort of equivalent. I'm inclined to think that the New Testament itself offers some clues for this reinterpretation: Matthew 25, I John 4:16, Mark 9:37.

To what Jesus do you point?

It will not do to try to strip away what the latest research may deem secondary, or to try to define a fixed core of teaching beneath and beyond the eschatological framework, or to try to advance toward some assured intention of Jesus himself before the church took over its interpretative role. It is not to the teacher, then, not to the historical Jesus. It is to the Christ of the New Testament, of the kerygma; the one whom the New Testament sees as the eschatological act of God, bringing the Kingdom, the new age, here and now into the midst of men's ordinary lives. What we have in the New Testament, I think, is a form of self-understanding, a way of being human, that is proclaimed by Jesus of Nazareth. It is that form or way that is accessible to us, even though we may never be able to discover whether or not Jesus embodied it himself. His own self-understanding or way of being human is probably irrelevant and certainly inaccessible to us. What he was is hidden; what he proclaimed, offered, defined, is not. In his baptism, his teaching, his healings, his passion, death, and resurrection—in all of it, there is a demand laid on us, or an offer tendered, and it is the task of the Christian to embody that offer in his world, being as candid as he can be about the difference between Jesus's world and his, Jesus's beliefs and his. The clue, then, is not "use my language and thought-forms"; it is not "follow in my footsteps" or "obey the will of God as I am doing," but "go thou and do likewise," whatever that might mean. Our theology must become just as "situational" as our ethics. My own feeling is that while the passion of Jesus will always bear a central position in our understanding, it is time for us to take note of his ministry of exorcism and healing as a significant contemporary model. We no longer are obliged to search out psychological explanations, or to reduce the miracles to stories about salvation or forgiveness, but can read them more naturally as instances where Jesus openly fought against the evils that afflicted men and women, and trained his disciples to fight in the same way. In the exorcisms and healings we can see, I think, something of the revolutionary Jesus that we cannot find in the passivity of his death or in his words about the Roman tax.

I don't think you have quite answered the question "why do you choose Jesus?"

This goes back to the matter of the radical theologian as a conservative, since he still asks the older question about the possibility of a Christian existence today. So one form of your question about Jesus is: "Why is it that you have chosen to remain a Christian in the midst of the religious revolution today?"

All right. As long as you don't evade the question about Jesus. Why have you so chosen? Is it not merely arbitrary, or a matter of vocational convenience or necessity?

Yes, the choice might be partly described as vocational. I find myself unable and unwilling to separate myself from Christianity because, in part, it is Christians (and Jews) who are raising the questions today that I hold to be most important. And I wish to stand in the midst of that community. We are what we are because of our choice of comrades.

Just what is that community? Is it the church?

It can be for some; it is not, on the whole, for me. Here the work of Charles Davis has been a great help, for he has raised the question (raised in another way by the Berrigans and Rosemary Reuther): is there anywhere a community in the midst of which we can continue to live as Christians? If so, as I believe, is it in any sense related to the church? I would say not, except in the most marginal and spiritual sense of that word. Then, is it not fated to be a very amorphous group of friends, whom you see and hear from now and then? I find that almost equally imperfect. Christianity has always meant space as well as time, community—even institution—as well as solitariness. I am a

Christian because I am deeply committed to many of the things that some Christians are committed to and know I cannot be without them. But I cannot now see in the church, even if renewed or underground, any trustworthy form for that new community.

Can you imagine yourself as non-Christian, or ex-Christian, or post-Christian?

No, none of them, though I feel sure I am leaving the wave of the future in saying that. I do not think that one can de-Christianize oneself by an act of the will. We are not only our present selves, we are both our memories and our hopes. And the Christian substance is too deeply engrained in my past, and in my expectations, to be readily dispensible. I was, and am, ordained, and I suspect I have a very high doctrine of sacramental grace lurking about.

Let's go back to my earlier question about Jesus. You answered the question about the vocational element in your decision to be a Christian. It still appears that there may be something arbitrary about your choice of Jesus as way, truth, and life.

I think I accept "arbitrary" as an adequate, if partial, description of the choice. It is arbitrary in that there are no inherent grounds in the object of that choice that compel my response. There is no special freedom there that I catch, that I cannot catch elsewhere; no unique ethic that I cannot find repeated or reproduced; no unique sonship or revelational power. Therefore, it is truly arbitrary. But isn't it the case that all truly human choices have this arbitrary character? If a decision flows inevitably from some rule, or some doctrine, it has lost its element of choice, and we say of a man so choosing, "He had no choice." So I am inclined to answer the question "Why Jesus?" not in terms of what justifies the choice, but of what consequences it makes possible in my life, and thus to let my life rather than my argument bear the burden of validation. I have been helped here by a passage from a book by Herbert Fingarette, *The Self in Transformation*:

> We flinch from this leap, this commitment without decisive justification. We would prefer to *know*. We

prefer security. And the heart of responsibility is
revealed when we see that, faced with anxiety and the
need for choice, precisely what we wish to know is what
we *cannot* know. We establish meaning and regulative
principle by our act—if we have the courage to accept
it and identify ourselves with the act and its import. [p.
101.]

Jesus gives me neither doctrine nor norm nor technique
for discipline. But he is in the world in such a way that he
readies me for whatever beliefs and actions and forms of
self-discipline I may be obliged to take on. Not the "only,"
not the "best," but the one, nonetheless. Sometimes this
means discerning Jesus in the world, and sometimes it
means becoming him in the world, but, in any case, he is
always between the Christian and his world. Elie Wiesel, at
the end of *The Gates of the Forest*, puts the Jewish equivalent
of this very beautifully:

> Whether or not the Messiah comes doesn't matter;
> we'll manage without him. It is because it is too late that
> we are commanded to hope. We shall be honest and
> humble and strong, and then he will come, he will
> come every day, thousands of times every day. He will
> have no face, because he will have a thousand faces.
> The Messiah isn't one man . . . he's all men. As long as
> there are men there will be a Messiah. One day you'll
> sing, and he will sing in you. [p. 225.]

*Very nice. I am still far from persuaded that you have
described anything that can be honestly called a Christian option.
Your relation to the Christian community seems accidental, and
your relation to Jesus both arbitrary and attenuated. Perhaps a
Jesus-humanism, but Christianity . . . ?*

You have put your finger on what is bound to be one of
the weak links in radical theology's chain. But one of the
basic questions that is undecided in theology today is
precisely the question about the definition of a Christian.
Perhaps it will turn out to be unimportant whether this
position ends up just inside or just outside the spectrum of

Christian possibilities. Perhaps for my generation it will prove to be sufficient to stay within, and for the next generation, warrant to move outside.

There will certainly be a very strong temptation, as you continue to insist on the contrality of Jesus, to reintroduce him as something like Christ or Lord.

True, though his own uneasiness with all such titles may prove to be helpful.

The alternatives to your project of staying within the Christian tradition appear to be, on the one hand, cutting the connection openly, and becoming a sort of ex-Christian secular humanist; and, on the other, finding some new way—necessarily non-theistic—into that region traditionally called the transcendent.

Right. There *is* the sacred, the holy, the transcendent. There are undeniable experiences even when one has given up the account of them in traditional theology. One simply has to insist on the fact that there need be no essential connection between such experiences and the idea of God. Melville drives this wedge between transcendence and God very nicely.

> This "all" feeling, though, there is some truth in. You must often have felt it, lying on the grass on a warm summer's day. Your legs seem to send out shoots into the earth. Your hair feels like leaves upon your head. This is the *all* feeling, But what plays the mischief with the truth is that men will insist upon the universal application of a temporary feeling or opinion. [Letter to Hawthorne, June 1(?), 1851.]

But of course your very success in developing a non-theistic interpretation—as in Buddhism and Confucianism, for example—only serves to call further into question the right of such an interpretation to say it is Christian.

That is so only if you assume that belief in God and Christianity are, by definition, inseparable.

What would a sacred event look like, as you try to imagine a non-theistic account of it?

I think I would try to keep the meanings of the various terms we've used pretty close together, and not—at least at first—make too many distinctions between the sacred, the holy, and the transcendent. There would be certain kinds of things that happen in human love and sexuality, in the experience of facing death, and certainly in the region of the arts, that all might be read, under certain conditions, as sacred events. To be seen as sacred, three things would have to happen. The experience would be one that comes to man, from outside him; it would have the character of a given, rather than an earned or expected thing. Second, it would come as something that he cannot control or measure. And finally, though this may be true only in the West, it should bear a claim or a proposed course of action within it. As in the word of Jesus, there should be a "go thou and do likewise."

The drug scene should be of some interest to you at this point.

Yes and no. LSD is inclined to produce a lot of religious language, and a lot of talk about the divine. Marijuana is different, I think, because taking pot is a social act, and it seems to produce something more like a sacramental community than a mystical vision. In general, I think, the drug scene belongs more in the post-Christian world, in which—after the death of God, and after the problem of being or staying a Christian or a Jew—the religious situation is much more fluid and open. One of the reasons I want to insist on my ethical test for experiences of the sacred is precisely here. To be a Christian is to insist of any religious experience, pharmacological or not, that, if it does not produce some new commitment to the alleviation of ugliness, injustice, suffering, or boredom in men's lives, it is worthless. I am sure that many of the recently religious young would argue with me at just this point of the ethical test. And it is because of my conviction of the validity of the ethical test that I am still unimpressed with the Jesus movement, except when it has helped young people get off of acid. This new Jesus has proved to be superbly marketable for Broadway, but in both his California-hip and his scrubbed form he appears to have created political reactionaries, racists, and sexist chauvinists. As a Black Panther leader recently said in Los Angeles: "Christers! Man, they hate blacks! Scratch the surface of any Jesus freak and you find a middle-class white supremacist pig." Groups of gay Christians have also begun to feel their venom.

One further question along these lines. You appear to be working with a curious contradiction in this whole project. On the one hand, you are quite conservative when it comes to defining the meaning of God. This doctrine must be defined rather narrowly within the mainstream of historical Christianity, and you want to criticize the contemporary revisionists like John A. T. Robinson, or John Cobb, or Harvey Cox, who, in general, have the same indictment of traditional theism that you do. But you insist that honesty requires either taking the whole thing or doing without altogether. On the other hand, you appear quite liberal, even permissive, when it comes to Jesus. His being the Christ, his filial dependence, his unique sonship—all these are relinquished, yet you still claim to be able to hold on to him, as a Christian. Won't you ultimately have to decide that you should be either conservative or permissive on both matters, rather than picking and choosing, as it serves your purpose of remaining both honest and Christian?

That is an absolutely critical question, and a good one. I don't want to answer it in the wrong way. One wrong way would be to say that radical theology is, after all, a holding operation, an interim stage in theological history, as the Christian era passes decisively into the post-Christian world. And thus we need a few conservatives refusing to go with the new religiosity, trying to reformulate some of the traditional questions about being a Christian. This may be partly true, but it has the same kind of dishonesty that I used to find myself criticizing in Marshall McLuhan, when he responded to criticism by saying that all of his ideas are probes, and none should be taken seriously. Another response, less wrong, perhaps, would be to admit candidly the force of the question and to say with impressive humility: "Yes, that is an inconsistency, and it is the one we have chosen to live with. It is no worse and no better than the flaws or gaps in other men's spiritual claims."

I think your question does have a straightforward answer, though I have by no means thought it through to the end. Your charge of inconsistency assumes a kind of logical equivalence between the idea of God and the person of Jesus. But the two realities, in the Christian tradition, are really quite different. Jesus was an historical person. He lived, taught, healed, and died. The church, from the resurrection on, tried to find proper theological interpretations of his meaning and message. These varied widely, depending on the heresies to be overcome, the resident culture, and needs of believing Christians. Over against this varied Christological history, Jesus's actual appearance stands in contrast. He was one who asked for discipleship, not theological credentials. He refused to accept the traditional terms placed on him by enthusiastic disciples and friends, and asked finally for ethical fruits rather than words of piety. So . . . So flexibility, or what you call permissiveness, seems to me to be built into the historical appearance of Jesus.

This is not the case with the idea of God. Of course it is true that the various doctrines of God reflect both the theological and human needs of the church, as it grows and changes. But there is, in the very concept of God, a fixity, the need for certain affirmations about him to be always the case, regardless of shifting needs. His answer to Job; his answer to Hosea, "I am God and not man"; his answer to Isaiah in the temple; to Augustine, to Luther, to Pascal. All these have a uniform character. There is something non-negotiable in the very idea of God that requires what you have called a conservative interpretation of how his name is to be properly uttered, just as there is something inherently flexible and freeing in the historical appearance of Jesus in the world, as difficult as that appearance is to get clear, that requires what you call a liberal or permissive approach.

Along such lines, I believe, your question can at least be faced, if not fully answered.

You've already mentioned, from time to time, the relation of radical theology to the other theological options today. What is your estimate of what the theological scene in Christianity will look like in the immediate future?

I am assuming that the present anti-theological mood of Protestantism will quickly pass. Relevance theology and involvement theology will make so many mistakes that serious theology will be forced back into the picture. The theological divergencies of the immediate future may be based on four key questions:

1. Is God possible? If so, in what form: traditional–orthodox, or revised–redefined?
2. Is church possible? As it is, or if renewed, how radically?
3. Is Christianity possible?
4. Is religion possible?

I think we are likely to see three rather large groupings, based on various combinations of answers to these key questions.

1. The first, and dominant grouping, will say "yes" to question (1). Evangelical Protestantism will continue to bear effective, and increasingly successful and sophisticated, witness to the traditional doctrine of God, while the ecumenical–liberal mainstream will develop various proposals for the redefinition of God: process theology, celebration and play theology, and the theology of the future, will all be heard from for some time. In general, this group will say "yes" to the church, though the more "revisionist" and radical the definition of God becomes, the greater will be the demand for church renewal and the more nontraditional will become the acceptable form of the church. The answer to question (3) will be "yes," and question (4) will increasingly receive

"yes" answers as we learn to live with the new religiosity of the young, and to suspect the tendentious and inadequate definitions of religion offered, once upon a time, by Barth and Bonhoeffer. Ecumenical theology, the Catholic–Protestant dialogue, student chaplains of a more traditional sort, most Black theologians will be working here with a mixture of a theology of the future, church renewal, and a secular involvement. The politics of this grouping will range from the conservative-becoming-liberal tone of the evangelicals, to the liberal and left-liberal views of the establishmentarians.

2. A second grouping, neither dominant nor dying, will contain those who have said "no" to question (1). On the whole, this will also entail "no" to question (2), though not to the idea of some kind of Christian community. This group says "yes" to (3) and, very likely, to (4). Some Blacks may come along. The politics will generally be radical, but not "crazy."

3. Group 2, radical theology, will be pushed much closer to 1 than heretofore, because of the emergence of a more radical theological tradition to its left, group 3. They will be defined by their "no" to question (3): Christianity and Judaism are not possible, certainly not necessary in their historic forms. This will entail a "no" to question (2), but a strong "yes" to (4) and "yes" to the question about God. There will be two distinct approaches, among these post-Christians, to the problem of God: one, the traditionalist wing, will be working on the development of a post-Christian theism or, more exactly, monotheism. They will include those with some connection, biographically or educationally, to groups 1 and 2, and those

two groups will give the post-Christian monotheists many of their converts. Out of them, or
perhaps independently of them, the post-
Christian polytheists will emerge, from those
theological observers most attuned to whatever still persists in the counterculture. Here
the world of rock, and pot, and the guru will
receive its theological formulation, and it will
be syncretistic, post-Christian and post-West-
ern, polytheistic, and probably white. The
politics here will be radical, and post-radical
disillusioned. The next journalistic theological
"controversy" will be created out of this movement. Groups 1 and 2, used to viewing each
other with alarm, will fall into each other's
arms, viewing 3 with joint alarm (no pun
intended), and the books and journals of the
late 1970s will spend a good deal of time and
space assuring us that both polytheism and the
conservative-evangelical reaction to it are both
dead.

This is a put-on.
You think so?
It should be fun.

II

God

Thanksgiving Day came and went without any fuss while Yossarian was still in the hospital. The only bad thing about it was the turkey for dinner, and even that was pretty good. It was the most rational Thanksgiving he had ever spent, and he took a sacred oath to spend every future Thanksgiving Day in the cloistered shelter of a hospital. He broke his sacred oath the very next year, when he spent the holiday in a hotel room instead in intellectual conversation with Lieutenant Scheisskopf's wife, who had Dori Duz's dog tags on for the occasion and who henpecked Yossarian sententiously for being cynical and callous about Thanksgiving, even though she didn't believe in God just as much as he didn't.

"I'm probably just as good an atheist as you are," she speculated boastfully. "But even I feel that we all have a great deal to be thankful for and that we shouldn't be ashamed to show it."

"Name one thing I've got to be thankful for," Yossarian challenged her without interest.

"Well . . ." Lieutenant Scheisskopf's wife mused and paused a moment to ponder dubiously. "Me."

"Oh, come on," he scoffed.

She arched her eyebrows in surprise. "Aren't you thankful for me?" she asked. She frowned peevishly, her pride wounded. "I don't have to shack up with you, you know," she told him with cold dignity. "My husband has a whole squadron full of aviation cadets who would be only too happy to shack up with their commanding officer's wife just for the added fillip it would give them."

Yossarian decided to change the subject. "Now you're changing the subject," he pointed out diplomatically. "I'll bet I can name two things to be miserable about for every one you can name to be thankful for."

"Be thankful you've got me," she insisted.

"I am, honey. But I'm also goddam good and miserable that I can't have Dori Duz again, too. Or the hundreds of other girls and women I'll see and want in my short lifetime and won't be able to go to bed with even once."

"Be thankful you're healthy."

"Be bitter you're not going to stay that way."

"Be glad you're even alive."

"Be *furious* you're going to die."

"Things could be much worse," she cried.

"They could be one hell of a lot better," he answered heatedly.

"You're naming only one thing," she protested. "You said you could name two."

"And don't tell me God works in mysterious ways," Yossarian continued, hurtling on over her objection. "There's nothing so mysterious about it. He's not working at all. He's playing. Or else He's forgotten all about us. That's the kind of God you people talk about—a country bumpkin, a clumsy, bungling, brainless, conceited, uncouth hayseed. Good God, how much reverence can you have for a Supreme Being who finds it necessary to include such phenomena as phlegm and tooth decay in His divine system of creation? What in the world was running through that warped, evil, scatalogical mind of His when He robbed old people of the power to control their bowel movements? Why in the world did He ever create pain?"

"Pain?" Lieutenant Scheisskopf's wife pounced upon the word victoriously. "Pain is a useful symptom. Pain is warning to us of bodily dangers."

"And who created the dangers?" Yossarian demanded. He laughed caustically. "Oh, He was really being charitable to us when He gave us pain! Why couldn't He have used a doorbell instead to notify us, or one of his celestial choirs? Or a system of blue-and-red neon tubes right in the middle of each person's forehead. Any jukebox manufacturer worth his salt could have done that. Why couldn't He?"

"People would certainly look silly walking around with red neon tubes in the middle of their foreheads."

"They certainly look beautiful now writhing in agony or stupefied with morphine, don't they? What a colossal, immortal blunder! When you consider the opportunity and power He had to really do a job, and then look at the stupid, ugly little mess He made of it instead, His sheer incompetence is almost staggering. It's obvious He never met a payroll. Why, no self-respecting businessman would hire a bungler like Him as even a shipping clerk!"

Lieutenant Scheisskopf's wife had turned ashen in disbelief and was ogling him with alarm. "You'd better not talk that way about Him, honey," she warned him reprovingly in a low and hostile voice. "He might punish you."

"Isn't He punishing me enough?" Yossarian snorted resentfully. "You know, we mustn't let Him get away with it. Oh, no, we certainly mustn't let Him get away scot free for all the sorrow He's caused us. Someday I'm going to make Him pay. I know when. On the Judgment Day. Yes, that's the day I'll be close enough to reach out and grab that little yokel by His neck and——"

"Stop it! Stop it!" Lieutenant Scheisskopf's wife screamed suddenly, and began beating him ineffectually about the head with both fists. "Stop it!"

Yossarian ducked behind his arm for protection while she slammed away at him in feminine fury for a few seconds, and then he caught her determinedly by the wrists and forced her gently back down on the bed. "What the hell are you getting so upset about?" he asked her bewilderedly in a tone of contrite amusement. "I thought you didn't believe in God."

"I don't," she sobbed, bursting violently into tears.

"But the God I don't believe in is a good God, a just God, a merciful God. He's not the mean and stupid God you make Him out to be."

Yossarian laughed and turned her arms loose. "Let's have a little more religious freedom between us," he proposed obligingly. "You don't believe in the God you want to, and I won't believe in the God I want to. Is that a deal?"

—Joseph Heller, *Catch-22*

Radical theology came proposing a debate about God, and has had the unintended and unhappy effect of neutralizing the very debate it proposed. At first it appeared that the critics of the death of God would be willing to talk about God. This is partly still the case, but even more it appears that the radicals, in abolishing God, have abolished talk about God. Protestants after the death of God have been unable to resist the temptation to fly to ethics, or church renewal, or eschatology, or play—not as a way of talking about God, but as a way of not talking. And radicals have had the eerie experience of being accused of being hung up on the problem of God, which is of course true, but which seems to be an odd kind of theological criticism to make. One gifted and influential secular theologian remarked, for example, that God-talk seemed to make sense on Mondays, Wednesdays, and Fridays, and seemed to make no sense at all on Tuesdays, Thursdays, and Saturdays. To the dowdy old radical theologian, this is a horrifying solution to a difficult problem; horrifying, because it is not a theological solution at all.

It appears that we need some ground rules for the game of talking about God. What is it that controls our attempts at reformulation or redefinition? Are we to be controlled by scripture, by tradition? What are the limits of freedom in renaming the Christian God, in giving the old name to some newly discerned truth or reality?

It should be noted that this question is a lively one only at the central and left-hand parts of the current theological spectrum. Such questions about rules for redefinition assume that a simple restoration of classical theism, or supernaturalism, or transcendence, will not suffice. Apart from the proponents of restoration, then, the field is in the hands of what might be called the "redefiners" and the "doers without." The first group includes nearly everyone of interest apart from the radicals, the second group is radical theology.

One of the points at which I first became aware of the influence of Karl Barth, or neo-orthodox theology, on the shaping of radical theology was in trying to face the criticism that radical theology, for all of its rhetoric about the death of God, was in reality nothing more than a negation of Barth, of only a single and conditioned theological construction, and not of the Christian God in general. This is an important criticism, and in a sense it is correct. Radical theology is, of course, part of the continuing criticism of the broadly based theology of the recent past, variously labeled neo-orthodox, neo-Reformation, ecumenical theology—the theology, however you name it, that still lies behind most of the ecumenical movement, the Catholic–Protestant dialogue, the movement of church renewal, the theology of the secular, the Bonhoeffer revival, the theology of hope. Radical theology is indeed a "no" to all that. But, in being a "no" to merely that, it is, I am convinced, a "no" to much more. For I would want to claim that one of the permanent and abiding achievements of that theological tradition was precisely its Biblical, historical, and systematic analysis of what having a God entailed.

Now all theologies are historically conditioned, yesterday's and tomorrow's, mine and thine. But none of them are wholly so, and one of the historian's functions is at this very point: the determination of just what are the abiding and what are the specious fruits of the theologies that come and go. Thus, while we may well want to reject

the specific theological proposals of liberalism, that movement did give us a respect for the historical method of
investigation that we cannot go back upon. In the same
way, one of the abiding results of this broad ecumenical,
neo-orthodox theological movement was its Biblical and
historical analysis of the doctrine of God. When these
theologians talked about God, they were talking properly
about what Christians have always meant by God. It is this
that one says "yes" to in faith, "no" to in unfaith.

Now whether I say "yes" or "no" is clearly a matter of my
free decision. But what I as a Christian am not free to do is
to alter the object in such a way that my resultant "yes" can
become more modern or relevant. I am not claiming it is at
all easy to state, in brief terms, this historical consensus
about God that I am claiming the neo-orthodox theological movement brought to us. I am certainly not claiming
that there is a single or a simple doctrine of God, nor that
the consensus can be easily formulated in terms of some
one category like holiness or transcendence. But if I
should be forced to state this consensus in an untechnical
way, it might well go something like this: "God may be said
to be—not a Being, not a Person—but perhaps an agency
or power not myself, not in me, in some sense over against
me, and real. He, or it, is such that it is appropriate and
possible to speak of his being the subject of verbs of acting,
loving, revealing, and of such a character that I may,
without distortion, address second-person singular language to him."

This is still highly generalized and would need both
expansion and precision before it could be fully service-
able. But if this is anything like an accurate description of
what Christians have meant when they have talked about
God, it appears to follow that, if Christians find they can
no longer mean this, they have forfeited their right to talk
about God at all. In any case, let us assume the working
validity of this statement of a consensus, and see what
follows in the contemporary debate between the "redefiners" and the "doers without."

Here we come to one of the classic texts of the modern world, Alice's discussion with Humpty Dumpty on language.

> "There's glory for you."
> "I don't know what you mean by glory," Alice said.
> Humpty Dumpty smiled contemptuously. "Of course you don't—till I tell you. I meant 'there's a nice knock-down argument for you.'"
> "But 'glory' doesn't mean 'a nice knock-down argument,'" Alice objected.
> "When *I* use a word," Humpty Dumpty said, in rather scornful tone, "it means just what I choose it to mean—neither more nor less."
> "The question is," said Alice, "whether you can make words mean so many different things."
> "The question is," said Humpty Dumpty, "which is to be master—that's all."
> [Lewis Carroll, *Through the Looking-Glass,* V]

Alice is insisting that words are our masters, that we have an obligation to past usage, that we are not utterly free to do with words what we will. If I am to make myself understood, I must pay some attention to the actual way in which a word has been used.

I propose to defend Alice on this theological issue, but Humpty Dumpty does have a point. Is there not a sense in which we must be the words' masters, in which we are obliged to reshape and restore a dying or flaccid language, with both new words and old words redefined? Could there be a Yeats or a Joyce or an Eliot, on Alice's terms? Could there be poetry at all? Perhaps not. But even so, theology is bound to be suspicious of Humpty's arrogant claims of mastery. Theology is never done for itself, but for a constituency, and this always means that communication comes before poetic power, healing comes before the need to purify the dialect of the tribe.

Today, as the post-radical debate about God takes its shape, radical theology is playing Alice's role in the midst of a host of gifted and articulate Humptys. (Radical theology as Tiny Alice?) And this is the claim radical theology insists on making: "The morality of language requires some sort of fidelity to the origin and history of a word—in this case the word God—and you are not free to put new content into the old word without control or limit. To say 'yes' to God involves in part saying 'yes' to the adequacy of the word in performing the functions it performed in its prime historical contexts. If today it does not perform those functions adequately, it will not do to keep the old word and give it new functions. The saying about new wine and old wineskins ought to guide us here. The old functions it once performed will have to be languaged in some other way, and such new demands made on us by the problem of believing in the modern world will require new words, not the careless restoration of the old. In both cases, having to do with the old needs and with the new, the old word, the old idea, the old God, is not available to us."

Radical theology, like Alice with "glory," holds that there is a definable shape to what Christians have meant by God, and that the ecumenical, Biblical, neo-orthodox theology gave a satisfactory formulation of that shape. It further holds, along with many of the other theologies of the center and the left, that it is precisely that formulation that is unbelievable today. It claims that what Christians have traditionally meant by God is unbelievable today, and that our primary task is therefore to examine the possibility of a Christianity without God.

But the post-radical discussion about God appears to be going with Humpty Dumpty, and Alice and her radicals cry out in protest. Everywhere we turn we find exciting and resourceful theological reappraisals that make Alice weep as deeply as they gratify the church. God, we are told, is the power of love at the heart of reality (John A. T. Robinson); the fact of the moral coherence of history (Schubert Ogden in his project of de-atheizing Sartre); not a presence but a promise, the power of the future, the guarantor of our confidence and hope (a whole host of Americans and Germans, Catholics and Protestants, conservative and revisionist theologians that might be described as the Bloch-heads). Or: transcendence is given in the experience of calling life into question or of making symbols (Michael Novak); God is the name for the processive or developmental character of reality (Leslie Dewart, Eugene Fontinell, Gregory Baum). Or, in the tour de force of Fritz Buri: "Whoever knows himself in his relativity as unconditionally responsible perceives in his existence that he is not merely held out into the nothing of a nameless secret but that he is related to a personal transcendence that calls to him and to which he responds." ("Toward a Non-Objectifying Theology," *Christianity and Crisis*, May 1, 1967, pp. 98–99.)

A great deal of effective theology is being done by Humpty Dumpty and the redefiners, and Alice and her radicals are deeply interested in it all. But a suspicion lurks that the proper theological name for all of these projects is, in fact, idolatry; and that, in a quite strict Biblical sense, absolutizing what is relative, taking a part (of the doctrine of God) and treating it as the whole. Is there not a sense in which one owes some sort of allegiance to the past contexts and meanings of the great words in our heritage? An allegiance which dictates, therefore, that if one today cannot assent to a moderately high proportion of the traditional meanings and contexts, one should be content to let the word go altogether, and do the theological work that remains to be done in some other way than by putting new wine into old wineskins.

I am persuaded that radical theology is right in its Puritan, almost effete, moralism of language, its unwillingness to allow the key words of our religious heritage, like God, to be used for anything that relevance or church renewal might require. Right, even though it means giving up a number of things, like church and prayer and immortality, which are ordinarily assumed to be inseparable from the Christian profession. But, however one

might be persuaded of his rightness, he is also fully aware
that it is quite possible that he is wrong. The issue may not
at all lie between the redefiners and the doers-without.
Perhaps there are no such foul lines in modern theology
that can be used to state what goes and what doesn't go in
talking about God. Perhaps we overestimate the fidelity
owed to past usage; there is, after all, something very
Protestant in this focus on some point in the past as a kind
of theological touchstone. Perhaps the Roman Catholic
revisionists are right in emphasizing the idea of the
development of doctrine as a sufficient theological instrument in relating the gospel to contemporary experience.
Perhaps the varieties of meaning of the word God are far
greater than the radicals have assumed; perhaps the
solution lies merely in moving from transcendence to
immanence, from providence to the suffering God, from
Lord to Comrade. Perhaps the Christian has a right to
speak about and to speak to God so long as he can discover
only the most tentative and modest kind of historical
justification, in Eckhart, say, or St. John of the Cross.

Or, along another line. Perhaps we will find that the
Bible itself is susceptible of more varied interpretations
than first seemed to be the case in those good old days
when "Biblical" and "God acts in history" had meanings we
were sure of. Erich Fromm has explored this possibility,
and his suggestions are worth looking into. In his book,
You Shall Be as Gods, he has claimed that the word God in
Hebrew scriptures has a number of varied functions to
perform, and that one of the central ones is the prohibition of idols. Fromm connects this anti-idolatry function to
the historical tradition of the nameless God, and comes up
with a definition of "belief" in God as the ability to assent
to any one of the primary functions that the word performs in scripture. Insofar as one would protest against
idolatry and blasphemy, he could be said to be a believer in
God.

> To which reality of human experience does the con-
> cept of God refer? . . . the acknowledgement of God

is, fundamentally, the negation of idols. . . . He becomes the nameless God, the God about whom no
attribute or essence can be predicated. This God
without attributes, who is worshiped "in silence," has
ceased to be an authoritarian God; man must become
fully independent, and that means independent even
from God. In "negative theology" as well as in mysticism, we find the same revolutionary spirit of freedom
which characterizes the God of the revolution against
Egypt. [Erich Fromm, *You Shall Be as Gods*, pp. 19, 42,
62, Holt Rinehart and Winston, New York, 1966.]

What would it mean to put this kind of question to the
New Testament? To ask what "God" means in the New
Testament would be to attend to the context of the word,
to see what functions it performs, what action it elicits or
recommends, what it does, where it places us. Look at
Jesus's words in Mark 9:37: "Whoever receives one such
child in my name receives me; and whoever receives me,
receives not me but him who sent me." It would appear, in
this place, that receiving the Father and receiving Jesus
(faith) is defined as receiving a child. Faith in God and
discipleship to Jesus both appear to be identified with a
certain mode of action, a form of being in the world. This
same process of redefinition appears to be going on in
chapter 4 of the first epistle of John, especially in that
portion of verse 16 which says that "he who abides in love
abides in God." If the phrase were reversed, we would be
obliged to read it in the traditional way: that a man fixed
upon God will naturally be free to love his brother. But
this is not what is being claimed; love of the brethren is the
meaning of love for God, the content of it, the definition
of what it is.

Matthew 25:31 ff., the parable of the Last Judgment, is
perhaps the most notable New Testament passage where
this worldly definition of faith is suggested. Here participation in the eschatological community is determined
by concrete human acts of service, not religious action or a
special religious language. Now in the New Testament
participation in the new age always presupposes faith, and

so we may be permitted to observe that the rewarded human actions are themselves forms of faith, not fruits of it, and that faith is once again defined as a way of being in the world.

This radicalized or ethicized approach to faith, therefore, may be something more than a contemporary requirement necessitated by the revolutions of the modern world—the way we are compelled to do our believing since Feuerbach, Nietzsche, and Freud. It may be possible to show that this movement has some faint beginnings in the New Testament itself, and thus to show that the "death of God" is a considerably more ancient event than our preoccupation with the nineteenth century has implied.

But even if such a faint support in the New Testament could be claimed, radical theology, while pleased, would still have to define itself as a theological venture committed to doing without the idea and reality of God as conceived by the mainstream of historic Christianity. It would still find itself saying that, whatever hope it may have of achieving a way back to Jesus, and a way forward to some form of Christian community, too much has happened to man's basic experience of being in the world to make possible a return to the Christian God. George Steiner has provided an admirable summary of some of the forms of this contemporary experience.

> This study of human experience and practice as convention, as a set of signals and "cultural phonemes," characterises much of what is at present most fashionable, but also most interesting, in the life of ideas. It relates, at least by metaphoric suggestion, the Crick-Watson account of the genetic code to the linguistic analyses of Noam Chomsky. It underlies both Marshall McLuhan's notion of the changes in human perception which follow on the changes in the nature and transmission of information and Levi-Strauss' work on the codified structures of man's imagination, myths, and sciences. The belief that "reality" is largely social convention is as marked in Foucault's *Histoire de*

la folie as it is in the argument of the new generation of historians of science that "empirical" discoveries are closely bound up with the verbal metaphors and psychological expectations current in a society at any given moment in its history. We see what we have been taught ("programmed") to look for. We find what we have been prepared to see. [George Steiner, "The Thinking Eye," *Encounter*, London, May 1967.]

This suggests why the world we live in cannot receive the name of the old God today. That name comes from another radically different conception of what it means to be in the world, and neither the device of the kernel and the husk (liberalism) nor demythologizing can effectively obscure the difference between the two worlds. The name of God was the proper name for man to use in that other time, and it is just our respect for that other time that compels us to leave the name there to do the work appropriate to it.

The debate between the redefiners and the doers-without is still in process. The radicals, in this debate, continue to ask why it is that we must live without God, and whether a life without God can be called Christian. They will also inquire what authentic speech about God was like when it was used, and under what conditions new speech about God might become possible once more. In the meantime, it is almost as if the only authentic word to the Christian God is "no"; as if the only way we can be faithful to what the Christian God was is to live in loving and responsible unbelief.

III

Fragments

To affirm the death of God is to be in a constant quizzical relationship to oneself, wondering always whether this is exactly what one wants to say.

For the death of God is like Silly Putty, or Hamlet's clouds. It is forever changing into something else, and new forms are always appearing.

As sickness serves to clarify what health means, so the death of God—as one really makes the attempt to live it out—serves to clarify what having a God really meant. Whether you are looking for a future resurrection or for present equivalents, it is always good to have in mind what the original was like.

Perhaps God is thus accessible to us only as dead.

Or, as Philip Rieff put it, perhaps Freud's nonexistent strong God is to be preferred to Jung's existent weak one.

Or: better one good god lost than a whole host of new and living ones. In the emerging struggle between the monotheists and the new polytheists, monotheism may be stretched to mean having one god, or less.

My students assure me that radical theology is hung up on God, and they're right. The Jewish-Christian God is far more deeply embedded in our language and action than we realize. To live after the death of God and to seek for real and living equivalents, to look carefully at those masks he wore: this is where radical theology differs so from atheism; atheism usually imagines that the project of doing without God is a relatively simple one.

Vocation. Whenever the idea of "job" or "work" shades, ever so slightly, into the idea of vocation, God is still present. Vocation presupposes that there is a real future, with a real space *out there* for you and me, and that the beginning of mature existence is to discern it, to work and train and postpone gratification so that you may come to fit that space. Here the theology of the future is right in seeing a connection between God and the future, but it is wrong if it assumes that the experience of having a future is a universal and natural one, and in arguing from that experience to the reality of God. Today, one sees in one's children, one's friends, one's students, the future losing its reality, its power to call and to claim. There is nothing, they say, *out there* with any power to draw us. Why they feel this, and whether they are right or wrong, is not easy to say. The "why" may be answered in terms of breakdowns of traditional symbols and institutions, of the information explosion through the media, the continuing numbing effect of a war which never began and may never truly end, the recollection of our leaders' rhetoric of defense of that war. It is hardly an accident that the experience of the death of God and the loss of a real future have come about at the same time. Maybe we'll find a way to recover a real future, and this may or may not mean we will have recovered God.

Guilt. The Reformation as normative event seems to be falling apart, and this is why appeals for a new Reformation all seem a little frantic. Guilt, in the Christian West, is about God, and requires Him for its formulation. Guilt is the sense of a violation of a value or standard that has come to me from outside myself, and in the presence of that violation my situation is one of deep instability so that I feel that amends must be made to something or someone. I cannot imagine myself living without the experience of guilt, but this hardly means I have any right to question the integrity of those who tell me that for them guilt is disappearing. I'll never forget an incident of a good many years ago, back in the Eisenhower era, in fact. These were college years without politics and without ferment, but years in which hordes of visiting speakers, religious and otherwise, were discoursing solemnly about the radical character of sexuality. Anyhow, I was on this sex circuit for a period, and at some campus I was busily taking sex seriously from a Christian standpoint. A wise student patiently consented to explain to me why my language made no impression on her. Sex is not truly part of the self, she assured me. It is simply a human activity to be used, and it can be used to harm others or it can be used to express something real. But, she said, I no longer feel "right" when I make use of my sexuality the way my parents advised me; and I no longer feel guilty when I use it in ways contrary to their advice. I murmured something about the neurotic dissociation of the self from the body. But that girl has become a groundswell today, and her sisters are active in the Women's Movement, for which the body is an external thing, outside yourself, which you are bound to control. The movement from "I am a body" to "I have a body" is the move from guilt to guiltlessness. There are still structured rules for what is and what isn't permitted in the guiltless community. But it has to do with the sanctions of the group, and with neither God nor the super-ego. I'm not at all sure that it even makes much sense to speak of the transition from a guilt culture to a shame culture. The guiltless ones appear to be doing without shame as well.

Limit. The disappearance of guilt as a form of the death

of God raises the question of the idea of limit or boundary. Nihilism, we have seen, is one of the consequences of the experience of the death of God, and it is a consequence that implies the abolition of all limits or boundaries to man's will or action. Camus wrestled with the problem of imposing a limit on the idea of rebellion without resorting to God. When God as limit or boundary or "nay-sayer" goes, we must become our own limit. When Ivan Karamazov cries, "If there is no God, then everything is permitted," he assumes that there are no other possible limits for man. It is strange to note that God can sometimes be the abolition of limits, in addition to the limiter. This is surely suggested by Nietzsche's "If there is a God, how can one tolerate not being God oneself?" All of this means that the question about the necessity of limits and the one about the necessity of gods are not the same question, however they have been joined in the Western world. We are learning to ask: in the time of the death of God, how are we to become limits and boundaries for each other? How are we to understand that form of human love that is contained in the idea of saying "no"? The teacher is his student's limit; the parent his child's; the lover his beloved's, the state the citizen's and the citizen the state's. Sometimes, someone else may be our proper limit, and sometimes no one can. This is when we become our own nay-sayer, and cry out, "thus far, and no further." The draft resistance movement perceived with considerable lucidity the relation of ethics and limit. A young man came to himself morally when he perceived that someone or something else, usually the state, had exceeded its limit. Good fences may make good neighbors, but today only man can make a fence.

Home. The Reformation meant the abolition of sacred space, but not really. A number of things have had to happen to us since then to bring us to the growing experience that there is really no place anywhere that, in itself, has any more claim on us than any other. "Be it ever so humble, there's no place called home." Familiar places

change, grow, deteriorate; we become more mobile and
transitory, and the death of God comes to live with us in
increasingly familiar ways. God seems embedded in the
ideas of home, fatherland, nation, so in the time of his
death no loyalty to any space can be assumed. It may be
won, or taken on as a strategy, or pretended, not given.

I have always been interested in what men mean when
they use the word "home." For many Southerners, and
perhaps New Englanders, it means the place where one
grew up, the place where parents may still be living. For
others, it means the present legal address. For others, it is
merely the place where one's wife and children happen to
be at the present moment. This whole issue distinguishes
Christians from Jews in interesting ways, for the Christian
has nothing in his experience parallel to the contemporary
Jew's relation to Israel. There has never been a special
place to which he has been trained to long to return.

The death of God means no home, no homeland, no
beloved nation. It is precisely this formulation of the
experience of the death of God that Herman Melville
made his own. He wrote in *Moby Dick*: "in landlessness
alone resides highest truth." The ideas of God and exile
have always been closely connected, but exile generally
means being driven away from your special place and
being unable to return. When the physical inability to
return is removed (as was the case with the reopening of
Jerusalem after the Six-Day War) one is no longer an exile.
But another kind of exile has emerged: not the inability to
return to the special place, but the experience of not
having any special place to return to or to stay in. This new
conception of exile, the sense in which, as Pete Seeger has
said, we are all exiles, leads to the possibility of expatriation. The death of God, the dissappearance of special
space, leads to the possibility of leaving where one is, not
because one is pulled by some alluring new sacred space,
but because one is driven out by something in the old,
familiar, desacralized place one lives in.

Now expatriation has a sinister and certainly an un-

American ring to it. It conjures up the poet fleeing a vulgar America to a more cultured Europe, or worse, the jet-setter looking for rarer and rarer thrills, and better and better tax relief. We generally admire one who chooses to leave his country only if we can convince ourselves that he has left tyranny for freedom, and we rightly reserve greater admiration for one who is actually driven out by tyranny or injustice because of his beliefs.

But expatriation, the choice to leave this country for another, is not in the American tradition at all. You don't desert a sinking ship, you hang in. Courage in America is defined as working within the system; bad guys work outside the system, good guys work within. "Responsible," as in the phrase "responsible dissent," generally means the way it has always been done, within the system, normal channels, keep it cool. Avoid the flamboyant gesture, breaking laws, and, above all, martyrdom and martyr complexes.

Yet, in spite of this, a growing number of men and women, young and not young, students and teachers, solid, conventional middle-class people, are finding themselves driven toward an act of expatriation they neither expected nor particularly wanted.

The external reason is in part the war in Vietnam and the kind of country we have become because of that war. If one was morally opposed to the war, the major problem became that of avoiding complicity in it. Add to this the feeling of powerlessness, of being unable to change anything, and add to this the experience of being manipulated by one of the best public relations firms in the country—the executive branch of the government—and you have some of the conditions for expatriation.

We have seen, in our cities, how violence has become the last language available to express the powerlessness of the poor. Expatriation might be seen as the violence of the middle class, the only language left. Expatriation assumes that there is no real resistance or underground in the homeland. There was, of course, an antiwar movement, and the draft resistance movement showed forth America's finest side. But this was a movement that belonged to those of draft age, and those of us beyond that age ran few risks in supporting them. In general, these young didn't need us to counsel them; they were counseling us by their acts. Expatriation may then be not only the violence of the middle class, but the resistance movement for the middle-aged and secure.

A moral act after the death of God is partly defined as putting yourself in certain places, with certain groups and against other groups, laying your body on the line, putting your money where your mouth is. The new expatriate appears to agree with his reactionary neighbor, who shouts, "If you don't like this country, get out; America, love it or leave it." But it is not a question of not liking or loving, but the subtler one of not being able to stay. This is rarely a move to a better job and more status (as with the European brain drain moving this way across the Atlantic), but usually the reverse: a move to something more insecure and marginal. And it is not a move *to* a better place, a new sacred space, but merely a move from this place which has lost its power to compel allegiance and respect. It is something like a civilized divorce; when the marriage has proved to be more damaging than healing, the case for bringing it to a close becomes plausible. It is something like leaving the priesthood or the church. One has to leave when one feels that to stay would mean being committed to more folly, more inanity, more destructiveness, than leaving would entail.

The potential expatriates during the duration of the war were not those who wished for what is now called an honorable settlement to the war. They were those who believed this country should lose the war, that such a war ought to be lost. And when one found oneself wishing for the defeat of one's own country, and found no means of working for that defeat, the only honorable thing that remained for many was to leave.

It is not that this is the only moral direction. It takes little moral courage to imagine expatriation; I am not at all sure I would have the courage to make this move myself. But something has clearly happened to America when the unthinkable can be conceived and even justified. The end of America, somehow. The end of the possibility of living here, of being an American. To live in the death of God is to go down even such unexpected and strange byways as this one.

The death of God may turn out to be false, or premature, or banal or too obvious to be of interest. But whatever it may turn out to be, true or false, obvious or sinful, it will certainly have proven itself as an enormously fruitful metaphor (or experience or event) through which to grasp some of the pieces of the contemporary world.

For we can already discern a specific culture of the death of God. When God dies, something must become mediatorial, incarnational. When mystery, grandeur, grace, no longer come in official ways, they must come unofficially. When there is no universal apolcalyptic vision, every man is his own apocalypticist.

Thus, we have had death of God films from Ingmar Bergman and Roman Polanski. More systematically, we have had in recent years specific attempts to interpret modern poetry, modern drama, and politics from the perspective of the death of God.

In two significant studies, J. Hillis Miller has offered a study of the movement from nineteenth- to twentieth-century poetry as a movement from the disappearance to the death of God (*The Disappearance of God* and *Poets of Reality*, The Belknap Press of Harvard University Press, 1963 and 1965). The writers of the mid-nineteenth century, Miller writes, speak of a God withdrawn from direct experience. He still exists, but withdrawn from nature and self, and the poetic project is to reunite the fragments, to bring God back to earth and to man.

But this invisible God proved unstable, and he gives way, in the twentieth century, to the dead God. And it is

the death of God that comes to be the starting point for
many twentieth-century writers. Nietzsche does not think
of himself as setting out to kill God; he merely finds him
dead. Not "I have killed him," but "we." Yet in a striking
passage Professor Miller shows how twentieth-century
man may be said to have become a deicide.

> Man has killed God by separating his subjectivity from
> everything but itself. The ego has put everything in
> doubt, and has defined all outside itself as the object of
> its thinking power. Cogito ergo sum: the absolute
> certainty about the self reached by Descartes' hyper-
> bolic doubt leads to the assumption that things exist,
> for me at least, only because I think them. When
> everything exists only as reflected in the ego, then man
> has drunk up the sea. If man is defined as subject,
> everything else turns into object. This includes God,
> who now becomes merely the highest object of man's
> knowledge. God, once the creative sun, the power
> establishing the horizon where heaven and earth come
> together, becomes an object of thought like any other.
> When man drinks up the sea he also drinks up God,
> the creator of the sea. In this way man is the murderer
> of God. [*Poets of Reality*, p. 3.]

For Miller it is inevitable that such a murderer of God
become a nihilist. Nothing has any value, save as man
values it; nothing has any reality, save as man experiences
it. The nihilist's will devours everything it touches, that its
emptiness may be assuaged.

Modern poetry, as Miller reads it, is the project of
escaping the nihilism occasioned by God's death by passing
through it. Curing the omnivorous ego swallowing up the
world by abandoning the ego's independence. Abandoning the presupposition of a self–world distinction that
nihilism always comes to grief upon. This new movement
of the self is both mystical, aesthetic, and ethical. Miller
calls it, in Wallace Stevens's phrase, walking "barefoot into
reality."

To walk barefoot into reality means abandoning the independence of the ego. Instead of making everything an object for the self, the mind must efface itself before reality, or plunge into the density of an exterior world, dispersing itself in a milieu which exceeds it and which it has not made. The effacement of the ego before reality means abandoning the will to power over things. This is the most difficult of acts for a modern man to perform. It goes counter to all the penchants of our culture. To abandon its project of dominion the will must will not to will. Only through an abnegation of the will can objects begin to manifest themselves as they are, in the integrity of their presence. When man is willing to let things be then they appear in a space which is no longer that of an objective world opposed to the mind. In this new space the mind is dispersed everywhere in things and forms one with them. [pp. 7–8.]

In the art of this new space, the dimension of depth has disappeared. The vertical line is dead, and we have only horizontals and surfaces. In the old space, the self was separated from its objects, and the objects were placed in a visual space. To be in one place is not to be in some other place, and space stretches out infinitely. Beyond, lurks the absent God; here, lurks the unknowable other self. In the new space, we touch and feel, rather than see, and the sense of endless space existing beyond us in mystery tends to vanish. "The mind, its objects, other minds, and the ground of both mind and things are present in a single realm of proximity" (p. 9).

To go back to the traditional picture of God, then, would be the impossible task of returning to a different experience of space and time. Such a God lived, and lived well, when both a visual space, near and far, and the stretch of time past, present, and future, dwelt comfortably with us. Thus, Miller suggests, "if there is to be a God in the new world it must be a presence within things and not beyond them" (p. 10). The poetry that particularly interests Miller, that of Wallace Stevens and William Carlos Williams, is precisely the poetry that celebrates the birth of the new palpable gods, the gods of this world.

Nihilism reaches its dead-end when men destroy themselves trying to become the old god. Nihilism is transcended when men are trained to touch, taste, and see in such a way that any ordinary thing at hand may become a new god for them.

If modern poetry, as read by Professor Miller, proposes a way beyond the nihilism attendant upon the death of the Christian God by a rendering of a new space and new gods, modern drama, according to Robert Brustein (*The Theater of Revolt*, Little, Brown, and Co., 1962) has the more limited task of exploring the meaning of that death—of rebelling against the old god and his surrogates—without trying to build anything new.

Brustein distinguishes between the traditional theater of communion, with secure spiritual foundations, and the modern theater, from Ibsen to Genet, characterized by what he calls revolt. "When Nietzsche declared the death of God," Brustein writes, "he declared the death of all traditional values as well. Man could create new values only by becoming God: the only alternative to nihilism lay in revolt" (p. 8). Brustein does recognize that modern drama occasionally tries to propose some quasi-religious alternatives to the displaced Christian God—Shaw's vitalism, Brecht's Communism, for example—but he sees these religious solutions generally as pretentious failures. The mood of despair with which the modern theater has ended, Brustein believes, is caused precisely by its failure to create a new sense of community, a religion for the post-Christian world.

Brustein's analysis of the forms of revolt that characterize the dramatists he considers most significant is a subtle one, and we need not go into it here. What he has done is to take a single complex idea, revolt or the death of God, and make it work as the central critical key by which to understand the movement of modern drama over the last one hundred years. It is something of a tour de force, and I am inclined to think that it works as well as any project could that tries to find a single metaphor for the explanation of such a complex body of material.

Brustein defends those dramatic artists who have the courage to look at the godless world without self-pity, and without longing for some new gods. For him, life is tragic, and rueful humanism is the only option for civilized men and women confronting meaninglessness and death. We were not surprised, then, when—more recently—he mounted an angry attack against such contemporary forms of theater of salvation as the Becks' Living Theatre. He perhaps should not be so surprised that the theater is attempting to explore the possibility of new gods, beyond both nihilism and tragic revolt. He wrote a book that showed precisely why people like the Becks were bound to emerge. Theater has been salvation—this is what Brustein's theater of communion was all about. But since, for him, there is no such thing as salvation, no old gods around, and no new gods possible, revolt remains the only authentic business for the playwright to be in.

Albert Camus's *The Rebel* was written in 1951, and this makes it very old, as far as fashions in ideas go. It was a book originally read by Christians as a sympathetic and persuasive attack on them, and it served, some time ago, to give many Christians a good conscience about their revolt against God and evil as a possible, and perhaps even a necessary, position to take. Today, we can return to it, read it less existentially, and be less threatened and defensive. For it is, however dated and however inept some of its philosophical analysis may be, part of what we are calling the culture of the death of God. It is really a book about the possibility of politics after the death of God, and there are few issues more in need of cool reflection than this one in our time.

This is not to say that Camus is likely to be of much use

to the young, or at least to the post-Christian mystics
among the young. No new gods are possible for him or
even necessary. This is because, in a curious way, he is very
dependent for his very conception of limited rebellion on
the Christian tradition. And that tradition lives on in an
important way in his thought. It is almost as if the
Christian God could become available to Camus only after
He died. For the rebel needs a personal God to fight
against. Only the Christian God can make a rebel. Camus
writes:

> The night on Golgotha is so important in the history of
> man only because, in its shadow, the divinity aban-
> doned its traditional privileges and drank to the last
> drop, despair included, the agony of death." [p. 32.]

This almost sounds as if the death of God commences with
the crucifixion, but I do not think that Camus intended to
say that. What he clearly does say is that Jesus raises within
the Christian tradition the possibility of authentic rebellion; but the church, with its rhetoric of resurrection,
erased it, and thus compelled rebellion to go underground
only to reemerge in Europe when the Christian tradition
began to crumble.

For Camus, as a good Frenchman, the death of God
begins in 1793 with the execution of Louis XVI. Here
God's representative on earth is killed, monarchy is abolished, and regicide and deicide become one. When there is
no king, there remains only a semblance of god in the
form of moral principles and absolutes. And in our time,
when principled absolutists improvise the ideologies of
totalitarianism both abroad and at home, even the Kantian
vestiges of deity disappear, and men are compelled to do
without both God and his moral shadows.

But, "with the death of God, mankind remains, and by
this we mean the history that we must understand and
shape" (p. 103). Thus, politics is the problem bequeathed
to us by the death of God. Can men live together without

destroying each other, when God as the limit, the imposer of value, disappears? Camus assumes that to be human is simply to believe that politics in its widest sense is possible. "The future is the only transcendental value for men without God" (p. 166). To believe in the future is to believe that there will be a future and that men still have a power to give it shape. The destructiveness of revolutionary violence and the death of the Christian God are Camus's two defining factors for the problem of men living together.

Rebellion is the primary ethical category for the man without God, rebellion against both God and tyranny. But this rebellion is limited in two ways. It is first of all a limited act in itself; rebellion affirms the existence of a boundary, a point beyond which I may not step. Everything is *not* permitted; to violate the freedom and integrity of my brother is not permitted. Why is it not permitted? Not, obviously, because God has given him a value or because Christ died for all men. But I am bound to respect my brother because he is part of the community I live in. Rebellion is limited, then, in this second sense. It is of instrumental, not ultimate value. Its function is to define the whole community of men. I rebel, therefore, we exist, he writes in his famous Cartesian parody. And we are alone. Yet somehow together (p. 104).

When Camus writes that rebellion cannot exist without a strange form of love, he makes visible what appears to be the only real moral absolute in his thought. In a world that can be divided between the victims and the executioners, I am bound to stand with and to love the victims. This, for Camus, is the action remaining to me; this is the form of politics possible, in the time of the death of God. I dare not try to become God, for that is nihilism, and men who try to become God turn out to be monstrous men. The death of God protects man, in a way, for there is no living God to try to become, and thus he writes that the single rule of life is "to learn to live and to die, and, in order to be a man, to refuse to be a god" (p. 306).

Poetry, drama, politics, each of these, and all of them, remain to us as models for answers we might be giving to the question about living after the death of God. Without God, or with new ones.

We can carry Camus's reflections on politics and the death of God a step further. Theodore Roszak has written: "We are long past the time for pretending that the death of God is not a political fact" (*Where the Wasteland Ends*, Doubleday, 1972, p. xxi). I first read this sentence at the time America was watching the prisoners-of-war from Southeast Asia returning home, stepping from the plane to the microphone and declaring their faith in Nixon, America, and God. It seemed to me that we should take these statements as heartfelt and sincere. The God of the white Christians had been in Vietnam, just as Mailer had written. He was on our side, and His message to our side was "kill, kill, kill."

The episode in Vietnam hadn't really been a war at all, and this is why it is so hard to deal with its deepest influences on us. Unlike a war, it had no clear beginning and no ending; the distinction between combatants and civilians never could be maintained, as Lieutenant Calley learned to his sorrow. Who were allies, who were enemies; where was victory, and where was defeat? This curious event had very little that a war was supposed to have. That is why the Pentagon so misconstrued it. It wasn't even a civil war, as it first appeared to some. It was, of course, a revolution to the Vietnamese people. But what was it, and what is it, to us? If this country is to face the terrible damage it has done to us, we must try to answer that question. I take seriously all those words of praise for God coming from the prisoners. The Vietnamese incident was really a religious event, part of the current history of the death of God in our time. It was conceived, at this end, by Christian men who felt that what they stood for was being called into question, and a substantial part of Christian America steadfastly defended it. It was in fact so obscene, so unthinkable, that its defenders for many years were driven to religious language to cover its obscenity, like a whore in a white wedding dress. We had to destroy a village in order to "save" it, and the event of Good Friday and the redemptive character of suffering somehow lurk in the distance. We went there, we stayed there, we bombed there—after all the other political defenses collapsed—because of a "commitment." To whom was never wholly clear. To the murdered Diem? To the corrupt generals Ky and Thieu? Or to the people—and, if that, what people? Did we consult them? Again, were we told all through the 1960s that we must stay lest the sacrifice of those already killed should prove to have been vain. Killing and genocide to justify deaths that had no justification except other deaths to follow. Again, lurking in the shadows is the great Jewish–Christian myth of sacrifice which affirms that the shedding of blood may, under some conditions, prove to be healing. Language so used, to such an end, is difficult to use again. Our Vietnam was a religious event, and politics and the death of God come together once again.

What we tried to call a war is "over," we are told. What we really mean, however, is that we are trying to forget it. But we cannot forget it as a religious event and should not. Amnesty for the resister and the deserter is not only politically, but psychologically, unthinkable. For to receive these young men back into our country would compel us to remember, and that is just what we do not wish to do. America cannot grant amnesty to the dissenters, because what it really wants is amnesty—which is not forgiveness but forgetting—for itself. They, the resisters, cannot accept our forgiveness, for they are aware of no sin committed, no necessary repentance, as a condition of forgiveness. If they returned, they would compel us to repent. And who is there here repenting and seeking forgiveness?

And so, as the war is forgotten, America readies itself for another religious revival, perhaps even a new Great Awakening. Oral Roberts is a guest star on *Hee-Haw*, while Billy Graham thinks up creative new answers to the problem of sex crimes and stands silent in the shadows of Watergate. Perhaps we will decide that the revival has in fact been going on for some time. Perhaps it began when we started the bombing of the north in 1965, and perhaps the real reason that old death of God movement began when it did is that it dimly saw God's hand in that bombing.

> And then, into this tasteless heap of gold and marble, He came, light and clothed in an aura, emphatically human, deliberately provincial, Galilean, and at that moment gods and nations ceased to be and man came into being—man the carpenter, man the plowman, man the shepherd with his flock of sheep at sunset, man who does not sound in the least proud, man thankfully celebrated in all the cradle songs of mothers and in all the picture galleries the world over.
> —Boris Pasternak, *Doctor Zhivago,*
> Pantheon, New York, 1958, p. 43

While radical theology, in its Christian form, goes to work on Christology (see, for an admirable start, John Phillips, "Radical Christology and the Death of God," *Cross Currents,* Summer, 1969; and Neill Hamilton, *Jesus for a No-God World,* Westminster Press, 1969), it should be attentive to the non-Christian (as well as Christian) resources in this task. I want to call attention to a particular kind of writing about Jesus that seems to be emerging in recent years in Europe. It might be defined as a search for a post-Christian Jesus. It comes not merely from ex-Christian humanists but from Marxists as well. It seems to be based on a common concern to find a way of stating just how Jesus has impressed himself on the consciousness of mankind, apart from those theological formulations Christians are supposed to require.

It is hard to know just why this genre seems more common in Europe than in America, and in continental Europe at that. Perhaps it is because the European intellectual has had an easier and more extended experience in

being away from the church than his American counterpart, and is thus more inclined to separate the Christian
intellectual tradition from sectarian allegiance or even
from "belief in God." He knows that the church is dead,
and is thus freer to examine the continuing influence of
Christian beliefs.

In any case, while it is not possible yet to write a *Quest for
the Post-Christian Jesus*, an outline for chapter one can be
tentatively put together. This material cannot be adopted,
without translation, by the Christian radicals. For one
thing, the European adherents are not necessarily without
God; and, for another, they are not deeply interested in
defining themselves as Christians. I would like to note,
very briefly, three of these representative figures.

The first, and most familiar, is the Italian novelist
Ignazio Silone. Readers of his fiction have often noted his
concern for finding a way for the ex-Catholic to remain
somehow faithful to what he has been. In *Bread and Wine*,
the revolutionary disguises himself as a priest, and nearly
becomes one in the quality of his actions. In his essays,
Silone has written, more than once, about the post-
Christian's allegiance to his past faith. In "The Choice of
Companions" (in the collection *Emergency Exit*) he tries to
state what the unshakable certainties are for man today.
They are, he declares, Christian certainties. We still preserve an assurance that we are free and responsible beings
and that "man has an absolute need of an opening into the
reality of others . . . [where] spiritual communication is
possible." From his assurance, he writes, comes a love for
the oppressed that no failure can shake.

Some years after this, Silone returned to the same theme
in an essay entitled "What Remains" (*Encounter*, December
1968). Here he sharply distinguishes his attempt to define
the nature of his Christian deposit from a desire to return
to the church. The latter rupture, he says, grows deeper
with the years. Fortunately, Jesus is always greater than
the church, and in this later essay it is clear that Jesus and
his message is the true content of his Christian allegiance.

"What is left," he writes, "is a Christianity without its myth, reduced to its moral essence, plus a great deal of respect and very little nostalgia for what has been lost on the way. To put it shortly but exactly, what is left is the Lord's Prayer. As to the Christian sense of brotherhood and devotion to the poor and humble, this is now translated for me into a fidelity to socialism."

In a passage from *Crowds and Power* (Victor Gollancz, London, 1962, p. 467) Elias Canetti gives his answer to the very problem that concerns Silone. What, he asks, remains of Christianity after the church is left behind? Or: what is still true about Jesus, after Christianity has lost its power to persuade?

> The image of him whose death Christians have la-
> mented for nearly two thousand years has become part
> of the consciousness of mankind. He is the dying man
> and the man who ought not to die. With the increasing
> secularization of the world his divinity has become less
> important, but he remains as an individual, suffering
> and dying. The centuries of his divinity have endowed
> the *man* with a kind of earthly immortality. They have
> strengthened him and everyone who sees himself in
> him. There is no-one who suffers persecution, for
> whatever reason, who does not in part of his mind see
> himself as Christ. Mortal enemies, even when both are
> fighting for an evil and inhuman cause, experience the
> same feeling as soon as things go badly with them. The
> image of the sufferer at the point of death passes from
> one to the other according to who is winning or losing
> and the one who in the end proves weaker can see
> himself as the better. But even one too weak ever to
> have acquired a real enemy has a claim to the image.
> He may die for nothing at all, but the dying itself
> makes him significant. Christ lends him his lament. In
> the midst of all our frenzy of increase, which includes
> men too, the value of the individual has become not
> less, but more. The events of our times appear to have
> proved the opposite, but even they have not really
> altered man's image of himself. The value that has
> been put on his soul has helped man to the assurance

of his earthly value. He finds his desire for indestructibility justified. Each feels himself a worthy object of lament; each is stubbornly convinced that he ought not to die. Here the legacy of Christianity, and, in a rather different way, of Buddhism, is inexhaustible.

Perhaps the most sophisticated and extended study of the post-Christian Jesus comes from the Polish philosopher Leszek Kolakowski in his essay "Jesus Christ, Prophet and Reformer" (*Tri-Quarterly*, Spring 1967). Kolakowski has been interested in Christian doctrine for a number of years, as readers of his striking earlier essay "The Priest and the Jester" will recall. In this essay on Jesus, he is not so much the Marxist, seeking political and historical equivalents for Christian dogma, but the post-Christian European asking about the universal meaning of Jesus.

Rather startlingly, Kolakowski rejects both Hegel and Nietzsche as guides in his search, preferring Pascal and Kierkegaard as models, even for non-Christians. Why? Because they tried to see Jesus as he really was; to ask about the historical reality and how it could be made contemporary. That is precisely Kolakowski's concern.

After a brief look at the New Testament story, Kolakowski concludes that "it is impossible to assert that Jesus made Christianity, if belief in Jesus' deity is to be among the foundations of Christianity." But, in any case, he has remained in our culture, even for those who cannot accept his deity or his supernatural mission. It is interesting to observe the five motifs in Jesus's ministry that Kolakowski chooses as central and abiding, and, above all, available to the non-Christian as well as the Christian.

(1) The abolition of law in favor of love
(2) The hope of eliminating violence from relations among people
(3) Man lives not by bread alone
(4) The abolition of the idea of the chosen people
(5) The essential misery of all that is temporal

Kolakowski acknowledges that no one of these themes is absolutely unique to Jesus. But it has been through him that they have been introduced into our experience, and the purpose of his essay is to insist that Jesus is not invalidated just because men do not believe in the God he believed in. The post-Christian world must avoid a crude and sterile atheism.

Perhaps, he notes, the Christian world may be able to reform itself. Perhaps "we can free ourselves from the dark nightmare of the clerical, fanatic and dull catechism, which for the last four centuries has oppressed and sterilized our national culture." But renewal of Christianity is not his concern, except to suggest that renewal can come only by attending to the five motifs he has cited. Because Jesus incarnated each of these five values in a unique and forceful life and death, he has become, for all men, "a model of that radical authenticity only in which every human being can give real life to his own values."

IV

Death

Would it not be better to give death the place in actuality and in our thoughts which properly belongs to it, and to yield a little more prominence to that unconscious attitude towards death which we have hitherto so carefully repressed? . . . We remember the old saying: *Si vis pacem, para bellum.* If you desire peace, prepare for war. It would be timely thus to paraphrase it: *Si vis vitam para mortem.* If you would endure life, be prepared for death.
—Sigmund Freud, *Collected Papers,* Vol. 4, pp. 316–317

Men can die without anxiety if they know that what they love is protected from misery and oblivion.
    —Herbert Marcuse, *Eros and Civilization,* p. 216

It was possible there was nothing more important in a man's life than the hour and the route and the power of his death, yes, certainly if his death were to launch him into another kind of life.
    —Norman Mailer, *Of a Fire on the Moon,* p. 35

The reality of God and the reality of death have always been closely related in Christian thought and experience, so much so that men have often been tempted to infer the former from the latter. Ludwig Feuerbach's project of identifying man and God was criticized by an orthodox theological writer who said Feuerbach ignored death and misunderstood evil. Apart from the question of the truth of the indictment, it does show that God and death have always had an intimate connection, and that radical theology, if it continues to propose the possibility of a Christianity without God, must have something to say about death.

One approach to the problem might entail the citation of some notable godless thinkers—Camus and Heidegger, say—who might be said to take death seriously. I propose here to work on the imaginative rather than the critical level. I suspect we know in our minds that faith in God does not always entail taking death seriously, as we know that godlessness does not necessarily lead to flight from death. But our imaginations are less deconverted than our intelligences, so I wish to offer at this point a modest exercise of the imagination.

I suspect that the clearest description of the literary form I have chosen would be a film scenario or, better, what the film people call a "treatment." A working title might be *The First Day of Dying,* and it is simply the presentation of three scenes from the first day in the life of a college student after she has learned from her physician that she is suffering from a fatal illness.

The first scene is the occasion of her learning about the nature of her illness, the consultation with the doctor; the second is a discussion with one of her professors; the third is with the young man she has been going with. I will make no attempts at realism: there are no names, no specific settings, no naming of the disease, no attempt to follow too scrupulously the psychology of grief.

In the first scene, which can be visualized anywhere, hospital, office, even restaurant, we are breaking into the middle of a conversation. The girl and her doctor have been sparring, and he has been making use of the ancient medical habit of offering assurance without making any statements of fact.

SCENE ONE

GIRL

Why can't you tell me what my chances are?

DOCTOR

Because we simply don't know enough to come up with the nice decisive answer you seem to expect. We can name the disease, we can make a very rough guess on the prognosis, and we can do a number of things to help you right now. We don't give up and we don't offer false hopes.

GIRL

Am I going to die?

DOCTOR

That's what we call a typical patient's question. We're all going to die.

GIRL

And that's what I call a typical doctor's answer. If I wanted little nuggets of homely wisdom, I'd ride around town and read the bulletin boards in front of the churches. Am I going to die as a result of this disease, soon . . . ?

DOCTOR

You just can't expect me to answer such a question. I don't know what you mean by soon.

GIRL

Doctor, I like you and I think you're very capable. But I must say you're almost as ready with the non-answers to questions as a politician or a clergyman.

DOCTOR

It's not as easy as you think to tell just how much a patient needs to know.

GIRL

So you sit there and play God and decide just how much of your precious wisdom your patients deserve to receive.

DOCTOR

My dear, only the saintly and the young imagine truth to be such a simple commodity. Look: when my word of truth to a seriously ill patient can actually hurt him physically, can even wipe out the will to live, what is truth in matters like this?

GIRL

An unfortunate question, considering the others in history who have asked it.

DOCTOR

You can't intimidate me; as a matter of fact I've always thought that Pilate probably really wanted an answer to that question, and that Jesus showed a kind of insensitivity, even self-centeredness, in refusing to come up with something. So I really have no qualms in putting Pilate's question to you, who seem to accuse me of being a stuffy, middle-aged phony placed on this earth to deceive lovely young girls like yourself who have terminal illnesses.

GIRL

You know, I prefer you angry to bland. The word I wanted to hear was "terminal." Is my illness, according to what you know at this time, a terminal one?

DOCTOR

Yes.

GIRL

A general sense of man's mortality and knowing that one is likely to die fairly soon are really quite different.

DOCTOR

I know. But we can still do a great deal.

GIRL

Except to answer my straightforward questions about death. Oh, I didn't really mean to accuse you of anything like dishonesty. I think I understand that truth isn't simple, especially truth about important things like love and sex and death. But I did want a little more candor than you were prepared to give me at first. Not a general proposition about man's mortality, but a word about me, my disease, my future. Now I have it.

DOCTOR

I'm a little surprised. Maybe I've been deceived by the old rhetoric about the generation gap. I really didn't expect that you'd be pinning me down the way you have. People your age are supposed to have the illusion of immortality, the idea that they can never die.

GIRL

I have that, I suppose, or had it. But I find that I am not exactly thinking about death right now, but about the curious feeling of not having a future. Most of my life up to now has been dominated by the idea that the present is to be sacrificed to the future. The past must be rejected, hometown, parents, and all that—but there isn't really any true feeling for the present, because we're all supposed to be getting ready for some mysterious tomorrow—work, or marriage, or the real world, or whatever they call it. I think I've made my peace with my past—it no longer bothers me much, or even interests me.

DOCTOR

And now, in addition to not having a past, you have— unexpectedly—no future.

GIRL

Most of my friends on campus talk a lot about the sense of unreality they have about the future. I'm sure the war used to be one of the causes of this. Now maybe it has something to do with our economic insecurity or disbelief in the government. I'm pretty straight, but I guess some of this disbelief may have rubbed off on me.

DOCTOR

So in some ways you may have begun to disbelieve in the future before we made this diagnosis.

GIRL

I think so. If believing in the future means a sense of a long white sheet of pure time, unrolled before me, clean and untouched and waiting for my little marks to be made—I've never felt that.

DOCTOR

No one feels that, really, if he's in his right mind. What did you mean when you said you'd made your peace with the past?

GIRL

Oh, nothing very fancy. I've been through the parent thing; rebellion is a drag. They don't bother me or understand me, and I don't bother or understand them, and I assume we love each other. I've never been terribly hung up by my past, but I may be just lucky.

DOCTOR

Maybe. But there is something very American, or at least very WASP-American, about not having a past. You have the feeling that many Americans really have no past, and are not guilty about the fact. This is one of the reasons that Freudian psychoanalysis has never penetrated as deeply into American culture as it has in Europe. It offers freedom from the past, the very thing many Americans have as a natural endowment, much to the frustration of Europeans and Asiatics, who call us shallow and optimistic.

GIRL

So, for one reason or another, I find myself without past and without future.

DOCTOR

What about the present? That you have not lost.

GIRL

I wonder if I can find it in time. Everything has always been "wait"—"postpone." After graduation, after vacation, after we're married, after I fall in love . . . Can getting ready to die bring me a present I was never taught to find?

DOCTOR

Why not? The past and the future have already lost some kind of reality for you. Maybe dying does have the power to make the present real and precious. Love does this; great art does, and I suspect some would say that God does too.

GIRL

I'm glad I didn't let you get away with your professional assurances. I think I really did want what I called the truth, and I think I want to get ready for—what's coming.

DOCTOR

Let me know what I can do. I'll be seeing you next week, in any case. And thank you for your honesty.

GIRL

I suppose I'd better find someone to talk to now, or I'll be tempted to cry, and I don't really think I'm ready for that yet.

SCENE TWO

The same day. The girl returns to the campus where she is a student, and we may assume she has had some time for reflection and grief to have their way. She has doubtless talked to some friends, and now she casts around for someone perhaps older, more authoritative. The Dean of Women she considers, and rejects, since the dean reduces all problems to either identity crisis or conflict between the generations, and the girl suspects that such approaches wouldn't help much. The College Chaplain is a possibility, but she discovers he is involved in conducting an informal seminar on the ethics of abortion.

So she is reduced to her professor of religion. The girl, we may assume, has some traditional religion; not much, and she is not sure whether it is something she can count on now or not. In any case, she is inclined to feel that what she now needs is someone who has a little more religion than she does. So this meeting is not wholly accidental. She has just started a course with this professor, and she does not know him well. She runs into him on the campus and uses as a pretext a question about a subject for the course term paper to open the conversation.

A word about the professor himself, before we break into the conversation. He is intelligent, fairly peculiar, and a believing Christian, unlike many professors of religion. He has just come from a tour of duty on the West Coast, so, as we might guess, his thing is erotic exuberance and sensory awareness. He is one of the house theologians for the Esalen Institute, and he is beyond politics, into salvation, and pretty sure that the orgasm is somehow the key to it all. A book of his, D. H. Lawrence— Demon or Saint, has just been accepted by Grove Press as part of their policy of publishing all good pornography, even Christian pornography. He is, of course, divorced, bearded, and attractive; and he was, of course, denied tenure at his previous institution because of some sort of irregular counseling techniques he tried with a female religion major in the office. But—he is a convinced Christian, and a fairly nice guy, for all of his lack of intellectual and sexual discipline. We are supposed to be ambivalent about him. His life is something of a mess, and he is something of a fake, but what he says may still be true. The moral is, I imagine, that the sincere gentleman may speak or teach nonsense or trivia, while the lecher or the phony may sometimes be right. He can be dressed in the latest hip professor style—beads, bellbottoms, whatever.

PROFESSOR

I see no reason why you shouldn't change your topic. It's

still early in the term. What was it you were planning to do?

GIRL

We'd decided on something about Constance Chatterley as a Christ-figure. But my interest has recently shifted from that.

PROFESSOR

Shifted from Jesus and sex? How wild! What else is there?

GIRL

I think I'd like to try something on death.

PROFESSOR

O.K. You can attack the idea of death in American culture——

GIRL

What I'm really interested in is the idea of immortality.

PROFESSOR

(The professor is thrown off his guard by this, as this is the first undergraduate he's ever met with an interest in this subject, and, since his subject is relevance, it is clear he hasn't thought about immortality for a long time.) George Orwell has an interesting remark somewhere. He says that the major problem of our time is the decay of the belief in personal immortality, and that it cannot really be faced until the prior problems of hunger and fear are faced. You might want to look that up—it's in one of his essays—and figure out how a non-Christian like Orwell could have come up with such an idea.

GIRL

(She now makes her move from term-paper questions to personal ones.) What do Christians say about immortality today?

PROFESSOR

Very little. We've rather carefully avoided the subject. You
know, other-worldliness is really out. You can find writers saying that Christians aren't really supposed to believe in that Greek idea of immortality, that the Christian
word on the subject is one about the resurrection of the
body.

GIRL

What does that mean?

PROFESSOR

Nothing, really, since most Christians north of the
Mason–Dixon Line don't believe in the resurrection of the
body either, except in some vague mythical way.

GIRL

Do you?

PROFESSOR

You stopped me to talk about your term paper, remember.

GIRL

Are you evading my question?

PROFESSOR

Partly. Why do you want to know what I believe? Can you
tell me that?

GIRL

No, but I would like to hear what you have to say.

PROFESSOR

All right, even though this is an odd time and place for
even a little lecture. Immortality is false if you take it to
mean "we don't die," or "there is no death." We do, and
there is. All of us die, and every part of us dies. Nothing in

us is immune. But immortality needn't mean that—even though it did for the Greeks. It can mean that death is not the end, that there is some kind of life beyond death. This is part of what the Christian hope means, and I think I believe it.

GIRL

You think? Aren't all Christians supposed to believe it?

PROFESSOR

I don't know. They say they do. I certainly don't find it easy to believe. Paul based his belief in life after death on Jesus' resurrection, and that little matter is hardly the easiest thing to hold on to. I find—do you really want to hear about my rotten little system of beliefs? It's not much, I'm afraid.

GIRL

Please go on.

PROFESSOR

The intellectual obstacles to this part of the Christian hope seem to me virtually insurmountable, and one always tries very hard not to kid oneself at this point. I rather doubt if my intellectual grasp of the Christian hope would help me much if I were facing death, someone else's or my own. But when my intellectual defenses are down: when I am making love, or listening to certain things in Mozart or Berlioz, or the Stones, then I tend not to take my intellectual reservations too seriously. Am I kidding myself—confusing the realm of the sensuous with the realm of faith? Or can sex and music really enable you to get at some truths that otherwise you're cut off from? I think so, and so I am a kind of believer after all. Do you know Donne's sonnet "Death Be Not Proud"?

GIRL

No.

PROFESSOR

Well, listen to it, for it's a lot sounder than my tentative claims.

Death be not proud, though some have called thee
Mighty and dreadful, for, thou are not soe,
For, those, whom thou think'st thou dost overthrow,
Die not, poore death, nor yet canst thou kill mee.

From rest and sleepe, which but thy pictures bee,
Much pleasure, then from thee, much more must flow,
And soonest our best men with thee doe goe,
Rest of their bones, and soules deliverie.

Thou art slave to Fate, Chance, kings, and desperate
    men,
And dost with poyson, warre, and sickeness dwell,
And poppy or charms can make us sleep as well,
And better than thy stroake; why swell'st thou then?

One short sleepe past, wee wake eternally,
And death shall be no more; death, thou shalt die.

GIRL

Lovely. The form and style persuade me, but the content turns me off.

PROFESSOR

Form and content, really? How about the medium being the message?

GIRL

Oh no, it won't work. When I descend from the bewitchment of the sound, I can see that it has all the theological sophistication of Billy Graham.

PROFESSOR

Well. There is certainly nothing sophisticated about the Christian hope for immortality. This is what I meant by my irresistible intellectual reservations. Perhaps this hope is available only to the childlike, and thus not to me, and perhaps not even to you. If you really want some intellectual noises from me, I can readily discourse on the fear of death in modern existentialism.

GIRL

I'm not—I wouldn't be—afraid of death, I think, and so I suppose existentialism is denied to me. And John Donne's confidence is far removed, so I guess I'm not much of a Christian.

PROFESSOR

I have the feeling we're not talking about a term paper any more.

GIRL

You're right, we're not. You've been counseling me.

PROFESSOR

Watch out, I'm known as the worst counselor in Christendom. I always make people listen to my problems. I can't have been much help.

GIRL

I don't know what I expected, but I think you have helped me.

PROFESSOR

Remember the poem, and let me know if I can do anything more.

SCENE THREE

The girl has been touched, not persuaded, by the odd, but not at all irresponsible, description of the Christian hope offered by the professor. And she is honest enough not to grasp at straws she feels

she has no right to. She is presumably still somewhat numb, since,
after all, her whole life and system of security has just been
overturned. Unable to believe in immortality, and unable or
untrained to think of any idea or cause worth dying for, she had,
up to the present, always felt that since life is all there is, nothing
could be worse than the loss of it. For this reason, she is somewhat
surprised to notice that she has not as yet been totally overwhelmed
by sorrow or grief or fear.

The third scene, that evening, is with her boyfriend. We
needn't know just how close they have been, whether they are, to
coin a phrase, "in love," whether, or how often, they have slept
together. She has already given him the details of the day's
activities when we break in.

BOY

Yes, I am surprised. I guess I expected to find you in less
control.

GIRL

Perhaps I did too. I haven't had much time to fall apart.

BOY

What's happened? What's it like? Are you afraid or bitter?

GIRL

A little, but less than I'd figured. More afraid of pain than
dying. Pain is something you know about already.

BOY

My philosophy teacher is convinced that all men fear
death, and that whoever says he doesn't is either lying or
repressing.

GIRL

I've heard that, and I don't believe it. It was very hard to
get the doctor to level with me, though when I went for
the first tests last week, I knew that something serious was
going on. He kept telling me why he couldn't say that I was
going to die.

BOY

We're all going to die.

GIRL

That was one of his approaches.

BOY

I feel very irrelevant, almost as if we are suddenly strangers. How can I help?

GIRL

Don't you want to walk away? I'm hardly what you could call a good catch.

BOY

I think that was my first temptation. I'm sure I'd thought of you as a girl I'd like to marry or live with, and now that's ruled out. But I don't want to run, and I don't want to pity.

GIRL

Good. I don't like pity, and I don't want it. I don't even think I need it. I think if you left me, or became suddenly cool and awkward, I really would fall apart. . . . Or if you stayed, just to be a friendly counselor.

BOY

I don't have anything to say.

GIRL

I don't think there is any advice to give. You've always been a wonderful listener, and I need you now just to help me understand what is happening. I've found out some strange things today. I can't believe in immortality, though that isn't much of a surprise. And God is either not there or not listening. But finding this out has somehow not bothered me. It's almost been a feeling of liberation. I seem to have come out from under a cloud of pressure that my life was determined by.

BOY

Pressure?

GIRL

All the virtues I was taught to value—achievement, competence, social responsibility—were based on a future time when there would be less tension, less pressure. I was always getting ready, just about to do or be something, in training. But never really doing. Never really getting hold of "now," today, the present.

BOY

So now that the future has been shortened, you no longer have to give up the present for it.

GIRL

I feel for the first time in my life that I am free to live in the present moment without some censor peering over my shoulder with advice about postponing gratification or delight. Does it make sense to say that one only learns to live when one is about to die?

BOY

It is supposed to be God who frees us from anxiety about the future.

GIRL

Dying has done what God doesn't do.

BOY

Or used to do, and cannot any more.

GIRL

My feeling for time is strange and quite exciting.

BOY

(Quoting.) "Time, that makes fools of us all, must have a stop."

GIRL

I'm not outside of time, but it certainly has lost its power to
control or bedevil me. I'm not even worried about whether
or not I'm losing my faith, if I ever had enough to lose.
Whatever I had or have, it doesn't seem to be either a help
or an obstacle.

BOY

God is not dead, he's just preoccupied with church matters.

GIRL

All I know is that each minute—just being here talking to
you—is much more precious, much more of a miracle,
than I've ever felt before.

BOY

Are we falling in love?

GIRL

I don't think so. It hardly seems important to ask. I think
I'd like to make love tonight.

BOY

Some sacraments still work. They say that health can be
fully valued only when it is lost, like innocence.

GIRL

I am beginning to live on the day I began to die. It is more
exciting than sad. The night sky looks like a Van Gogh
painting, and you in your silence seem wiser and more
wonderful than I've ever imagined.

V

Mailer

Religion in America, and probably in the Western world at large, is in an usually rapid period of ferment, change, and decay. It may even be possible to speak of a religious revolution, perhaps inside, certainly outside the traditional religious institutions. Many of its components everybody knows: the counterculture, drugs, the turn toward the East, rock music, the new Jesus. But one central figure of this revolution, I suspect, does not come from any of these chic communities. He comes from Brooklyn and his name is Norman Mailer. It is as a representative of this revolution that I wish to attend to him.

Oddly enough, one may need to justify the project of taking Mailer seriously as a religious and theological presence. As a matter of fact, the very idea of "seriousness" follows him around everywhere. It was the theme dominating his mayoralty campaign in New York City in the summer of 1969. "Is he serious?" was a question often asked, especially by reporters. I don't see that such a question, applied to his religious writing, is either important or answerable. The point is, he is to be taken seriously, and, if this means taking him more seriously than he takes himself, so much the worse for us all.

In all of his writing, in one way or another, Mailer has

been out to capture God, and this would be true even if he hadn't been telling us for years of this obsession. In his report on the 1972 Democratic convention he recalled that "once, how many years back, he had thought to himself, 'The world's more coherent if God exists. And twice coherent if He exists like us.'" (*St. George and the Godfather*, New American Library, p. 29). Let me set down, by way of introduction, three themes that weave in and out of his writing over the last decade or so and which will make out a case for taking him seriously. The first comes from a 1958 interview (*Advertisements for Myself*, Signet, pp. 337 ff.) in which he is discussing the meaning of Hip. Hip is dominated, he writes, by a vision that is going to influence our religious thinking for a hundred years. It is that "God is in danger of dying" (p. 341), no longer all powerful, but still in combat with evil. We must become fellow voyagers, heralds of this dying God, not trying to win back his omnipotence for him, but fighting with him and for him in his weakness.

This may be Mailer at his most mystical-Jewish, for here he has touched one of the main motifs in the creation myth of Lurianic cabala, when it speaks of the God in exile from himself and of man's need to rescue himself by rescuing the embattled God. This is apparently a theme that refuses to let Mailer go; it appears again and again. In his report on *Apollo 11*, he refers to the 1958 interview and reflects:

> Heroism cohabited with technology. Was the Space Program admirable or abominable? Did God voyage out for NASA, or was the Devil our line of sight to the stars? [*Of a Fire on the Moon*, p. 81]

The second theme is found in the 1966 preface to the collection of papers, *Cannibals and Christians*. Here Mailer brings to the surface a metaphor that has continued to dominate his thinking: the metaphor of disease, cancer, plague.

Well, it has been the continuing obsession of this writer that the world is entering a time of plague. And the continuing metaphor for the obsession—a most disagreeable metaphor—has been cancer. . . .

The difficulty—for one can always convince the literary world to accept a metaphor if one remains loyal to it—is that my obsession is not merely an obsession, I fear, but insight into the nature of things, perhaps the deepest insight I have, and this said with no innocence of the knowledge that the plague can have its home within. . . . [p. 2]

In a modern world which produces mediocrities at an accelerating rate . . . a world of such hypercivilization is a world not of adventurers, entrepreneurs, settlers, social arbiters, proletarians, agriculturists, and other egocentric types of a dynamic society, but is instead a world of whirlpools and formlessness where two huge types begin to reemerge, types there at the beginning of it all: Cannibals and Christians.

We are martyrs all these days. All that Right Wing which believes there is too much on earth and too much of it is second-rate, all of that Right Wing which runs from staunch Republicanism to the extreme Right Wing, and then half around the world through the ghosts of the Nazis, all of that persecuted Right Wing which sees itself as a martyr, knows that it knows how to save the world: one can save the world by killing off what is second-rate. So they are the Cannibals— they believe that survival and health of the species comes from consuming one's own, not one's near-own, but one's own species. . . .

Then come our Christians. They are the commercial. The commercial is the invention of a profoundly Christian nation—it proceeds to sell something in which it does not altogether believe, and it interrupts the mood. We are all of us Christians: Jews, liberals, Bolsheviks, anarchists, Socialists, Communists, Keynesians, Democrats, Civil Righters, beatniks, ministers, moderate Republicans, pacifists, Teach-inners, doctors, scientists, professors, Latin Americans, new African nations, Common Marketers, even Mao Tse-tung. Doubtless. From Lyndon Johnson to Mao Tse-tung, we are all Christians. We believe man is good if given a chance, we believe man is open to discussion, we believe science is the salvation of ill, we believe death is the end of discussion; ergo we believe nothing is so worthwhile as human life. We think no one should go hungry. So forth. What characterizes Christians is that most of them are not Christian and have no interest left in Christ. What characterizes the Cannibals is that most of them are born Christian, think of Jesus as Love, and get an erection from the thought of whippings, blood, burning crosses, burning bodies, and screams in mass graves. Whereas their counterpart, the Christians—the ones who are not Christian but whom we choose to call Christian—are utterly opposed to the destruction of human life and succeed within themselves in starting all the wars of our own time. . . . [pp. 3, 4.]

Most of what the world calls Christians are in fact Cannibals, and most of what Mailer calls Christians are as corrupt in their impotence as are the Cannibals in their power. Man should be neither Cannibal nor Christian; in 1958 he was saying that the hipster presented a third way out. By 1966 the solution was vaguer; the novelist, he said, may become a physician.

But what kind of physician? Mailer wavers. At times, he believes only in the diagnostic radiologist who reveals the trouble; at other times, he believes in the surgeon who can remove it. As novelist, Mailer is the diagnostician: as journalist, he is the healer. As novelist, he knows how to locate the cancer, as journalist (and as campaigner?) he seems to have a nose for the grace of life.

The third theme is the theme of grace. Mailer has often written about this. It figures importantly (as we shall observe) in *The Armies of the Night*, and in his mayoralty campaign:

Who is to say that the religious heart is not right to think the need of every man and woman alive may be to die in a state of grace, a grace which for atheists and

agnostics may reside in the basic act of having done
one's best, of having found some part of a destiny to
approach, and having worked for the view of it?
[*Existential Errands*, p. 329. Little, Brown & Co., 1972.]

What does Mailer believe his theological constituency to
be? Not those who believe there is already an undiseased
religion, politics, or art that can save them. Not those
content with what is given. His audience, he writes, is "that
audience which has no tradition by which to measure their
experience but the intensity and clarity of their inner lives"
(*Cannibals and Christians*, p. 220).

These themes, joined with others, constitute a genuine,
passionate, and prototypical religious vision. No, not vision, but rather journey; for movement in time and space
is an important part of Mailer's religious thought. From
World War II to the Pentagon steps, on to Houston and
the moon, and—most recently—to Miami and a post-
nomination party after the close of the 1972 Democratic
convention, Norman Mailer has been up to something.

It is not wholly accidental that his first novel, *The Naked
and the Dead*, contains both a conventional conception of
the relation of the novelist to his material and a fairly
conventional set of theological reflections. The novelist
stands apart from his characters, and so does the God of
the novel. The future seeds of some later concerns can be
seen in the character that seemed to interest him the most,
the reactionary General Cummings, who remarked that, if
there is a God, He is just like him (p. 183) and that "man
had to destroy God in order to achieve Him, equal Him"
(p. 392.)

In the journalism and the fiction of the fifties, these
themes are carried along, and some new things are added.
In a 1955 interview (*Advertisements for Myself*, p. 247)
Mailer declares that he believes in God, but that it is a
wholly personal confession having nothing to do with
organized religion. By 1958 the attack on organized
religion is escalated (*ibid.*, pp. 337 ff.); he calls it "one of

the great enemies of our time," one of the "murderers of
the senses" (p. 345).

Mailer's debate with God, from *The Naked and the Dead*
onward, rarely deals with Jesus; Mailer is, after all, a Jew,
even though he clearly wishes part of the time he were
Irish. But since the discovery of Jesus is a central part of
both his Pentagon experience of 1967 and his meditation
on the space program in 1969–1970, it should be observed
that there is a preparation for it in the fifties. Lanny, in
Barbary Shore, longs for drunkenness so she can feel like
the crucified Christ, whom she believes was a happy man.
She receives Mikey's sexual advances passively, as a "sweet
suffering Jesus upon the cross" (p. 107). This theme is
picked up, modestly, in *The Deer Park*, in Eitel's idea for a
film scenario about a kind of Miss Lonelyhearts–saint–
counselor whose passive suffering redeems those who
come to him for help.

This theme is important only in retrospect; Mailer's
major theological focus in the fifties and sixties remains on
God. It is in *The Deer Park* (1955) where we find, for the
first time, I believe, a move beyond the private belief in
God coupled with an attack on organized religion. It is an
identification of God and the Devil, a conception of an evil
God, a beast who devours men or makes His own children
into devourers. Faye, in that novel, finds himself en-
tertaining such an hypothesis: God is the Devil, the earthly
Devil is really God dethroned; and this Devil–God is
winning the world, except for the few "who saw the cheat
that God was not God at all" (p. 281). It may be that Mailer
knows that this perception is shared by an earlier religious
revolutionary, whom he resembles, and not only physically. It was Luther who said that "one does not know
whether God is the devil or the devil God" (H. Grisar,
Luther, vol. V, p. 352). The Devil–God is clearly the God of
the Christians for Mailer, the omnipotent one whose
power to effect good has become so negligible that He has
turned to evil as a more successful way of manifesting
power.

In 1963 (*The Presidential Papers*), Mailer is still working this theme when he remarks that W. B. Yeats's poem "The Second Coming" is the greatest poem of the century precisely because of its description of the great beast–God lumbering toward Bethlehem to be born, to correct the twenty centuries of Christian deception.

This beast–God is one of the leading characters in Mailer's novel *Why Are We in Vietnam?*; indeed, the answer to the question of the novel's title is surely: "Because Christians still, alas, worship the evil God."

> For the lights were talking to them, and they were going with it, near to, the lights were saying that there was something up here, and it was really here, yeah God was here, and He was real and no man was He, but a beast, some beast of a giant jaw and cavernous mouth with a full cave's breath and fangs, and secret call: come to me. They could almost have got up and walked across the pond and into the north without their boots, going up to disappear and die and join that great beast . . . for God was a beast, not a man, and God said, "Go out and kill—fulfill my will, go and kill . . ." [*Why Are We in Vietnam?* pp. 202, 203.]

There is a second theme, superimposed on and interwoven with the theme of the evil God, that is the basis for Mailer's more "believing" statements about God in recent years. This is the Manichaean (or Lurianic) theme of the weak God, of human life as a battleground for the cosmic struggle between the powerful Devil and the weak and needy God. The God of the Christians has become evil, and is by no means dead. Indeed, he should be killed. But there is another God—in danger of dying—who needs us desperately. Mailer first makes this point, as noted above, in 1958, and it surfaces his debate with William Buckley in 1962 (*The Presidential Papers*, pp. 162 ff.). Here he refers to two views of God, or two Gods, which lead to two different views of society. One God is a conservative who creates the form of society we now have, and one should neither tamper with Him nor with the society. It is

this God, presumably, who has become discredited, as He
has moved from the omnipotence of good to the omnipotence of evil, and become the Killer. The second God,
and this will become almost obsessive, is locked in combat
with an apparently more powerful Devil (perhaps the
demonized God of the Christians, and, if so, we have a
contemporary Gnostic battle between two parts of God
Himself), and society is the battlefield. Man must seek to
discern the weak God, to become His agent and to seek to
shift the wealth and power of the nation so that men may
be liberated from the Devil's grasp.

What is our proper obedience to the weak God? This is
the theological question Mailer asks in his reflections on
the moon shot. He is deeply ambivalent about the whole
space program. He is unable to decide whether we are
going up there to help the weak God or to destroy Him.

> For the notion that men voyaged out to fulfill the
> desire of God was either the heart of the vision, or
> anathema to that true angel in Heaven they would
> violate by the fires of their ascent. [*Of a Fire on the
> Moon*, p. 105.]

The same dualism appears more recently:

> For he [Bertolucci] begins *Last Tango* with Brando
> muttering two words one can hardly hear. They are:
> Fuck God. The unmanageable in oneself must now
> offer advice. If Bertolucci is going to fuck God, let him
> really give the fuck. Then we may all know a little more
> of what God is willing or unwilling to forgive. That is,
> unless God is old and has indeed forgot, and we are
> merely out on a sea of human anality, a collective Faust
> deprived of Mephisto [God?] and turning to shit.
> [Norman Mailer, "A Transit to Narcissus," *The New
> York Review of Books*, May 17, 1973, p. 10.]

Again, the Jewish Mailer surfaces. The weak God of the
cabala is yoked to the ambiguity of *Genesis*: the warning
against pride, the advice of the serpent to become like

gods, the divine condemnation of Babel, versus the equally divine commandment to be sovereign over the creation, to subdue it and use it for man.

We need to ask about the reasons, if any, for this shift from the idea of the evil God to be killed, to the idea of the weak God to be helped. I suspect there are two possible explanations. First, the shift appears to be related to a shift from a deep pessimism about the possibility of political change to a faint optimism or hope, and thus it would be a fair guess to say that the early days of Kennedy's presidency lie behind both the hope and the theological shift. And Mailer seems to have a heightened artistic as well as political confidence during this time. In a 1962 interview he claims he is no nihilist. He admits that all legal structures appear to him bad, but he states that they can be dissolved by art, by the word. (It can be noted, however, that by and large Mailer's novels have come from his periods of political pessimism, while his best essays and journalistic pieces seem to emerge from times of greater hope.)

The only kind of hero that Mailer could conceive, prior to Kennedy's victory, was an existentialist hero fully at home with his own violence and candid about it (remember his affection for Sonny Liston during this period), and thus a hero who could only serve to lead us more deeply into our incurable disease. Kennedy became a possibility for cure and thus a theological vision emerged to give form to the hope. After Kennedy's death, and with the escalation of the Vietnamese war, the old political pessimism was to return, and the hopeful polarity between God's minority and the Devil's majority was to be transformed into the struggle between the Christians and Cannibals, both equally diseased. In such a world, the only proper work is that of the artist, expressing and exposing our cancer.

But, in 1967, Mailer is persuaded to join the March on the Pentagon and thus to set aside both his artistic vocation and (it turned out) his theological pessimism. This experience leaves him with some hope, and has some striking political and theological consequences. And it appears that this combination of dualistic theology and confidence in some form of rational politics by no means disappeared. Mailer has since made a most distinguished, if unsuccessful, bid for political office; and, a little earlier, he had reported on the 1968 conventions.

Yet, in *Miami and the Siege of Chicago*, Mailer allows very little of this theological undercurrent to show. What there is showing is clearly Manichaeism. At the close of the convention that nominated Mr. Nixon, he cites the remark of John Updike (though he could easily have quoted himself) that God may have withdrawn his blessing from America, thereby freeing the demons of the left and of the right to do their work. Perhaps, he adds, if Nixon could ever grow into an authentic leader, we would have some proof that the blessing had not wholly been withdrawn. But he left Miami (and presumably Chicago as well) unclear: "He had no idea at all if God was in the land or the Devil played the tune."

But we must return to the problem of the transition, in the early sixties, from the killer-God to the weak God who is to be sought out and helped. There is a second explanation for this transition besides the move from political despair to hope. It is to be found in Mailer's experience with drugs.

He tells us in 1962 that he finds himself fascinated by mysticism; that he is not animal enough to be a natural mystic; that he discovered, to his horror, that he could get no mystical experiences of his own without drugs. The resultant relationship between the new weak God and drugs remains somewhat obscure; it may be that the drugs led him to suspect that there may be something there besides the killer-God, but also that a thing you can only find with drugs is a thing you do not deserve. So the new theology becomes a means of dealing with the problem of the present but suffering God when drugs are given up. In his 1968 *Playboy* interview, Mailer develops the relation

between drugs and the weak God in an astonishing way:
drug use has become blasphemy, and the decisive argument against them is theological. Drugs, he states, lead
man to use time in the wrong way; to exhaust or to
mortgage the future in a way no man has a right to do.

> If his own future has already been used up in one or
> another mysterious or sinister sense, then maybe pot is
> drawing it out of the very substance of what I may as
> well confess I call God. . . . During the time the addict
> has some of his most intense and divine experiences, it
> is because he is literally imbibing the very marrow and
> nutrient of existence. But since I do not believe that
> God is necessarily inexhaustible, the drug addict may
> end up by bleeding Him. [*Existential Errands*, p. 248.]

Mailer's problem is never "Does God exist?" It is always
"How?", "In what form?", "What are we to do about it?"
This is how he puts it in a *Paris Review* interview, sometime
prior to 1966:

> But I will say one thing, which is that I have some
> obsession with how God exists. Is He an essential god
> or an existential god; is He all-powerful or is He, too,
> an embattled existential creature who may succeed or
> fail in His vision? [*Cannibals and Christians*, p. 214.]

But in *An American Dream* (1965), it is clear that the
existential, embattled God has captured Mailer's imagination, and that he is no longer interested in polemics against
omnipotence. The singer Cherry tells Rojack that she is
sure God is weaker simply because she is so unhappy. But
He is doing his best, even though He knows much less
than the Devil does.

> I think I decided some time ago that if there is a God
> and He's all-powerful, then His relation to us is
> absurd. . . . If the only world we have is one of abys-
> mal, idiotic disproportions, then it becomes too dif-
> ficult to conceive of an all-powerful God who is all

good. It is far easier to conceive of a God who died or who is dying or who is an imperfect God. But once I think of an imperfect God, I can begin to imagine a Being greater than ourselves, who nonetheless shares His instinctive logic with us. We as men seek to grow, so He seeks to grow; even as we each have a conception of being—my conception of being, my idea of how we should live, may triumph over yours, or yours over mine—so, in parallel, this God may be engaged in a similar war in the universe with other gods. We may even be the embodiment, the partial expression of His vision. If we fail, He fails, too. He is imperfect in the way we are imperfect. He is not always as brave or extraordinary or as graceful as He might care to be. This is my notion of God and growth. The thing about it that gives me sustenance is that it enables me to love God, if you will bear these words, rather than hate Him, because I can see Him as someone who is like other men and myself except more noble, more tortured, more desirous of a good that He wishes to receive and give to others—a tortuous ethical activity at which He may fail. Man's condition is, then, by this logic, epic or tragic—for the outcome is unknown. It is not written. [*Existential Errands*, pp. 252–253.]

We will note, in a moment, the affinity Mailer has for Catholicism, so it will be appropriate here to cite a passage on this same theme in which a very Protestant, very supernatural conception of God is in evidence, a God who does not fulfil nature, but who drives men deeply beyond nature into something like grace.

There are times when He has to exploit us; there are times when we have to exploit him; there are times when He has to drive us beyond our natural depth because He needs us—those of us, at least, who are working for Him. [*Ibid.*, p. 253.]

Just what does Mailer mean by working for Him? In *The Presidential Papers* (1963, pp. 157 ff.) he tries to interpret his own inability to complain or to act at the time of the

Cuban missile crisis. If God (and he means the real, weak God) is defined as our courage, perhaps the Devil is our cowardice, and when we did not protest the game our government was playing with us, when we simply sat around and waited for the news, what we really did was to kill the God of courage in us, because "it is too frightening to keep Him alive" (p. 160). It appears, then, that to work for this God is to act with confidence that something may come of it, and to work for the Devil is to withdraw, to wait, and sometimes even to write. A deep mistrust of the novelist's work is suggested, therefore, in the comment (which first appears to be mere bravado, but which on closer look is more like terror) that he may be working for the Devil. "I sometimes suspect every novelist is a Devil's helper. The ability to put an eye on your own heart is icy" (*Existential Errands*, p. 253). It is the wild, fearless, demonic, novelist–Mailer that has to be tamed; the Beast, as he calls it, that recognizes the existence of nothing beyond himself (*The Armies of the Night*, p. 13). Of this wild Mailer he writes that "sin was his favorite fellow, his tonic, his jailer, his horse, his sword . . ." (*ibid.*, p. 14). The novelist–Mailer still must serve the evil God, the old omnipotent one, while some other kind of visible action in the world is called forth by his obedience to the weak God. Until he went on the Pentagon March, Mailer did not really know what that other kind of visibility might be like. He did not realize that it was political, in quite a conventional sense. Hence, the summer of 1969.

But before this time, he dimly sensed that the new God, the weak God, demanded something of him. Here is one of his most elusive attempts to make this point, in a self-interview from *Cannibals and Christians* (pp. 365–366):

INTERVIEWER

Yes. I follow that. When you speak of the surrender of souls, it is as if you make the totality of them synonymous to God.

MAILER

They are not synonymous. There is the Spirit and the Vision as well. You must account for the Spirit and the Vision.

INTERVIEWER

But souls are the essence of God? His *élan vital*? His flux?

MAILER

They are His present tense. His moral nature exists, you remember, not in the soul but in the Vision. Good. I will give you a scheme. It will make you happy. Vision is the mind of God; soul, His body; and Spirit is what He has left behind. Literally. It is His excrement.

INTERVIEWER

So bad as that?

MAILER

Not so bad. Moral nature resides after all in the Spirit as well as the Vision.

INTERVIEWER

In the Spirit? In God's excrement? In the Devil?

MAILER

Think of this Devil as the echo of history, the lore of the past, the mansions of philosophy, as the blunt weight of every problem which has been solved and every lie which has succeeded. Think of this Devil as the spirit of magic and the dead spirit of institutional life, as mass communication, and the passing of the guards. Everything rich, hideous, poor, proud, nauseating and marvelous goes into that excrement, but it is God's excrement—it is more so. So take Spirit and pose it upon the Vision of the future—between just these two leviathans, at their junction, is moral nature. Of course this moral nature, this junction, is being rotted by the plague.

There *is* something the "moral nature" of man can undertake, but Mailer's political pessimism during the presidency of Johnson makes him very obscure about what it might be. Sometimes he feels that our only health is our disease, and that we must simply let our cancer of plague take its course. Indeed, he takes this metaphor of disease so seriously, so literally, that he can even protest against the use of antibiotics to arrest our actual diseases. This formulation of man's hope he calls the restoration of the metaphor, a location of hope in disease itself. (See the interesting analysis of this on pages 309–310 of *Cannibals and Christians.*) Sometimes he defines the action demanded by the weak God more precisely:

> Sometimes I think God may have lost his way. . . . He could be too far behind. We could have been too slow. Too many of us might have died, too many surrendered. God no longer knows whether to reduce our migrations to the family plot or encourage the most exceptional surrealist journey. [*Cannibals and Christians*, pp. 362–363.]

Who God is, then, is no abstract question for Mailer. It is a problem that can be verified only by finding the right journey to take. He concludes his essay on sex by making the same point: "And who was there to know that God was not the greatest lover of them all? . . . (Unless dear God was black and half-Jewish and a woman, and small and mean as mother-wit. We will never know. until we take the trip. . . .)" (From "The Prisoner of Sex," *Harper's*, March 1971, p. 92.) But the journey need not be an inner or a symbolic one. When Mailer went to Washington, it was the weak and needy God that sent him, but it almost seems as if he did not find God at all, but rather Jesus. A strange thing to find in Washington, that persistent goal of every liberal schoolboy and -girl during some high school spring vacation.

One minor task remains before we follow him to the

Pentagon steps. As everyone knows, Mailer has written a great many words about violence and sex, but I did not feel there was anything worth saying again on these matters until we had first looked at his theological pilgrimage. That pilgrimage has been given something of a form: we have discerned a purely personal confession of a belief in God, a slight but significant attention to the suffering Jesus, the motif of God the Great Beast and the motif of the weak God in danger of dying unless we come to his aid. Both politics and drugs, we observed, appear to have something to do with this dialectic between God the Beast and God the weakling.

Now we must ask: What is the relation of this theological passion in Norman Mailer to the interest he takes in sex and violence?

Throughout his writing, nearly from the start, there is the conviction that human extremities bring one closer— but to what? Sometimes just to self-awareness, to reality, or to guilt. If we have a soul, he writes in *Cannibals and Christians*, "some of us come close to it only through pain." His work, he writes, from *Barbary Shore* on, has been concerned with "the mysteries of murder, suicide, incest, orgy, orgasm, and Time" (*Advertisements for Myself*, p. 97). "Orgasm is the moment when you can't beat life," he comments in the *Playboy* interview. The existentialist is, for Mailer, the man who knows his own desires and rages. Rojack, in *An American Dream*, has based his professional career on the belief that magic, dread, and the perception of death are the roots of human action. (Mailer doesn't bring the theme of death to the fore after this, though, as the passage from his book on the moon shot at the beginning of the previous chapter hints, it may be a theme he is ready to return to. Fear of death seems to be the one point of connection he can achieve with the space heroes.) Or, again:

> Without guilt, sex was meaningless. One advanced into
> sex against one's sense of guilt, and each time guilt was

successfully defied, one had learned a little more about
the contractual relation of one's own existence to the
unheard thunders of the deep. [*The Armies of the Night*,
p. 24.]

If this were all, we would be bound to conclude that it is
impossible to connect the sex–violence interest to the
theological matters we are investigating. But there is
something more. At the close of *The Deer Park*, the lonely
hero is arguing with God. "Would you agree that Sex is
where the vision begins?" (I am quoting from the drama-
tized version of the novel; "vision" reads "philosophy" in
the novel itself.) Mailer had God reformulate the question;
I think God would answer, the hero says, that sex is time
and "Time is the connection of new circuits." But doesn't
this mean that sex as time really captures something? No,
God seems to reply, "opening up new circuits" will have to
do for a mechanical American brain like yours. And then
Sergius says:

> Then for a moment in that cold Irish soul of mine a
> glimmer of the joy of the flesh comes back to me, rare
> as the eye of the rarest tear of compassion, and we
> laugh together after all, for to hear that Sex is Time
> and Time the connection of new circuits is a part of the
> poor odd dialogues which give hope to us noble
> humans for more than one night. [*The Deer Park*,
> dramatized version, Dell, p. 190.]

But to what God do the circuits connect? Isn't it to the evil
God? Aren't the circuits really designed to further the
novelist's vision, and isn't the novelist in the hands of the
Devil? In any case, this view of sex seems to fit, in time and
coherence, with the idea of God as the Evil Beast, and to
make sex the revivification of man when there is nothing
but violence and hopelessness in the political world outside. Sex makes possible an ambivalent service to the evil
God, makes possible the work of the novelist. It is, then, to
this evil God, the Christian God, the source of wars, space

programs, and mechanized, mediocre men, that the orgasm points; just as journeys deliver us into the hands of the other God.

> . . . the Lord, Master of Existential Reason was not thus devoted to the absurd as to put the orgasm in the midst of the act of creation without cause of the profoundest sort, for when a man and woman conceive, would it not be best that they be able to see one another for a transcendent instant, as if the soul of what would then be conceived might live with more light later? ["The Prisoner of Sex," *Harpers*, March 1971, p. 60.]

Sex, like drugs, appears to weaken the good God that is in every man.

The connection between God and evil returns as a fundamental theme in Mailer's report on the 1972 Democratic Convention. He remarks of the young people supporting McGovern at the convention that they knew nothing of transcendence; so he hated them. And, at a private party after the nomination with the McGovern party, he felt there was "insufficient evil in the room" (*St. George and the Godfather*, p. 86). No transcendence seems equivalent to no evil.

When Mailer is invited by a friend to join the Pentagon March, he is first inclined to refuse. After all, isn't it true that one's own literary work is the only true answer to the war in Vietnam? But he feels uncomfortable with that answer and decides to go. We may have a clue to that refusal, for we have seen that Mailer is deeply ambivalent about the novelist's role: he sees the novelist as somehow a servant of the Devil, and still suspects that only sex or violence can remove the novelist's blocks. Yet the war which he wishes to protest is itself violence, so the other Mailer, the anti-novelist, the servant of the weak God, rather than the evil one, must once more step to the fore.

The crisis of the novelist's role in America is enlarged, at this point, into a vision of the crisis of Christianity in America today. We have already seen, in the passage on Cannibals and Christians, how he has described the relation between Christianity and the war, and other passages make this point.

> Christianity, the gentlest of religious professions, is the most militant and warlike of religions, the most successful and Faustian of religions. [*Playboy,* January 1968, p. 78; reprinted in Mailer's *Existential Errands.*] So in the seed of Christianity was an origin of technology, and even conceivably an origin of human mediocrity. ["The Prisoner of Sex," *Harper's,* March 1971, p. 83.]

The Washington visit embodied this critique of Christianity. The Christian God is not dead for Mailer, but very much alive and very evil. Christianity is achieving its historical fruition by fighting the war in Vietnam. The corruption of the old heroic faith and heroic God is combined with the manipulations of technology and is creating a new kind of anti-heroism of passivity. So Western post-Christians are inevitably flirting with Oriental, as well as pharmacological, forms of passivity, and this appears to leave them more than a little susceptible to manipulation by the wielders of technological power.

Here is Mailer's most precise description of the relation of Christianity to the Vietnamese war:

> He came at last to the saddest conclusion of them all, for it went beyond the war in Vietnam. He had come to decide that the center of America might be insane. The country had been living with a controlled, even fiercely controlled, schizophrenia which had been deepening with the years. Perhaps the point had now been passed. Any man and woman who was devoutly Christian, and worked for the American Corporation, had been caught in an unseen vise whose pressure could split their mind from their soul. For the center of Christianity was a mystery, a son of God, and the center of

the corporation was a detestation of mystery, a worship of technology. Nothing was more intrinsically opposed to technology than the bleeding heart of Christ. The average American, striving to do his duty, drove further every day into working for Christ, and drove equally further each day in the opposite direction— into working for the absolute computer of the corporation. Yes and no, 1 and o. Every day the average American drove himself further into schizophrenia; the average American believed in two opposites more profoundly apart than any previous schism in the Christian soul. Christians had been able to keep some kind of sanity for centuries while countenancing love against honor, desire versus duty, even charity opposed in the same heart to the lust for power—that was difficult to balance but not impossible. The love of the Mystery of Christ, however, and the love of no Mystery whatsoever, had brought the country to a state of suppressed schizophrenia so deep that the foul brutalities of the war in Vietnam were the only temporary cure possible for the condition—since the expression of brutality offers a definite if temporary relief to the schizophrenic. So the average good Christian American secretly loved the war in Vietnam. It opened his emotions. He felt compassion for the hardships and the sufferings of the American boys in Vietnam, even the Vietnamese orphans. And his view of the war could shift a little daily as he read his paper, the war connected him to his newspaper again: connection to the outside world, and the small shift of opinions from day to day are the two nostrums of that apothecary where schizophrenia is treated. America needed the war. It would need a war so long as technology expanded on every road of communication, and the cities and corporations spread like cancer; the good Christian Americans needed the war or they would lose their Christ. [*The Armies of the Night,* pp. 188–189.]

The war equals Christians equals Christ equals the evil God. And yet, what Mailer sees and finds in Washington is something very theological. For what he finds is, strictly speaking, grace, and hope, and Jesus. A new kind of

suffering heroism to replace the dying Faustian heroism of
the old Christianity, and, we may conjecture, to replace
the sex–violence-induced heroism of the novelist who set
aside his work in New York to make the journey that
turned into a pilgrimage.

Grace, hope, and Jesus. What seems to be fundamental
for Mailer is the actual sight of the students coming
forward to offer or burn their draftcards on that Friday.
Here is a kind of courage that the novelist had never really
dealt with (except, as we have noted, very tentatively in
Barbary Shore and *The Deer Park*). It was the way they
moved, the way they looked, and it led Mailer to utter a
very characteristic remark: "one has ultimately, it may be
supposed, to believe in some kind of grace" (*The Armies of
the Night*, p. 74).

Mailer, we have already noted, has always been fascinated by the idea of grace. Just before Washington, he
spoke on a platform with Robert Lowell; he saw a grace in
Lowell that he could not find in himself, and he was led to
guess that no protest march could produce the kind of
grace that should be present in any cause for which one is
willing to die (*Ibid.*, p. 18). Some years before, when Mailer
was playing with the distinction between Hip and Square,
the Protestant was Square, the Catholic Hip, and grace was
again the difference. Grace seems to mean, then and now,
the opposite of earnestness or effort, a sort of lightness,
gayety, bravado. Not pardon but power. Could it be that
his perception of this grace in the draftcard burning that
October Friday marked some kind of fulfillment of
Mailer's life-long struggle with the idea of power, a
struggle that begins with his affection for Cummings and
Croft in *The Naked and the Dead*, and moves through Sonny
Liston, Jack Kennedy, Rojack, D. J., and Robert Lowell to
the hundred-odd who burned their cards? Mailer has
always seemed to want to be either Black or Irish or both,
and now it is possible. His mayoralty campaign seems to
confirm this.

This perception of grace becomes enriched and colored

by the idea of hope. The next morning, at breakfast in a
Washington hotel before the march, Mailer is with Lowell
and Dwight Macdonald. They speak together of what they
had witnessed the day before, "the unspoken happy
confidence that politics had again become mysterious, had
begun to partake of Mystery; that gave life to a thought
that the gods were back in human affairs" (*The Armies of
the Night*, p. 88). Not merely that politics had become
possible, though that was partly it; but that a politics was
once more possible that had some grace or mystery in it.
We no longer have to chase after the Evil God, we no
longer have to perform calculated acts of sellout to the
Devil to analyze our disease or madness or cancer. We can
move from diagnosis to cure. We can become wounded
surgeons after all. The gods, or at least the suffering god
who needs us, are back again.

And so is Jesus. For if one Jesus or Christ is fighting the
war in violence, another one is fighting against the war in
suffering. So Mailer, the defrocked Irish priest, the prank-
ster deeply serious, speaks to the reporters after his brief
imprisonment following his Saturday arrest.

> The sum of what he had done that he considered good
> outweighed the dull sum of his omissions these same
> four days. So he was happy, and it occurred to him that
> this clean sense of himself, with a skin of compassion at
> such rare moment for all . . . this sense of nice ex-
> pectation and shining conception of his wife, and
> regrets for the guards, and pride in the prisoners, too
> much, much too much, it must come crashing soon,
> but still—this nice anticipation of the very next moves
> of life itself (and all for just an incredibly inexpensive
> twenty-four hours in jail) must mean, indeed could
> mean nothing else to Christians, but what they must
> signify when they spoke of Christ within them, it was
> not unlike the rare sweet of a clean loving tear not
> dropped, still held, oh he must be salient now, and
> deliver the best of himself to these microphones and
> reporters. . . .

So he made the following speech:

"Today is Sunday, and while I am not a Christian, I happen to be married to one. And there are times when I think the loveliest thing about my dear wife is her unspoken love for Jesus Christ." Unspoken it was, most certainly. She would wonder if he was mad when she read this, for outside of her profound observance of Christmas Eve and her dedication to decorating a Christmas tree, they never talked about such matters. As a child, she had rarely gone to church, but he knew what he meant—some old pagan spirit of her part-Swedish blood must have carried Christ through all the Southern exposures of her mixed part Indian blood, crazy American lass, one-time mouther of commercials on television, mother of his two—would they be mighty?—boys, angel or witch, she had a presence like silver, she was on all nights of the full moon near to mad, and he loved her for that quality he could never explain—her unexpected quixotic depths of compassion, yes the loveliest thing about his dear wife was her unspoken love for Jesus Christ.

"Some of us," said Mailer to the reporters and the photographer and the microphone, "were at the Pentagon yesterday, and we were arrested in order to make our symbolic protest of the war in Vietnam, and most of us served these very short sentences, but they are a harbinger of what will come next, for if the war doesn't end next year," then said he, feeling as modest as he had felt on the steps of the Department of Justice, "why then a few of us will probably have to take longer sentences. Because we must. You see, dear fellow Americans, it is Sunday, and we are burning the body and blood of Christ in Vietnam. Yes, we are burning him there, and as we do, we destroy the foundation of this Republic, which is its love and trust in Christ." He was silent. Wow. [*The Armies of the Night*, pp. 213–214.]

The students with their grace, the Quaker pacifists, refusing clothing and food in a Washington cell—these had brought mystery, hope, grace itself, the weak God who needs us, and the love of Christ, back into the world.

If there are saints, and there are, who can dare not to venture to be one?

> Whole crisis of Christianity in America that the ·military heroes were on one side, and the unnamed saints on the other! Let the bugle blow. The death of America rides in on the smog. America—the land where a new kind of man was born from the idea that God was present in every man not only as compassion but as power, and so the country belonged to the people; for the will of the people—if the locks of their life could be given the art to turn—was then the will of God. Great and dangerous idea! If the locks did not turn, then the will of the people was the will of the Devil. Who by now could know where was what? Liars controlled the locks. [*The Armies of the Night*, p. 288.]

The Pentagon, source of so much destructiveness to the bodies and souls of men, was able to give Mailer a secret that he still today continues to wrestle with, like his ancestor Jacob by the river: the search for America and the search for God are one search.

At the close of the 1960s, Mailer went to Houston to continue the search. He found our old friends, the two gods, at work on the space mission. Was the space program a voyage dictated by the same killer-God at work in Vietnam? Or was it a glorious search for the weak god, our courage, who needs our help as much as we need his? Oddly enough, Houston had a Jesus, too; but it was the bloodthirsty American Jesus at work in Vietnam, not the gentle hero visible on the Pentagon steps. Houston's Jesus was bad news, so Mailer was down. For what Houston's Jesus did, to or for Mailer, was to abolish the mythic connection between the sins of the father and the children. And then something happens.

> So that love on the cross which had requested that the sons not pay for the sins of the fathers had opened a hair-line split which would finally crack the walls of taboo. And the windowless walls of technology came through that gap. [*Of a Fire on the Moon*, p. 140.]

Jesus, the bearer of technology. Jesus the enemy. After
Apollo 11, God is alive and mad, and Jesus is transforming
us all into plastic robots.

But this is not quite all we know about the most recent
parts of this journey. Back Mailer goes to Democratic
Miami in 1972. No transcendence; no evil in the room,
and he hates it. But, at the end of the week, something else
happens, and a part of the old Pentagon vision returns.

> In America, the country was the religion. And all the
> religions of the land were fed from that first religion
> which was the country itself, and if the other religions
> were now full of mutation and staggering across de-
> serts of faith, it was because the country had been false
> and ill and corrupt for years, corrupt not in the age-old
> human proportions of failure and evil, but corrupt to
> the point of terminal disease, like a great religion
> foundering.
>
> So the political parties of America might be the true
> churches of America, and our political leaders the
> popes and prelates, the bishops and ministers and
> warring clergymen of ideologies which were founded
> upon the spiritual rock of America as much as any
> dogma, and so there was a way now to comprehend
> McGovern and enter the loneliness which lived in his
> mood, for he inhabited that religious space where men
> dwell when they are part of the power of a church and
> wish to alter that church to its roots. For yes, the
> American faith might even say that God was in the
> people. And if this new religion, not 200 years old, was
> either the best or the worst idea ever to shake the
> mansions of eschatology in the world beyond, one
> knew at least how to begin to think of McGovern; if he
> had started as a minister in the faith of his father, he
> had left that ministry to look for one larger. [*St. George
> and The Godfather*, pp. 87–88. Cf. pp. 154–155.]

Norman Mailer, the left-conservative become reluctant
religious revolutionary, is at the height of his powers. He
has forced us to become his comrades as we stagger
forward into what may be a terrible spiritual future.

VI

Jesus

When the Lamb opened the seventh seal, there was silence in heaven for about an hour.

—Revelations 8:1

The meaning is not in the words, but between the words, in the silence.

—N. O. Brown

I did not enter into silence . . . silence captured me.

—Ezra Pound, on returning, after forty years, to Paris

And the high priest stood up in the midst, and asked Jesus, "Have you no answer to make? What is it that these men testify against you?" But he was silent and made no answer.

—Mark 14:60–61

So he [Herod] questioned him at some length but he made no answer.

—Luke 23:9

But he gave them no answer, not even to a single charge; so that the governor wondered greatly.

—Matthew 27:14

He [Pilate] entered the praetorium again and said to Jesus, "Where are you from?" But Jesus gave no answer.

—John 19:9

I have yet many things to say to you, but you cannot bear them now.

—John 16:12

> And behold, a Canaanite woman from that region
> came out and cried, "Have mercy on me, O Lord, Son
> of David; my daughter is severely possessed by a
> demon." But he did not answer a word.
>   —*Matthew* 15:23

This play (the form is really that of a television play)
appears to be about war and resistance. So it is, in a way,
but it is really about silence and Jesus. I once distinguished
between two different ways given us to know Jesus—
between the active and critical task of discerning Jesus in
the world and the passive but equally moral task of
becoming Jesus in the world. Both of these tasks remain to
us, but this play is concerned with the more passive of the
two possibilities. As the comments on Norman Mailer
suggested, I am persuaded that whatever fresh reap-
propriation of the meaning of Jesus Christians manage to
make today will come from something beyond our struggles with exegesis, demythologizing, and the historical and
systematic work in Christology that is always necessary.
What that something beyond is is suggested in the phrase,
so often spoken and heard today, "laying your body on the
line." This is a phrase from the world of action and ethics,
but it is laden with ancient overtones of sacrifice and
crucifixion. The contemporary world of action may have a
few suggestions for Christians who are seeking a renewed
grasp on the life and the death of Jesus.

Thus, this play is about "being" or "becoming" Jesus in
the world. About *imitatio Christi.* Now, there are many
things one simply cannot imitate, when confronted by
what we know of Jesus. We who are not Jews cannot
imitate his Jewishness. We cannot imitate his location in
time and space. There are many things he did not do that
we need to do. And, in this dangerous task, we must
choose very precisely what about him we are attempting to
respond to. In the cited New Testament passages, I have

indicated that one special element in the life of Jesus, in his
Passion primarily, interests me here. His silence. That part
of his passivity and nonresistance that found him refusing
to speak. Jesus rarely answered any question directly, and
he occasionally did not answer at all. This play is an
exercise in silence, an attempt to see what it would feel like
and mean.

The time is vaguely future, the late eighties or early
nineties, and this only to take any obscuring present
references out of the picture. The setting is the town
house of Dr. Thomas Westerman in the Georgetown
section of Washington, D.C. Two areas will be used. The
first is a section of the front hall, with a door leading
outside and another door leading into Westerman's study.
Next to the study door is a small table, with phone and
chair. Here the military guard is posted.

The second area is Dr. Westerman's study itself. He is a
scientist, he teaches at the university, and serves the
government in a number of advisory capacities. It is a
spacious, cluttered room; large desk with books and
magazines scattered about. Along the back wall, behind
the desk, is a contemporary videotape recording and
playback system, with screen. No very obvious attempt
should be made to suggest the future time, except perhaps
some slight hints in clothing and furniture design.

SCENE ONE

*It is evening. The front door to the house opens and Dr.
Westerman enters, accompanied by an army guard. Front door is
closed. Guard, efficient without being rough, unlocks study door,
nods to the doctor for him to enter, checks the small telephone table
for messages.*

GUARD
We've put yesterday and today's news broadcasts on your
viewer, Doctor. You can look at them whenever you like.
(Doctor enters his study, acknowledges guard's words with a nod

or a look. After Westerman has entered, guard locks the study door from the outside.)

WESTERMAN
(Looks around his study, fascinated by the prospect of being under restraint in his own home. Checks his desk for mail, and then sets his videotape player in motion, sitting at his desk to watch.)

TV ANNOUNCER *(on the screen)*
Good evening, ladies and gentlemen. Here is the local news. Last night, at the end of a student peace rally at the University, the distinguished Nobel Prize winner and biologist, Dr. Thomas Westerman, was detained for questioning by Department of Justice officials. This was, as far as we have been able to determine, the first arrest made under the provisions of the new National Interests Act, signed into law by the President just last month. We have a portion of Dr. Westerman's address at the rally on videotape.

WESTERMAN *(on screen at rally)*
It's good to see so many of you here at the rally tonight, even though this business of demonstration and protest meeting seems so futile and irrelevant. After all, some of us have been meeting, marching, destroying draft records, and getting arrested, off and on, for over twenty years, in an effort to protest our country's criminal policy of aggression on the Asiatic mainland. The sum total of this whole story of dissent has been to send some of our best young people to jail, and to harden and make more self-righteous the policies and the policy-makers. Today, with this new National Interests Act in effect, it may be dangerous as well as admirable for you to attend such meetings as this one. I am not a pacifist, as many of you know, and I have never argued that all wars, everywhere and all the time, are equally foolish. Tonight, we're meeting to go on record as declaring that our government's adventures in Asia, its pretense that the war is "ended," its bombing

policies and apparently programed massacre of civilians, are not only obscene and immoral, but are in direct violation—do you want to hear this again?—of the Geneva and Hague conventions, both part of our law through Senate ratification; the United Nations Charter prohibiting the bombing of a foreign territory without a declaration of war; the Kellogg-Briand Treaty; the principles of the Nuremberg and Tokyo war crime tribunals; and finally, God help us, in violation even of the Army's Field Manual. We have been war criminals for many years, all in the name of honor, and we are impotent witnesses to the moral disintegration of a very great nation. Look at the millionaires this war has spawned, look at the contempt once-friendly nations hold us in. We have been saying "no," and we have been impotent; we have tried violence, and we have hurt our cause; we have been guilty of civil disobedience, and have been arrested. What is left to us—treason, expatriation, martyrdom?

TV ANNOUNCER *(on screen)*

Shortly after these words were spoken, as he was leaving the auditorium at the University, Dr. Westerman was detained for questioning by the Justice Department. Here, on tape, is a portion of an interview with Dr. Westerman immediately following the preliminary hearing last night, after the arrest.

WESTERMAN *(on screen)*

(The scene is just outside the door of the hearing room, and Westerman is shown with a civilian guard. A number of reporters are surrounding him, shouting questions, and he is speaking mainly to one reporter with a microphone. The crowd is noisy and hectic, but Westerman appears calm and untroubled.)
(To the reporter.) Yes, I believe the hearing is completed for the present.

REPORTER *(on screen)*

Are you free to go home, doctor?

WESTERMAN *(on screen)*

Apparently not. I've refused to post bail, and I take it I'm to spend the night somewhere in this building.

REPORTER *(on screen)*

Are they planning to enforce the new National Interests Act in your case?

WESTERMAN *(on screen)*

I wouldn't be surprised.

REPORTER *(on screen)*

Would that involve a charge of treason?

WESTERMAN *(on screen)*

I believe it might. I am not familiar with the new law in any detail, but my lawyer is busily filling in the gaps for me. I am convinced that the law is a terrible one, and represents a regrettable and probably dangerous turn in our national life.

REPORTER *(on screen)*

Do you still intend to speak in public against the wars in Asia?

WESTERMAN *(on screen)*

(He now speaks to the whole group of reporters, gathered around, as the scene becomes somewhat quieter.) I've written out a statement that I'd like to read, if I may. *(He pulls a rumpled sheet of paper from his pocket.)* "I have been objecting to our Asian military adventures, and to our government's pious defenses of them ever since we first sent troops and bombers to the Asiatic mainland over twenty years ago. As a government advisor I have, up to now, been allowed to disagree with our foreign policy in public. Now, the government has added a corrupt law to a corrupt foreign policy, and has virtually defined any criticism or disagreement as contrary to our national interest, encouraging to

our enemies who might otherwise capitulate or negotiate, weakening of our military effort. In effect, treason. As far as I can tell, disagreement with a government policy, if it can be shown contrary to national interest, has become a capital offense—treason in time of war. If this is what is going on, then something quite tragic has taken place in America. For me, speeches, articles, words of any kind, have ceased to have any effect. I have persuaded no one except perhaps for a few of my students, who hardly needed me to tell them what was obvious. I am, therefore, choosing at this moment, having broken the new law, to begin a period, not of speaking out, but of silence. Both as a means of further disassociating myself from both the secret and open wars we are waging, and as an occasion for taking thought and meditation. I will make no further attempt to explain, to justify my silence, or to defend myself against treason, if that is to be the charge. For a reference, may I suggest the book of the prophet Isaiah, chapter fifty-three, verse seven."

(There is considerable consternation as Westerman concludes. Some reporters rush away with the story; the one he originally spoke to approaches him with his microphone.)

REPORTER *(on screen)*

Dr. Westerman, could you tell us what you expect to accomplish by this means of protest? *(Westerman looks at the reporter kindly, without a flicker of response, and turns to his guard as a signal that he is finished. The scene ends with all the reporters breaking away.)*

TV ANNOUNCER *(on screen)*

The Old Testament passage that Dr. Westerman cited, Isaiah fifty-three, seven, reads as follows: "He was oppressed, and he was afflicted, yet he opened not his mouth; like a lamb that is led to the slaughter and like a sheep that before its shearers is dumb, so he opened not his mouth." I have in the studio this evening, to comment on this event, the Reverend Doctor Roger Rinde, distinguished leader in

the ecumenical movement, chaplain to the United States
Senate, and friend of the President. Dr. Rinde is also a
friend and neighbor of Dr. Westerman. Dr. Rinde, what
do you think about Dr. Westerman's decision to keep
silence, particularly in reference to the Biblical passage?

RINDE *(on screen)*

The decision surprised me, quite frankly. Thomas and I
have often talked about the problems of Asia. We disagree, of course, but I never expected such an extreme act
from him.

TV ANNOUNCER *(on screen)*

Doesn't that Old Testament passage refer to Christ?

RINDE *(on screen)*

That's not quite the way to put it. The passage is from a
section describing the suffering servant who is, in the Old
Testament, a person or a personified nation, whose suffering is supposed to redeem Israel and the world. Christians
have usually taken this figure as being fulfilled in the life
and death of Jesus, but I don't think the author of the
passage is making any prediction about the Messiah.

TV ANNOUNCER *(on screen)*

So you don't feel that Dr. Westerman is in any way
identifying himself with Jesus.

RINDE *(on screen)*

Oh, I hardly think so. Westerman is not a religious man in
any of the usual senses of that word.

TV ANNOUNCER *(on screen)*

Do you agree with his protest?

RINDE *(on screen)*

By no means. He can do whatever he wants, but he seems
to have violated a law and perhaps even committed

treason, and I for one could not countenance anything that breaks a law.

TV ANNOUNCER *(on screen)*
Thank you, Dr. Rinde. Well, there is the Westerman story, as far as we know it tonight. Let me recapitulate. Last night, after addressing a rally at the University, Dr. Thomas Westerman, the Nobel Prize biologist and government advisor, was interrogated by Justice Department officials concerning possible violations of the National Interests Act recently signed into law. After his initial interrogation, he met with reporters and publically made a vow of silence, refusing to defend or justify his position. After spending last night in detention, he was further interrogated, and it is reported that later this evening he will be returned to his home in Georgetown under house arrest. Apparently, further investigations will be . . . *(At this point, Westerman rises from his chair and switches off the videotape recorder. The door to the hall opens, and the guard sticks his head in.)*

GUARD
Hey doctor, somebody from the Department of Justice is on the phone. Do you want to take it here or in the hall? *(Westerman walks out of his study, past the guard without noticing him, starts pulling off his tie, as if going to bed. The guard returns to the phone in the hall.)* No sir, he's not coming to the phone. He's going to bed, I guess. No, not a word, as far as I can tell.

SCENE TWO

A day or two later, afternoon. Dr. Westerman is in his study reading. There is a knock on the door, and the guard shows in a Mr. Strype. He is young, intelligent, probably law school, looking like a New Frontiersman or Nixon junior staffer. He has been assigned the task of discrediting Westerman and breaking his

vow of silence and, if possible, obtaining some sort of retraction.
He begins warily and acts as if he does not expect a reply at first,
pausing just briefly when a reply might be expected. But he is not
accustomed to failure, so at the end of the interview his aplomb
does get somewhat ruffled.

MR. STRYPE

Dr. Westerman, I'm Bill Strype from Justice. Actually, I do
liaison work with State and my special assignment right
now is with some of the legal problems connected with the
new emergency legislation, like the National Interests Act.
(Westerman gives a smile of recognition.) We wanted to be
quite clear that you understood our attitude to your arrest,
why it has taken place, and what is likely to come from the
later hearings. Our government has, as you know, accepted the responsibility for the defense of freedom
throughout the world, and particularly for the military
containment of Chinese and other forms of communism
in Asia. Ever since we sent troops and began to bomb
North Vietnamese military emplacements in North and
South Vietnam some twenty years ago, this has been our
firm policy. We are persuaded that only a show of force,
military force, is capable of dissuading the Chinese, and
their allies, from their expansionist aims. You are perfectly
aware that our commitment in Asia entails a very limited
use of power. No nuclear weapons, no civilian or village
bombing. Specific defensive reactions against guerrilla
troops or supply routes or transportation centers. Restraint, and always the promise to withdraw whenever the
enemy gives evidence that it is willing to withdraw. The
President has often had to resist strenuous pressure from
the Pentagon who have been pushing for an all-out
military victory for many years. We have brought home
our ground troops; our casualties are way down. Vietnam-
ization has largely succeeded. Of course, we have no
intention of going back on our commitments to the
Vietnamese government and people. If we did that, we'd
make a mockery of the sacrifices our young men have

already suffered. But we are not asking for a conventional military victory, only an honorable end to the fighting *(Westerman is interested in Strype's rather moderate line, and notes his assurance. He is interested to see just what approach he plans to take.)*

At one time I myself would have been inclined to support a unilateral withdrawal of our forces, but I have been persuaded by our experts that this would have serious domestic consequences. Look, can you imagine what would happen in this country if we completely withdrew from all the areas where we are fighting? South Vietnam, Laos, Cambodia, Thailand, would all become bloodbaths, and the Communists would easily take over, even if general elections were held. If we pulled out, and if any of these countries went Communist, the radical right in this country would have a field day. We would have become responsible for a series of Communist takeovers, the murder of thousands of friends in Asia, and I suspect we would see a resurgence of the radical right, even neofascism here, that would make the Goldwater or Wallace episodes in the past look like tea parties. A defense of unilateral withdrawal seems to me to play directly into the hands of the right.

(Westerman is fascinated by this point, though not convinced, since he has heard it before. He remains thoughtful and attentive, and might get up from his chair to pour some coffee for both of them, always courteous. Some slight irritation begins to appear in Strype as he continues.)

It seems to me that you intellectuals ought to be more appreciative of our limited use of power. Only power can persuade the Communists, and their national liberation movements, that guerrilla wars cannot succeed, and thus that compromise and negotiation alone can settle the issues. They must be persuaded that military force will still be used, so long as they refuse to withdraw and stall on the Paris talks. This, along with the domestic problem, is why unilateral withdrawal has been rejected. And this is why our overall strategy entails not only the actual use of force, but also the presentation of a national consensus concerning that use. The enemy must not see us as divided in our aims. Now this, quite frankly, raises some problems at precisely the point where your arrest is involved. What is the role of dissent in a society engaged in this sort of complex war? *(Westerman may well appear somewhat sad to see an attractive and able young man committed to such a set of ideas, and he may find his silence a rather frustrating experience at this point.)* Of course, even during wartime, a government needs responsible criticism. Dissent is always the lifeblood of a democracy. And responsible criticism and dissent, I suppose, can be defined as that which lies within the national interest. Now, I do not think that most mass meetings or student demonstrations, particularly those covered by the press and TV, can be defended as appropriate structures of dissent. Ideals have a curious way of serving self-interest, so you must excuse me if I am a little suspicious when college students decide they'd rather not get killed in Asia and defend themselves with high-flown antiwar slogans. Pacifism looks pretty good when the war in question might get you. Our policy is a complex one, then. Limited use of military force, backed by a nation so united that the enemy can never hope for any softening of our national resolve. We are so convinced that this combination of limited force and national unity will shorten the war, and ultimately save lives, that we have reluctantly consented to admit some temporary state-of-emergency legislation, prohibiting certain forms of public criticism of our foreign policy. National interest, for a brief period only, requires a certain limitation of criticism, and a modest expansion of the category of treason. Your address the other evening would have been perfectly appropriate in a classroom, or spoken to a group of friends in this room. But given the setting of the student rally, it fell, unfortunately, under the domain of the new National Interests Act. For the duration of our Asiatic problem, treason is to be defined somewhat more loosely than previously as any public act deliberately undertaken with the purpose of weakening our country's military or psychological posture. Mass meetings of the kind you addressed are not now in the national interest. For however well meant your intentions and however earnest the students may think themselves to be, such meetings actually work against the very goal you and we have in common—the goal of peace with honor. I'm prepared to assume, and I've been instructed to say this to you by my superiors at the Department of Justice, that if your decision to speak at the meeting was made without full knowledge of the detailed provisions of the National Interests Act, we are willing to call off any further hearings, to lift the house arrest, and to let the matter drop. All we'd require is some kind of public disavowal of the more inflammatory portions of your address. *(Here Strype for the first time sees that he is not likely to win. Without replying, Westerman indicates his unequivocal rejection of any deal. Foreseeing his failure, from here to the close of the interview, Strype is less assured and more irritated.)*

Of course, if your address and your support of the student rally was made with reasonable knowledge of the import of the new laws, and if you are not inclined to give us a disclaimer, then the situation becomes more serious. You will have broken a law, encouraged others to do the same, and weakened respect not only for our government of law but for authority in general. I frankly can't see a hell of a lot of difference between lawlessness in the streets and the refined lawlessness of you intellectuals who seem to think you can break any law that doesn't suit you. You seem to feel that your good conscience is the only important fact in the picture. In any case, the situation is now this. If you won't give us the disclaimer we want, then I don't see how we can avoid bringing the provisions of the National Interests Act into play. This may well involve a treason charge, and, in effect, treason in time of war. I trust I need not remind you what sort of punishment generally goes with wartime treason.

(After this threat, Strype looks for some sort of reaction, some weakness from Westerman. Finding none, he walks quickly to the door, knocks for the guard to open it, and quickly leaves.

Westerman remains, reflective. We shift to the hall, outside the study door, as Strype is leaving the house. Mrs. Westerman meets Strype in the hall.)

MR. STRYPE

Mrs. Westerman?

MRS. WESTERMAN

Yes.

MR. STRYPE

Your husband is a very difficult man.

MRS. WESTERMAN

I rather expected you'd find him so.

MR. STRYPE

He is in trouble, you know.

MRS. WESTERMAN

Yes, we know that. *(She sees him out the front door, and goes over to the study door, indicating to the guard that she'd like to be let in. She goes in, and the scene shifts back to the study. She goes up to her husband with some quiet gesture of affection. He speaks to her, since vows of silence, they have decided, ought not to apply to wives.)*
How did it go? Was that the man from Justice?

DR. WESTERMAN

Yes. He was quite effective.

MRS. WESTERMAN

What's going to happen?

DR. WESTERMAN

He offered to drop the proceedings if I would make a public retraction of what he called the more inflammatory parts of my talk.

MRS. WESTERMAN

And if not—

DR. WESTERMAN

Just some dark hints about bringing the full force of the law to bear.

MRS. WESTERMAN

Are you sure you want to go on with this, Thomas? I'm a little frightened.

DR. WESTERMAN

I am too, my dear. And I know this whole business is going to be harder on you than on me. But if I thought you weren't with me—

MRS. WESTERMAN

It's all right. I just feel a little shut out and irrelevant. The usual woman's complaint. Was it difficult not to answer back?

DR. WESTERMAN

At first, but it got easier. You know, it is almost as awkward to speak to you now as it was to keep silence when Syrype was here. I feel as if those few words I do speak should be chosen with great care. I need you, I see, both to help me keep silence, and to help me break it. Silence by itself is terribly lonely, and often exhilarating. I realize I still need to be assured that I'm doing the right thing. You know, the phrase that kept haunting me all afternoon was Pascal's terrible cry, "the silence of these infinite spaces terrifies me."

SCENE THREE

A few days later, late afternoon. Westerman is sitting in his study listening to some music on his tape recorder, jazz piano perhaps.

Without a knock, the guard opens the study door, and Dr. Rinde enters. Rinde is the churchman and friend of Westerman's we have already met in the television interview in scene one. Westerman turns the music down, but not off, and greets his friend silently.

DR. RINDE

Hello, Thomas. I brought along your mail from the University. No one had collected it since the arrest. I—I thought I'd just look in to see how things are going. *(He refers to the pile of mail he has just brought.)* You might be interested in the *Time* and *Newsweek* stories on your arrest. Not too flattering. *(He leafs through a magazine, and reads:)* "Can a Secular Man Play Jesus?" *(The lack of response makes him uneasy.)* You're probably going to have dinner soon, and I don't want to bother you. *(Westerman waves him to a seat, or gives him some assurance to set him at ease, to show he is glad to see a friend. But Rinde is not at ease.)* I should confess, Thomas, that this visit isn't wholly personal. I've had several calls from the Attorney General's office in the last day or two. I need hardly tell you that they're upset at what they call your uncooperative attitude. I tried to explain to them that your silence was not just surliness or publicity-seeking, but a real attempt to make a point, however one might disagree with it. *(There are awkward pauses before nearly every sentence now.)* Thomas, I don't understand what you think you're doing. You're in real trouble. They are a bit embarrassed that the new law has to go to work on someone of your stature right off the bat, but if you think that your distinguished name will get you off the hook you're mistaken. They're preparing an indictment, and no one can guarantee what sort of punishment may be involved if you're found guilty. Do you understand what I'm saying? Can I make some appeal to your responsibility to Jean and the children? Or to your research and teaching? If I could only persuade you how serious matters really are!

(Westerman wants to show that he is listening, and that he is

*grateful even for the rather stiff show of affection from a friend.
He crosses to him, touches him on the shoulder, and walks past
him to the window. Rinde now sees that he will have no effect in
breaking the vow of silence by appeals to friendship. So he
changes his attack, slightly.)*

Thomas. Some of us are wondering about the psychological implications of all this. That Old Testament passage and all this talk in the press about Jesus complexes.
And this silence, your refusal to defend yourself, your
stubbornness in turning down the most generous com-
promises. Look. I've just received some pretty firm assurances, from quite high up, that if you would offer a
private retraction of your university address, and promise
to stay away from peace rallies for twelve months, the
demand for a public retraction will be dropped and the
investigation will be quietly shelved. There is some feeling
at Justice that the initial arrest was perhaps a bit over-
enthusiastic, and they'd like just a little help from you in
getting off the hook. Dammit, Thomas, they don't want to
prosecute, but they don't much like your forcing them to
do so. *(Rinde's voice is uneasy, perhaps threatened, not quite
angry.)* Are you out for martyrdom? It really doesn't
become you. Have you thought that the man who thinks
he is a martyr may turn out to be a self-righteous prig? Are
you so sure that you are right and the rest of us immoral
time-servers?

*(Westerman looks carefully at Rinde to see if he knows that he
has projected his own guilt onto him. He sees a man who knows
that he has compromised his beliefs and his profession for some
years, and who probably will never forgive Westerman for
bringing this awareness in the open. There is a long pause here as
the flustered Rinde tries to determine the effect of his attack.
Westerman is calm, but uneasy mainly because Rinde is so
uneasy. Westerman walks over to his audiotape player and turns
up the jazz music that has been playing low throughout this scene.
He does this not to dismiss Rinde, but to give him an excuse to
leave if he wants it. He does, and Rinde picks up the cue.)*

I must go, Thomas, I shouldn't have come. I can't stand

it in here. It's too . . . unreal. Something frightening has
happened to you. You're not only stubborn and wrong; I
think you're a little mad. The martyr's mantle doesn't
become you; you're communicating nothing, you're bearing witness to nothing, you're throwing away the work of a
lifetime, and doing violence to yourself, your family, and
(painfully) your friends. *(Rinde quickly leaves, after the business of knocking on the study door for the guard to open it. The
door to the hall is left open; the study is quite dark in the late
afternoon, the hall is brightly lit. We hear Rinde leaving by the
front door of the house; Mrs. Westerman enters the study and the
study door is closed. Westerman is standing at the window,
watching Rinde leave, clearly moved by Rinde's visit and
outburst. His wife stands beside him, and he speaks, partly to
himself and partly to her.)*

DR. WESTERMAN

I'm loveless, I'm a fool. I'm wrong. I don't care about you.
I have a martyr complex, and I've committed treason. Yet I
know I'm not wrong. I certainly don't feel as if I've
rejected you. And I simply have never worried about
martyr complexes. Perhaps I am a fool, that may be
needed now. Perhaps I have committed treason, perhaps
that's what I meant to do all along. I can't turn back. *(To
his wife.)* Do you understand? *(Mrs. Westerman's response is
ambiguous. She wants to indicate her full support, yet there is a
bewilderment or bitterness somewhere that she is afraid to
articulate. She leaves it unspoken, but he sees it and is worried.)*
Forgive them all, even though they know what they're
doing. *(They stand together for a moment at the window, Dr.
Westerman rapt and remote. She touches him on the arm, and
leaves him alone in the study.)*

VII

Self

In the fateful, epoch-announcing words of Nietzsche's Zarathustra: "Dead are all the gods." One knows the tale; it has been told a thousand ways. It is the hero-cycle of the modern age, the wonder-story of mankind's coming to maturity. The spell of the past, the bondage of tradition, was shattered with sure and mighty strokes. The dream-web of myth fell away. . . .

It is not only that there is no hiding place for the gods from the searching telescope and microscope; there is no such society any more as the gods once supported. The social unit is not a carrier of religious content, but an economic-political organization. Its ideals are not those of the hieratic pantomime, making visible on earth the forms of heaven, but of the secular state, in hard and unremitting competition for material supremacy and resources. . . .

The problem of mankind today, therefore, is precisely the opposite to that of men in the comparatively stable periods of those great co-ordinating mythologies which now are known as lies. Then all meaning was in the group, in the great anonymous forms, none in the self-expressive individual; today no meaning is in the group—none in the world: all is in the individual. . . .

The hero-deed to be wrought is not today what it was in the century of Galileo. Where then there was darkness, now there is light; but also, where light was, there now is darkness. The modern hero-deed must be that of questing to bring to light again the lost Atlantis of the co-ordinated soul.

Obviously, this work cannot be wrought by turning back, or away, from what has been accomplished by the modern revolution; for the problem is nothing if not that of rendering the modern world spiritually significant—or rather (phrasing the same principle the other way round) nothing if not that of making it possible for men and women to come to full human maturity through the conditions of contemporary life. . . . The national idea, with the flag as totem, is today an aggrandizer of the nursery ego, not the annihilator of an infantile situation. Its parody-rituals of the parade ground serve the ends of Holdfast, the tyrant dragon, not the God in whom self-interest is annihilate. And the numerous saints of this anticult—namely the patriots whose ubiquitous photographs, draped with flags, serve as official icons—are precisely the local threshold guardians (our demon Sticky-hair) whom it is the first problem of the hero to surpass.

Nor can the great world religions, as at present understood, meet the requirement. For they have become associated with the causes of the factions, as instruments of propaganda and self-congratulation. (Even Buddhism has lately suffered this degradation, in reaction to the lessons of the West.) The universal triumph of the secular state has thrown all religious organizations into such a definitely secondary, and finally ineffectual, position that religious pantomime is hardly more today than a sanctimonious exercise for Sunday morning, whereas business ethics and patriotism stand for the remainder of the week. Such a monkey-holiness is not what the functioning world requires; rather, a transmutation of the whole social order is necessary, so that through every detail and act of secular life the vitalizing image of the universal god-man who is actually immanent and effective in all of us may be somehow made known to consciousness. . . .

But there is one thing we may know, namely, that as the new symbols become visible, they will not be identical in the various parts of the globe; the circumstances of local life, race, and tradition must all be compounded in the effective forms. Therefore, it is necessary for men to understand, and be able to see, that through various symbols the same redemption is revealed. "Truth is one," we read in the Vedas; "the sages call it by many names." A single song is being inflected through all the colorations of the human choir. General propaganda for one or another of the local solutions, therefore, is superfluous—or much rather, a menace. The way to become human is to learn to recognize the lineaments of God in all of the wonderful modulations of the face of man. . . .

The descent of the Occidental sciences from the heavens to the earth (from seventeenth-century astronomy to nineteenth-century biology), and their concentration today, at last, on man himself (in twentieth-century anthropology and psychology), mark the part of a prodigious transfer of the focal point of human wonder. Not the animal world, not the plant world, not the miracle of the spheres, but man himself is now the crucial mystery. Man is that alien presence with whom the forces of egoism must come to terms, through whom the ego is to be crucified and resurrected, and in whose image society is to be reformed. Man, understood however not as "I" but as "Thou": for the ideals and temporal institutions of no tribe, race, continent, social class, or century, can be the measure of the inexhaustible and multifariously wonderful divine existence that is the life in all of us.

The modern hero, the modern individual who dares to heed the call and seek the mansion of that presence with whom it is our whole destiny to be atoned, cannot, indeed must not, wait for his community to cast off its slough of pride, fear, rationalized avarice, and sanctified misunderstanding. "Live," Nietzsche says, "as though the day were here." It is not society that is to guide and save the creative hero, but precisely the reverse. And so every one of us shares the supreme ordeal—carries the cross of the redeemer—not in the bright moments of his tribe's great victories, but in the silences of his personal despair.

—Joseph Campbell, *The Hero with a Thousand Faces*
(Bollingen Series XVII, 1949, pp. 387–391)

In every age man faces a pervasive theme which defies his engagement and yet must be engaged. In Freud's day it was sexuality and moralism. Now it is unlimited technological violence and absurd death. We do well to name the threat and to analyze its

components. But our need is to go further, to create
new psychic and social forms to enable us to reclaim
not only our technologies, but our very imaginations,
in the service of the continuity of life.
     —Robert Jay Lifton, *Death in Life, Survivors of
Hiroshima* (Random House, New York, 1967, p. 54)

"New consciousness," "a consciousness revolution,"
"Protean man," "the counterculture." The issue suggested
by these phrases has been with us for nearly a decade. For
a while, in the early sixties, it was hidden, hinted-at,
thought about by some teachers and parents, written
about in occasional articles, academic and journalistic.
Then, somewhere around 1969, the counterculture became a media event and books, cover stories, articles—
praise, blame, and ambivalence in equal measure—flowed
into our living rooms. Theodore Roszak, Charles Reich,
Jean-François Revel, and William Irwin Thompson became our definitive guides through the media or fashion-
able phase of this complex event. George Steiner even
connected the new consciousness to the death of God.

> If the gamble on transcendence no longer seems worth
> the odds and we are moving into a utopia of the
> immediate, the value-structure of our civilization will
> alter, after at least three millennia, in ways almost
> unforeseeable. [*Bluebeard's Castle*, Yale University Press,
> 1971, p. 93.]

But media events die almost as fast as they get born.
This has already been the case with "the death of God"
and with "making the university more responsive to
human needs." The new consciousness and the counterculture are now on a downward spiral, and we can even
begin to talk about the "unmaking of the counterculture,"
the "decline of the new consciousness," the "end" of
Protean man. Indeed, we may even expect the end of the

counterculture to become itself a media event as interesting as its beginning. We have already experienced the zonked-out despair of Haight-Ashbury and Telegraph Avenue.

In 1969, the first Whole Earth Catalog appeared, with its statement of purpose on the inside front cover: "We *are* as gods and might as well get good at it."* All right. As a response to the death of God, that sounded plausible, and—in 1969—we almost took it seriously. But in 1972, when *The Last Whole Earth Catalog* appeared, with the same ringing statement of purpose, what had appeared plausible before somehow became either archaic and camp, or frightful. We remembered how Woodstock became Altamont, how Janis Joplin and Jimi Hendrix died, how Charles Manson had become a god, knowing good and evil. Today we see the mute despair overtaking the new consciousness, we watch economic anxiety cutting into the celebration of life. And we recall Camus's almost forgotten words: "In order to be a man, I refuse to be a god."

But it is the nature of a media event to die. Perhaps now we can begin to sort out what the new consciousness really means. Only when an event is liberated from its media phase can it be understood. Prior to that liberation, everything is gossip or journalism. But even media events leave, sometimes, a genuine deposit behind, and so it may be time to ask ourselves just what we have learned from the rise and fall of the counterculture.

It is not the right time, nor do I have the expertise, to

---

*Surely the Jesus movement (as well as the Children of God, Hare Krishnas, and the Divine Light Mission) lies dormant in these words. Midwestern and Southern fundamentalism had to join together with California hip culture, as improbable as it seemed at the time. Peter Marin's stunning analysis of the new Jesus is already an important document interpreting the decline of the counterculture ("Children of Yearning," *Saturday Review*, May 6, 1972). It is instructive to compare the mood of euphoria captured in the documents from the period I am studying with Marin's vivid portrait of demoralization and despair retreating into passivity and silence. Yet, for all that, Marin's response to the consciousness revolution is by no means purely negative. Our new consciousness, he writes, "has not released us from the demons of the age but has simply brought us face to face with them."

offer a full explanation of that rise and fall. What I propose here is something more modest. I have tried to assemble some of the relevant texts from the early, pre-media explosion, pre–Charles Reich phase of the movement. A chrestomathy, if you like, from the 1960s (and before) to offer a perspective and some evidence as a contribution to the larger task of interpretation that still remains to be done.

At the close of the chapter, after the texts have been assembled, my own response to the problem of religion and the new consciousness will be in the form of a tale, a short story.

A. SOME BACKGROUND PREPARATIONS

With William Blake we must begin. Death of God, radical politics, new consciousness—many things today seem to begin with him. The following are the "Proverbs of Hell" from "The Marriage of Heaven and Hell," and they will do as well as anything to remind us why we seem to be rereading him.

> In seed time learn, in harvest teach, in winter enjoy.
> Drive your cart and your plow over the bones of the dead.
> The road of excess leads to the palace of wisdom.
> Prudence is a rich ugly old maid courted by Incapacity.
> He who desires but acts not, breeds pestilence.
> The cut worm forgives the plow.
> Dip him in the river who loves water.
> A fool sees not the same tree that a wise man sees.
> He whose face gives no light, shall never become a star.
> Eternity is in love with the productions of time.
> The busy bee has no time for sorrow.
> The hours of folly are measur'd by the clock, but of wisdom: no clock can measure.
> All wholesome food is caught without a net or a trap.
> Bring out number, weight & measure in a year of dearth.
> No bird soars too high, if he soars with his own wings.

A dead body revenges not injuries.

The most sublime act is to set another before you.

If the fool would persist in his folly he would become wise.

Folly is the cloke of knavery.

Shame is Pride's cloke.

Prisons are built with stones of Law, Brothels with bricks of Religion.

The pride of the peacock is the glory of God.

The lust of the goat is the bounty of God.

The wrath of the lion is the wisdom of God.

The nakedness of woman is the work of God.

Excess of sorrow laughs. Excess of joy weeps.

The roaring of lions, the howling of wolves, the raging of the stormy sea, and the destructive sword, are portions of eternity too great for the eye of man.

The fox condemns the trap, not himself.

Joys impregnate. Sorrows bring forth.

Let man wear the fell of the lion, woman the fleece of the sheep.

The bird a nest, the spider a web, man friendship.

The selfish, smiling fool, and the sullen, frowning fool shall be both thought wise, that they may be a rod.

What is now proved was once only imagin'd.

The rat, the mouse, the fox, the rabbet watch the roots, the lion, the tyger, the horse, the elephant, watch the fruits.

The cistern contains: the fountain overflows.

One thought fills immensity.

Always be ready to speak your mind, and a base man will avoid you.

Every thing possible to be believ'd is an image of truth.

The eagle never lost so much time as when he submitted to learn of the crow.

The fox provides for himself, but God provides for the lion.

Think in the morning. Act in the noon. Eat in the evening. Sleep in the night.

He who has suffer'd you to impose on him, knows you.

As the plow follows words, so God rewards prayers.

The tygers of wrath are wiser than the horses of instruction.

Expect poison from the standing water.

You never know what is enough unless you know what is more than enough.

Listen to the fool's reproach! it is a kingly title!

The eyes of fire, the nostrils of air, the mouth of water, the beard of earth.

The weak in courage is strong in cunning.

The apple tree never asks the beech how he shall grow; nor the lion, the horse, how he shall take his prey.

The thankful reciever bears a plentiful harvest.

If others had not been foolish, we should be so.

The soul of sweet delight can never be defil'd.

When thou seest an Eagle, thou seest a portion of Genius; lift up thy head!

As the caterpiller chooses the fairest leaves to lay her eggs on, so the priest lays his curse on the fairest joys.

To create a little flower is the labour of ages.

Damn braces. Bless relaxes.

The best wine is the oldest, the best water the newest.

Prayers plow not! Praises reap not!

Joys laugh not! Sorrows weep not!

The head Sublime, the heart Pathos, the genitals Beauty, the hands & feet Proportion.

As the air to a bird or the sea to a fish, so is contempt to the contemptible.

The crow wish'd every thing was black, the owl that every thing was white.

Exuberance is Beauty.

If the lion was advised by the fox, he would be cunning.

Improvement makes strait roads; but the crooked roads without Improvement are roads of Genius.

Sooner murder an infant in its cradle than nurse unacted desires.

Where man is not, nature is barren.

Truth can never be told so as to be understood, and not be believ'd.

Enough! or Too much.

There was so much of the anti-Apollo, so much of the Dionysian, in the new spirituality, that it is well to recall Nietzsche's definition in *The Birth of Tragedy* of the Dionysian experience as that moment in which "the state and society, and, in general, the gaps between man and man give way to an overwhelming feeling of oneness which leads back to the very heart of nature." And Norman Brown's definition:

> Dionysus does not observe the limit, but overflows; for him the road of excess leads to the palace of wisdom; Nietzsche says that those who suffer from an overfullness of life want a Dionysian art. Hence *he does not negate any more*. This, say Nietzsche, is the essence of the Dionysian faith. Instead of negating, he affirms the dialectical unity of the great instinctual opposites: Dionysus reunifies male and female, Self and Other, life and death. . . . Nietzsche was right in saying that the Apollonian preserves, the Dionysian destroys, self-consciousness. [*Life Against Death*, p. 175.]

It is obvious why Charles Baudelaire should find his way to this point. The following is a passage from his work "The Poem of Hashish" (1860; *My Heart Laid Bare and Other Writings*, ed. Peter Quennell, Weidenfeld and Nicholson, London, 1950).

> Let us now see what happens to such a personality when driven to desperate extremes by hashish. Let us follow the procession of the human imagination to its last and most magnificent altar, to the individual's belief in his own godhead. . . . Shall I explain how, under the dominion of the poison, our man soon makes himself the centre of the universe? How he becomes a living and outrageous personification of the proverb which says that desire knows no barriers? He believes in his own virtue and genius: can the end not be guessed? All surrounding objects are so many suggestions provoking in him a world of thought, all more highly coloured, more vivid and more subtle than ever before and clad in a veneer of magic. "These magnificent cities," he tells himself, "with their superb buildings echelonned as if on a stage—these handsome ships swaying on the waters of the harbour in nostalgic idleness, seeming to express my very thought: 'When shall we set out for happiness?'—these museums crammed with lively shapes and intoxicating

colours—these libraries where all the works of Science and the dreams of the Muses are assembled—these massed instruments speaking with a single voice—these enchanting women, made still more charming by the science of self-adornment and the demureness of their glances—all these things were created for me, for me, for me! For me humanity has worked, been martyrised and immolated—to provide pasture, pabulum to my implacable appetite for emotion, knowledge and beauty!"

Let us hasten on and cut the story short. Nobody will be surprised that a final, supreme thought bursts from the dreamer's brain: "I have become God!"; that a wild and ardent shout breaks from his bosom with such force, such projectile power that, if the wishes and beliefs of a drunken man had any effective virtue, this shout would bowl over the angels scattered on the paths of Heaven: "I am a God!"

Coming closer to our time, yet still part of the background, the following extracts seem to belong.

And Jesus was risen flesh-and-blood. He rose a man on earth to live on earth. The greatest test was still before him: His life as a man on earth. Hitherto He had been a sacred child, a teacher, a messiah, but never a full man. New, risen from the dead, He rises to be a man on earth, and live His life of the flesh, the great life, among other men. This is the image of our inward state to-day.

This is the image of the young: the Risen Lord. The teaching is over, the sacrifice is made, the salvation is accomplished. Now comes the true life, man living his full life on earth, as flowers live their full life, without rhyme or reason except the magnificence of coming forth into fulness.

If Jesus rose from the dead in triumph, a man on earth triumphant in renewed flesh, triumphant over the mechanical anti-life convention of Jewish priests, Roman despotism, and universal money-lust; triumphant above all over His own self-absorption, self-

consciousness, self-importance; triumphant and free
as a man in full flesh and full, final experience, even
the accomplished acceptance of His own death; a man
at last full and free in flesh and soul, a man at one with
death; then He rose to become at one with life, to live
the great life of the flesh and the soul together, as
peonies or foxes do, in their lesser way. If Jesus rose as
a full man, in full flesh and soul, then He rose to take a
woman to Himself, to live with her, and to know the
tenderness and blossoming of the twoness with her; He
who had been hitherto so limited to His oneness, or
His universality, which is the same thing. If Jesus rose
in the full flesh, He rose to know the tenderness of a
woman, and the great pleasure of her, and to have
children by her. He rose to know the responsibility and
the peculiar delight of children, and also the exaspera-
tion and nuisance of them. If Jesus rose as a full man,
in the flesh, He rose to have friends, to have a
man-friend whom He would hold sometimes to His
breast, in strong affection, and who would be dearer to
Him than a brother, just out of the sheer mystery of
sympathy. And how much more wonderful, this, than
having disciples! If Jesus rose a full man in the flesh,
He rose to do His share in the world's work, something
He really liked doing. And if He remembered His first
life, it would neither be teaching nor preaching, but
probably carpentering again, with joy, among the
shavings. If Jesus rose a full man in the flesh, He rose
to continue His fight with the hard-boiled convention-
alists like Roman judges and Jewish priests and
money-makers of every sort. [D. H. Lawrence, "The
Risen Lord," from *Assorted Articles*, Random House,
New York, 1930.]

The cultural era is past. The new civilization, which
may take centuries or a few thousand years to usher in,
will not be *another* civilization—it will be the open
stretch of realization which all the past civilizations
have pointed to. The city, which was the birth-place of
civilization, such as we know it to be, will exist no more.
There will be nuclei of course, but they will be mobile

and fluid. The peoples of the earth will no longer be
shut off from one another within states but will flow
freely over the surface of the earth and intermingle.
There will be no fixed constellations of human aggre-
gates. Governments will give way to management,
using the word in a broad sense. The politician will
become as superannuated as the dodo bird. The
machine will never be dominated, as some imagine; it
will be scrapped, eventually, but not before men have
understood the nature of the mystery which binds
them to their creation. The worship, investigation and
subjugation of the machine will give way to the lure of
all that is truly occult. This problem is bound up with
the larger one of power—and of possession. Man will
be forced to realize that power must be kept open,
fluid, and free. His aim will be not to possess power but
to radiate it. [Henry Miller, *Sunday After the War*, New
Directions, New York, 1944, pp. 154–155.]

B. TWO LITERARY CRITICS SEE IT COMING

In the years just before we began to talk directly about
the new consciousness, literary critics began to engage the
problem of the modern as a special problem. This was the
time, prior to the serious disturbances on the college
campuses, when the demand for relevance was being
raised by students in a relatively modest way. Two literary
critics of great distinction responded to this demand, and
through their words we can see the more radical demands
for a new consciousness taking shape. The importance of
Lionel Trilling and Irving Howe is that they are both
ambivalent about the new environment in which literature
is studied, both deeply uneasy with the idea of literature as
salvation or guide to life.

The fact is that the student today is at liberty to choose
between two cultural environments. One of them can
no doubt be described in terms not unlike those that
Sidgwick and Arnold used of the class-bound England

of a century ago—it is perhaps less proud and less self-praising but we can take it to be Philistine and dull, satisfied with its unexamined, unpromised beliefs. The other environment defines itself by its difference from and its antagonism to the first, by its commitment to the "sources of life," by its adherence to the imagination of fullness, freedom, and potency of life, and to what goes with this imagination, the concern with moralized taste and with the styles which indicate that one has successfully gained control of the sources of life or which are themselves a means of gaining that control.

As thus described, the second environment would seem to be the more appealing of the two. It is here that art resides, and where art is, life is—surely that is true? But as we watch the development of the second cultural environment, we become less and less certain that it is entirely free of the traits that we reprobate in the first, which may have led us to wish to unfit our students for it. This second environment must always have *some* ethical or spiritual advantage over the first, if only because, even though its influence and its personnel do indeed grow apace, it will never have the actual rule of the world; if its personnel sometimes dreams of rule, it yet knows that it would become bored by the dreary routine that rulers must submit to: the blame for the ugly actualities of rule will therefore always rest on Philistine shoulders. But as our students find it ever easier to take their places in the second cultural environment, as they are ever surer of finding comfort and companions in it, we have to see that it shows the essential traits of any cultural environment: firm presuppositions, received ideas, approved attitudes, and a system of rewards and punishments. The student who decides to enter this second environment, if he considers it from the distance of some provincial city or town, or of a family strong in whatever class feelings it may have, may understandably take his steps toward it in a dramatic mood, in the belief that he ventures into the uncharted fearsome territory of freedom. In point of fact, as his teachers must know if they have any right sense of our life at the present time, he is joining one of the two established cultural parties. If the one he has chosen is in the minority, the party of opposition, this has its recognized advantages. . . .

But some teachers will not be content to see things so. If they believe that education has the power (and duty) to act as "a counter to the trivializing forces of our society," they may feel that the teaching of literature is no longer able to bring that power to bear. If they are aware of the existence of the two environments, they may even be disposed to think that in the very structure of the second there exists a trivializing force. And although these teachers may feel this the more in the degree that the curriculum responds to the demand, made in the interests of "relevance" and "immediacy", that it deal with modern literature, they will not easily recognize this connection or, recognizing it, they will be puzzled to account for it if they are themselves young or relatively young people who have responded strongly to the great classic literature of modern times. The literature itself is not trivial. But there has grown out of this literature, or around it, a cultural environment which might well lead some serious teachers to think twice before undertaking to prepare their students to enter it. . . .

Modern literature (it need scarcely be said again) is directed toward moral and spiritual renovation; its subject is damnation and salvation. It is a literature of doctrine which, although often concealed, is very aggressive. The occasions are few when criticism has met this doctrine on its own fierce terms. Of modern criticism it can be said that it has instructed us in an intelligent passivity before the beneficent aggression of literature. Attributing to literature virtually angelic powers, it has passed the word to the readers of literature that the one thing you do not do when you meet an angel is wrestle with him. [Lionel Trilling, *Beyond Culture*, The Viking Press, New York, 1965, pp. 226–228, 228–229, 231.]

Let me push ahead a bit further, and list several traits of "the modern hero," though not in the delusion

that any fictional character fulfills all or even most of
them:

The modern hero is a man who believes in the
necessity of action; he wishes, in the words of Malraux,
to put "a scar on the map." Yet the moral impulsions
that lead him to believe in action, also render him unfit
for action. He becomes dubious about the value of
inflicting scars and is not sure he can even locate the
map.

He knows that traditionally the hero is required to
act out the part of bravery, but he discovers that his
predicament requires courage. Bravery signifies a
mode of action, courage a mode of being. And since he
finds it difficult to reconcile the needs of action with
those of being, he must learn that to summon courage
he will have to abandon bravery. His sense of the
burden he must carry brings him close to the situation
described by William James: "Heroism is always on a
precipitous edge, and only keeps alive by running.
Every moment is an escape."

He knows that the hero can act with full power only
if he commands, for his followers and himself, an
implicit belief in the meaningfulness of the human
scheme. But the more he commits himself to the
gestures of heroism, the more he is persuaded of the
absurdity of existence. Gods do not speak to him,
prophets do not buoy him, nor doctrines assuage him.

The classical hero moved in a world charged with a
sense of purpose. In the early bourgeois era, the belief
in purpose gave way to a belief in progress. This the
hero managed to survive, if only because he often saw
through the joke of progress. But now his problem is
to live in a world that has moved beyond the idea of
progress: and that is hard.

The modern hero often begins with the expectation
of changing the world. But after a time his central
question becomes: can I change myself? He asks, in the
words of Hermann Hesse's Demian, "I wanted only to
try to live in obedience to the promptings which came
from my true self. Why was that so very difficult?"

If the modern hero decides the world is beyond

changing, he may try, as in the novels of Hemingway, to create a hermetic world of his own in which an unhappy few live by a self-willed code that makes possible—they tell themselves—struggle, renewal, and honorable defeat.

Still, the modern hero often continues to believe in the quest, and sometimes in the grail too; only he is no longer persuaded that quest is necessarily undertaken through public action and he is unsure as to where the grail can be found. If he happens to be an American named Jay Gatsby, he may even look for it on the shores of Long Island. There is reason to believe that this is a mistake.

The modern hero moves from the heroic deed to the heroism of consciousness, a heroism often available only in defeat. He comes as a conqueror and stays as a pilgrim. And in consciousness he seeks those moral ends which the hero is traditionally said to have found through the deed. He learns, in the words of Kyo Gisors in Malraux's *Man's Fate*, that "a man resembles his suffering."

The modern hero discovers that he cannot be a hero. Yet only through his readiness to face the consequences of this discovery can he salvage a portion of the heroic. . . .

In its multiplicity and brilliant confusion, its commitment to an aesthetic of endless renewal—in its improvisation of "the tradition of the new," a paradox envisaging the limit of *limitlessness*—modernism is endlessly open to portraiture and analysis. For just as some of its greatest works strain toward a form freed from beginning or end, so modernism strains toward a life without fixity or conclusion. If, nevertheless, there is in literary modernism a dominant preoccupation which the writer must either subdue or by which he will surely be destroyed, that is the specter of nihilism. [Irving Howe, "The Idea of the Modern" in *Literary Modernism*, edited by Irving Howe, Fawcett Premier Book, New York, 1967, pp. 35–37.]

Trilling and Howe are surely correct in discerning a religious nihilism latent in the needs and demands of the young they have so faithfully instructed. In the new consciousness, both the religious and the nihilistic elements came to the fore. Religion and nihilism, in classroom or street, are threatening enough separately, but when they come together, we will not be surprised to find something like a revolutionary situation at hand.

Irving Howe has been a particularly interesting observer of the emerging alternative culture. He is a stern critic of it, but he does not distort his description to make criticism easier. At the close of his 1968 article on the New York intellectuals, he puts together some observations on the new breed.

> There is a rising younger generation of intellectuals: ambitious, self-assured, at ease with prosperity while conspicuously alienated, unmarred by the traumas of the totalitarian age, bored with memories of defeat, and attracted to the idea of power. This generation matters, thus far, not so much for its leading figures and their meager accomplishments, but for the political–cultural style—what I shall call the new sensibility—it thrusts into absolute opposition both to the New York writers and to other groups. It claims not to seek penetration into, or accommodation with, our cultural and academic institutions; it fancies the prospect of a harsh generational fight; and given the premise with which it begins—that everything touched by older men reeks of betrayal—its claims and fancies have a sort of propriety. It proposes a revolution, I would call it a counterrevolution, in sensibility. Though linked to New Left politics, it goes beyond any politics, making itself felt, like a spreading blot of anti-intellectualism, in every area of intellectual life. Not yet fully cohered, this new cultural group cannot yet be fully defined, nor is it possible fully to describe its projected sensibility, since it declares itself through a refusal of both coherence and definition. . . .
>
> The new intellectual style, insofar as it approximates a politics, mixes sentiments of anarchism with apologies for authoritarianism; bubbling hopes for "participatory democracy" with manipulative elitism; un-

qualified populist majoritarianism with the reign of the cadres. . . .

Perhaps the most sophisticated and currently popular of anti-democratic notions is that advanced by Herbert Marcuse: his contempt for tolerance on the ground that it is a veil for subjection, a rationale for maintaining the *status quo*, and his consequent readiness to suppress "regressive" elements of the population lest they impede social "liberation." . . .

In the *Kulturkampf* now emerging there are issues more consequential than the political ones, issues that have to do with basic views concerning the nature of human life.

One of these has been with us for a long time, and trying now to put it into simple language, I feel a measure of uneasiness, as if it were bad form to violate the tradition of antinomianism in which we have all been raised.

What, for "emancipated" people, is the surviving role of moral imperatives, or at least moral recommendation? Do these retain for us a shred of sanctity or at least of coercive value? . . . Do moral principles continue to signify insofar as and if they come into conflict with spontaneous impulses, and more urgently still, can we conceive of moral principles retaining some validity if they do come into conflict with spontaneous impulses? Are we still to give credit to the idea, one of the few meeting-points between traditional Christianity and modern Freudianism, that there occurs and must occur a deep-seated clash between instinct and civilization, nature and nurture, or can we now, with a great sigh of collective relief, dismiss this as still another hangup, perhaps the supreme hangup, of Western civilization? . . .

By contrast, the emerging new sensibility rests on a vision of innocence: an innocence through a refusal of our and perhaps any other culture, an innocence not even to be preceded by the withering away of the state, since in this view of things the state could wither away only if men learned so to be at ease with their desires, all need for regulation would fade. . . .

The new sensibility posits a theory that might be called *the psychology of unobstructed need*: men should satisfy those needs which are theirs, organic to their bodies and psyches, and to do this they now must learn to discard or destroy all those obstructions, mostly the result of cultural neurosis, which keep them from satisfying their needs. . . .

The new sensibility is impatient with ideas. It is impatient with literary structures of complexity and coherence, only yesterday the catchwords of our criticism. It wants instead works of literature—though literature may be the wrong word—that will be as absolute as the sun, as unarguable as orgasm, and as delicious as a lollipop. It schemes to throw off the weight of nuance and ambiguity, legacies of high consciousness and tired blood. It is weary of the habit of reflection, the making of distinctions, the squareness of dialectic, the tarnished gold of inherited wisdom. It cares nothing for the haunted memories of old Jews. It has no taste for the ethical nail-biting of those writers of the Left who suffered defeat and could never again accept the narcotic of certainty. It is sick of those magnifications of irony that Mann gave us, sick of those visions of entrapment to which Kafka led us, sick of those shufflings of daily horror and grace that Joyce left us. It breathes contempt for rationality, impatience with mind, and a hostility to the artifices and decorums of high culture. It despises liberal values, liberal cautions, liberal virtues. It is bored with the past: for the past is a fink.

Where Marx and Freud were diggers of intellect, mining deeper and deeper into society and the psyche, and forever determined to strengthen the dominion of reason, today the favored direction of search is not inward but sideways, an "expansion of consciousness" through the kick of drugs. The new sensibility is drawn to images of sickness, but not, as with the modernist masters, out of dialectical canniness or religious blasphemy; it takes their denials literally and does not even know the complex desperations that led them to deny. It seeks to charge itself into dazzling sentience through chemicals and the rhetoric of violence. It gropes for sensations: the innocence of blue, the ejaculations of red. It *ordains* life's simplicity. It chooses surfaces as against relationships, the skim of texture rather than the weaving of pattern. Haunted by boredom, it transforms art into a sequence of shocks which, steadily magnified, yield fewer and fewer thrills, so that simply to maintain a modest *frisson* requires mounting exertions. [Irving Howe, *Decline of the New*, Harcourt, Brace, and World, New York, n.d., pp. 248–256 (selections).]

Less than a year later, Howe realized that the movement he had described existed not only in the narrow intellectual climate of urban America, but was a sign of a wider transformation and shift in cultural style. He outlines this transformation, including some points from the earlier essay, and some new ones.

A willed and self-conscious and generational break, defined as a clash between young and old more insistently than any similar phenomenon of recent times.

A revolt against the drive to success and against the ethic of work. (The two are by no means the same, though part of the present confusion is that they are often taken to be the same.)

Indifference to the "idea" as well as the established institutions of the working class—something radically new among new radicals.

A strong inclination toward absolutist morality, sometimes absolutist moralism, by means of which elements of belief and feeling usually attached in the past to religion are now directed toward politics.

A strong revulsion against traditional ideas concerning education, which in extreme instances takes the form of antirationalism.

A recurrent impulse toward utopian communitarianism, the effort to realize in the small those visions of the good society that have not been realized in the large.

A feeling shared by many young people throughout the world that their generation comes to maturity at a point which signifies a major turning point in the history of Western culture. [Irving Howe, "Nixon's Dream—and Black Reality," *Dissent,* March–April 1969.]

C. THE YOUNG TALK, AND ARE TALKED ABOUT

From the start it was clear that there was a political and a consciousness wing to the counterculture. Young men and women themselves moved back and forth between the poles, as their despair or modest hope happened to lead them. At the close of the pre-media phase of the movement, the phase I am especially interested in here, Theodore Roszak stated why he thought the two poles were really one.

> We grasp the underlying unity of the counter cultural variety, then, if we see beat-hip bohemianism as an effort to work out the personality structure and total life style that follow from New Left social criticism. At their best, these young bohemians are the would-be utopian pioneers of the world that lies beyond intellectual rejection of the Great Society. They seek to invent a cultural base for New Left politics, to discover new types of community, new family patterns, new sexual mores, new kinds of livelihood, new esthetic forms, new personal identities on the far side of power politics, the bourgeois home, and the consumer society. When the New Left calls for peace and gives us heavy analysis of what's what in Vietnam, the hippy quickly translates the word into *shantih*, the peace that passes all understanding, and fills in the psychic dimensions of the ideal. If investigating the life of *shantih* has little to do with achieving peace in Vietnam, perhaps it is the best way of preventing the next several

Vietnams from happening. [*The Making of a Counter Culture*, p. 66.]

A year later, Charles Reich was, of course, to see the matter differently, and to urge a post-Marxist, Che Guevara–like priority of consciousness over political structure.

Here are two statements of a confessional nature from this generation which was so curiously instructing the rest of us at this time; one, very sophisticated; the second, off the cuff.

We nurtured a daring premise: we were of historical moment, critical, unprecedented, containing within ourselves the fullness of time. Some great wind was brewing as we breathed; not a new generation, but a new notion of generation with new notions of its imperatives. We would not default, succumb to the certainties of age, gulp pills, compromise maturely, lubricate our adulthoods with facile resignations. We would not be normal. For normality was now disease—hacking coughs, quilted stomachs and cold loins, the sniveling bitterness of diminished hopes—and if we were to live propitiously in our era, we would have to define normality anew. We might say no, after long childhoods of indulgence, to the sudden demands for our complicity. We might not, on schedule, relinquish our freedom. We might remain forever infants, joyous beggars, dependent on the system, refusing our contributions yet ready enough to consume. Though distribution was presently askew, or demented, technology has already created wealth enough to sustain us all. . . . Or so we mused when we were on, and up. When we were off, and down, we could envision ourselves forty-year-old waifs, with pee stains on our underwear, drifting without callings in a society we could neither convert nor make sense of. For in a single day we could waver between something like optimism and a despair so deadly it seemed there was no acre of earth where we would be permitted to

gather with those we loved and share a creditable
life—a despair that suggested we were the first generation that could imagine declining its bid to inherit the
earth. . . . We needed new definitions of livelihood, of
maturity and enjoyment, but we could scarcely imagine change so gargantuan it seemed close to reversal,
so inaccessible to legislation or "programs" as to demand a radicalism of messianic proportions. America
injured us into black experiments, futile bouts; our
fists sank into her fat, and disappeared. Some of us
were beautiful before going over the edge. The personal histories of friends, and their friends, merged
with our own; we shared a common genealogy, and we
would share a common fate. One, brimming with
compassion, marched and organized. As he ascended
ghetto stairwells a kind of targetless hate began to
spread inside him, a guilty helplessness, and dread. He
was neither poor nor black. He could not pay his dues
with nightstick scars, even assuming he could find
someone to administer them. His hair and eyes grew
wild, but some vestigal love of country froze him in the
anarchist's posture. He became an armchair kamikaze;
talked of confrontation, interests, guns, resistance,
plotted strikes on Lockheed and, at last, provoked a
beating from the law in a Westchester shopping center
so suburban ladies might see that it could happen
there, and to a nice Jewish boy. Succumbing to the
romance of guerrilla-hood, he laughed at talk of Asian
peasants or disenfranchised Blacks, crying that each
injustice was but a single head of the Hydra that had to
be stilled by a sword through the heart. One day, he
was gone, some said to Cuba. Another, with a foot
already inside the academy, gave away what he had,
wandered barefoot and penniless through Mexico,
smoked ganja in Jamaica with Ras Tafarians and
charas in Calcutta with poets; became an animal,
howled through the woods of western Pennsylvania,
was loved across the boundaries of class and burned
for a time with the conviction that it was all *there*, laid
out for him, the occult feast, the rites of exploration.
"I'm running a whole different flick," he said. Some-

times he talked ideas that unhinged our knees, sometimes his silence was so wise we swore we'd never speak
again. And while our leaders reassured positions, he
reassessed for us the meat of consciousness, to make
our lives organic, of a piece. Some months ago he
turned vegetable, but until he could no longer wipe
himself after toilet, we thought we must also cast off
what we still clung to, and follow him. We had sent
them out to reconnoiter galaxies, and they, as it
happened, plunged too far. We lost radio contact.
They lost ground control. We could no longer interpret their fitful vibrations. . . . Those of us with nerve
endings less exposed hung back, holding our acts
together, but making little waves. Teen-agers ran a
gigantic import industry. (How can you venerate government and law when you commit a felony every
day?) Black sophomores propped their black feet up
on the prexy's walnut desk. Wheeler-dealer heads took
Wall Street for a ride. Ecstatic communitarians
grooved to divine potato patches. Children invented
music that didn't go Bingo-Bango. They didn't know
much; they were suckers for fakery. But we were slow
to call any experiment excessive. Within ambient disorder, each seemed somehow appropriate. We felt
ourselves growing into the people our parents had
warned us about. The woods already burning, they
spent their strength clucking over our eccentricity.
And there were ever reassurances: we would learn;
we'd soon be out on the field with the team from
V.I.S.T.A. or Dow. Meanwhile, we dug in for the
longest "adolescent phase" since adolescence was invented a century ago. Bleak signals flashed across our
skies. Legions of our most promising would surely
disappear into the prisons. In the Fifties, we never
guessed the phonies could become so dangerous.
Many wouldn't stick it out. They'd learned why Lao-
Tze hopped upon his ox, at last, and rode out beyond
the Great Wall. Many others, perhaps stronger and
finer, perhaps not yet placing the problems at so
terrible a depth, might begin their thousand pinpricks,
launch forays into the barren democratic sensibility. By

their refusal, their mischief, their infiltration, great numbers could begin to conceive of something more decent than submitting to the culture. There was that vague and fragile chance, and although I had contempt for much of my generation spawned, I could not see another chance anywhere I looked. [Jacob Brackman, "My Generation," *Esquire*, October 1968.]

The second confession comes from an interview conducted by *The New York Times* with a group of young men and women just after their return from the Woodstock Music and Art Fair in Bethel, New York, in the summer of 1969.

Judy: I just had a feeling that, wow, there are so many of us, we really have power. I'd always felt like such a minority. But I thought, wow, we're a majority—it felt like that. I felt, here's the answer to anyone who calls us deviates.

Q.: Was that before you heard any music?

Judy: I never made it to the concert. I never heard any music at all.

Q.: The whole weekend?

Judy: Yeh. The whole weekend.

Q.: Were you sorry then that you went?

Judy: Oh, definitely not . . .

Q.: Do you want a family?

Judy: One child. Just, you know, to procreate. But I don't want a family because I don't want to get into that much responsibility. I want to be able to move. I want to be able to leave at any time. I don't want that much restriction.

Q.: Do you think this attitude is widespread among your generation? Do you feel yourself different from us?

Judy: We're more oriented to the present. It's like do what you want to do now. It's almost a rushing thing. And it's bad.

Q.: Why bad?

Judy: Because it seems like, well, you can never stay one

place very long. The kids that you know go off. If you
stay anywhere very long you get into a planning thing.
If you get a job, if you keep it, it seems like, Oh hell,
what am I going to do? You know, I've been here this
long and I've got money—what am I going to do? Save
it? What for? So you just move on . . .
Q.: Was there much touching?
Judy: People were hanging on the cars and everybody
was hanging on to each other so they wouldn't fall off
and this might have been touching. But the most
amount of touching was through other people's eyes.
They touched you and felt you just through the eyes.
[*The New York Times*, August 29, 1969.]

Leslie Fiedler, in an important early essay, saw what was
coming.

The new irrationalists, however, deny all the apostles
of reason, Freud as well as Socrates; and if they seem to
exempt Marx, this is because they know less about him,
have heard him evoked less often by the teachers they
are driven to deny. Not only do they reject the Socratic
adage that the unexamined life is not worth living,
since for them precisely the unexamined life is the only
one worth enduring at all. But they also abjure the
Freudian one: "Where id was, ego shall be," since for
them the true rallying cry is, "Let id prevail over ego,
impulse over order," or—in negative terms—"Freud is
a fink!"

But what the students were protesting in large part,
I have come to believe, was the very notion of man
which the universities sought to impose upon them:
that bourgeois–Protestant version of Humanism, with
its view of man as justified by rationality, work, duty,
vocation, maturity, success; and its concomitant understanding of childhood and adolescence as a temporarily privileged time of preparation for assuming those
burdens. The new irrationalists, however, are prepared to advocate prolonging adolescence to the grave,
and are ready to dispense with school as an outlived
excuse for leisure.

The new young celebrate disconnection—accept it as one of the necessary consequences of the industrial system which has delivered them from work and duty, of that welfare state which makes disengagement the last possible virtue, whether it call itself Capitalist, Socialist or Communist. "Detachment" is the traditional name for the stance the futurists assume; but "detachment" carries with it irrelevant religious, even specifically Christian overtones. The post-modernists are surely in some sense "mystics," religious at least in a way they do not ordinarily know how to confess, but they are not Christians.

The young to whom I have been referring, the mythologically representative minority (who, by a process that infuriates the mythologically inert majority out of which they come, "stand for" their times), live in a community in which what used to be called the "Sexual Revolution," the Freudian-Laurentian revolt of their grandparents and parents, has triumphed as imperfectly and unsatisfactorily as all revolutions always triumph. They confront, therefore, the necessity of determining not only what meanings "love" can have in their new world, but—even more disturbingly—what significance, if any, "male" and "female" now possess. For a while, they (or at least their literary spokesmen recruited from the generation just before them) seemed content to celebrate a kind of *reductio* or *exaltatio ad absurdum* of their parents' once revolutionary sexual goals: The Reichian-inspired Cult of the Orgasm.

All of us who are middle-aged and were Marxists, which is to say, who once numbered ourselves among the last assured Puritans, have surely noticed in ourselves a vestigial roundhead rage at the new hair styles of the advanced or—if you please—delinquent young. Watching young men titivate their locks (the comb, the pocket mirror and the bobby pin having replaced the jackknife, catcher's mitt and brass knuckles), we feel the same baffled resentment that stirs in us when we realize that they have rejected work. A job and unequivocal maleness—these are two sides of the same Calvinist coin, which in the future buys nothing.

We have, moreover, recently been witnessing the development of a new form of social psychiatry (a psychiatry of the future already anticipated by the literature of the future) which considers some varieties of "schizophrenia" not diseases to be cured but forays into an unknown psychic world: random penetrations by bewildered internal cosmonauts of a realm that it will be the task of the next generations to explore.

In any case, poets and junkies have been suggesting to us that the new world appropriate to the new men of the latter twentieth century is to be discovered only by the conquest of inner space; by an adventure of the spirit, an extension of psychic possibility, of which the flights into outer space—moonshots and expeditions to Mars—are precisely such unwitting metaphors and analogues as the voyages of exploration were of the earlier breakthrough into the Renaissance, from whose consequences the young seek now so desperately to escape. ["The New Mutants," *Partisan Review*, Fall 1965.]

Several years later, and many cultural miles away from Leslie Fiedler, Dr. George Wald, in a March 4, 1969, address at M.I.T., put his finger on a decisive and central element in the new consciousness—the disappearance of the future.

How real is the threat of full scale nuclear war? I have my own very inexpert idea, but realizing how little I know and fearful that I may be a little paranoid on this subject, I take every opportunity to ask reputed experts. I asked that question of a very distinguished professor of government at Harvard about a month ago. I asked him what sort of odds he would lay on the possibility of full-scale nuclear war within the forseeable future. "Oh," he said comfortably, "I think I can give you a pretty good answer to that question. I estimate the probability of full-scale nuclear war, provided that the situation remains about as it is now, at two per cent per year." Anybody can do the simple calculation that shows that two percent per year means that the chance of having that full-scale nuclear war by 1990 is about one in three, and by 2000 it is about 50–50.

I think I know what is bothering the students. I think that what we are up against is a generation that is by no means sure that it has a future.

I am growing old, and my future so to speak is already behind me. But there are those students of mine who are in my mind always; there are my children, two of them now seven and nine, whose future is infinitely more precious to me than my own. So it isn't just their generation; it's mine too. We're all in it together.

Are we to have a chance to live? We don't ask for prosperity, or security, only for a reasonable chance to live, to work out our destiny in peace and decency. Not to go down in history as the apocalyptic generation.

And it isn't only nuclear war. Another overwhelming threat is in the population explosion. That has not yet even begun to come under control. There is every indication that the world population will double before the year 2000; and there is a widespread expectation of famine on an unprecedented scale in many parts of the world. The experts tend to differ only in their estimates of when those famines will begin. Some think by 1980, others think they can be staved off until 1990, very few expect that they will not occur by the year 2000.

That is the problem. Unless we can be surer than we now are that this generation has a future, nothing else matters. [As reprinted in *The National Catholic Reporter*, March 19, 1969.]

The changes were seen from every perspective; from the academy, and from the ghetto.

It is among the white youth of the world that the greatest change is taking place. It is they who are experiencing the great psychic pain of waking into consciousness to find their inherited heroes turned by events into villains. Communication and understand-

ing between the older and younger generations of
whites has entered a crisis. The elders, who, in the
tradition of privileged classes or races, genuinely do
not understand the youth, trapped by old ways of
thinking and blind to the future, have only just begun
to be vexed—because the youth have only just begun
to rebel. So thoroughgoing is the revolution in the
psyches of white youth that the traditional tolerance
which every older generation has found it necessary to
display is quickly exhausted, leaving a gulf of fear,
hostility, mutual misunderstanding, and contempt.
[Eldridge Cleaver, *Soul on Ice*, McGraw-Hill Book
Company, New York, 1968, pp. 69–70.]

D. GLIMPSES OF THE NEW PSYCHE

There is a reason why political revolution in our time
requires not merely an ideology, but a new mode of
consciousness. The reason is technology. Technology cannot be resisted by conventional strategies of dissent. It has
the impalpable power to gobble up and neutralize most of
what we say or do along conventional political lines.
Theodore Roszak's book *The Making of a Counter Culture*
had the great advantage of making this clear.

Ironically, it is the American young, with their un-
derdeveloped radical background, who seem to have
grasped most clearly the fact that, while such immediate emergencies as the Vietnam war, racial injustice, and hard-core poverty demand a deal of old-style
politicking, the paramount struggle of our day is
against a far more formidable, because far less obvious,
opponent, to which I will give the name "the technocracy"—a social form more highly developed in America than in any other society. The American young have
been somewhat quicker to sense that in the struggle
against this enemy, the conventional tactics of political
resistance have only a marginal place, largely limited to
meeting immediate life-and-death crises. Beyond such

front-line issues, however, there lies the greater task of altering the total cultural context within which our daily politics takes place. [Theodore Roszak, *The Making of a Counter Culture*, pp. 4–5.]

Roszak further notes that technology is nourished by a myth—he calls it the myth of objective consciousness. We might call it the idea of the separate self, the self–world distinction. And so he clearly sees that, to get at the real enemy, we must get at its operative myth.

Thus, if we probe the technocracy in search of the peculiar power it holds over us, we arrive at the myth of objective consciousness. There is but one way of gaining access to reality—so the myth holds—and this is to cultivate a state of consciousness cleansed of all subjective distortion, all personal involvement. What flows from this state of consciousness qualifies as knowledge, and nothing else does. . . .

When, therefore, those of us who challenge the objective mode of consciousness are faced with the question "But is there any other way in which we can know the world?", I believe it is a mistake to seek an answer on a narrowly epistemological basis. Too often we will then find ourselves struggling to discover some alternative method to produce an accumulation of verifiable propositions. The only way we shall ever recapture the sort of knowledge Lao-tzu referred to in his dictum "those who know do not speak," is by subordinating the question "how shall we know?" to the more existentially vital question "how shall we live?" [Theodore Roszak, *The Making of a Counter Culture*, pp. 208–233.]

The new consciousness, secure in its largely white and middle-class status, eschewed the Protestant work ethic for celebration. "Repressive" was the worst that could be said of persons and institutions. Abolition of repression, then, and if there must be a choice between Apollo and Dionysius, Dionysius (or Orpheus) it must be.

The replacement of the pleasure principle by the
reality principle is the great traumatic event in the
development of man. . . .

[Freud's] work is characterized by an uncompromising
insistence on showing up the repressive content of the
highest values and achievements of culture. . . .

As the family becomes less decisive in directing the
adjustment of the individual to society, the father-son
conflict no longer remains the model conflict. . . . The
technological abolition of the individual is reflected in
the decline of the social function of the family. . . .

In a repressive civilization, death itself becomes an
instrument of repression. Whether death is feared as a
constant threat, or glorified as supreme sacrifice, or
accepted as fate, the education for consent to death
introduces an element of surrender into life from the
beginning—surrender and submission. . . . In contrast, a philosophy that does not work as the hand-
maiden of repression responds to the fact of death
with the Great Refusal—the refusal of Orpheus the
liberator. [Herbert Marcuse, *Eros and Civilization*, Vin-
tage Books, Random House, New York 1962, pp. 14,
16–17, 87, 216.]

Many have seen, and none more clearly than Robert Jay
Lifton, that what is really at issue in the new consciousness
is the very idea of selfhood. What we want, he seems to say,
is not merely a revised, reformed, or expanded conception
of self, but something like a total abolition of what we in
the West have so long taken for granted. This is the
consciousness revolution at its most radical, and most
dangerous.

I should like to examine a set of psychological patterns
characteristic of contemporary life, which are creating
a new kind of man—a "protean man." As my stress is

upon change and flux, I shall not speak much of "character" and "personality," both of which suggest fixity and permanence. Erikson's concept of identity has been, among other things, an effort to get away from this principle of fixity; and I have been using the term self-process to convey still more specifically the idea of flow. For it is quite possible that even the image of personal identity, in so far as it suggests inner stability and sameness, is derived from a vision of a traditional culture in which man's relationship to his institutions and symbols are still relatively intact—which is hardly the case today. If we understand the self to be the person's symbol of his own organism, then self-process refers to the continuous psychic recreation of that symbol. . . .

I do not mean to suggest that everybody is becoming the same, or that a totally new "world-self" is taking shape. But I am convinced that a new style of self-process is emerging everywhere. It derives from the interplay of three factors responsible for human behavior: the psychobiological potential common to all mankind at any moment in time; those traits given special emphasis in a particular cultural tradition; and those related to modern (and particularly contemporary) historical forces. My thesis is that this third factor plays an increasingly important part in shaping self-process. . . .

I would stress two historical developments as having special importance for creating protean man. The first is the world-wide sense of what I have called historical (or psychohistorical) dislocation, the break in the sense of connection which men have long felt with the vital and nourishing symbols of their cultural tradition—symbols revolving around family, idea systems, religions, and the life cycle in general. . . .

The second large historical tendency is the flooding of imagery produced by the extraordinary flow of post-modern cultural influences over mass communication networks. These cross readily over local and national boundaries, and permit each individual to be touched by everything, but at the same time cause him

to be overwhelmed by superficial messages and un-
digested cultural elements, by headlines and by endless
partial alternatives in every sphere of life. . . .

The protean style of self-process, then, is characterized by an interminable series of experiments and
explorations—some shallow, some profound—each of
which may be readily abandoned in favor of still new
psychological quests. The pattern in many ways resembles what Erik Erikson has called "identity diffusion,"
and the impaired psychological functioning which
those terms suggest can be very much present. But I
would stress that the protean style is by no means
pathological as such, and, in fact, well may be one of
the functional patterns of our day. It extends to all
areas of human experience—to political as well as
sexual behavior, to the holding and promulgating of
ideas and to the general organization of lives. . . .

What has actually disappeared—in Sartre and in
protean man in general—is the classic superego, the
internalization of clearly defined criteria of right and
wrong transmitted within a particular culture by parents to their children. Protean man requires freedom
from precisely that kind of superego—he requires a
symbolic fatherlessness—in order to carry out his
explorations. But rather than being free of guilt, we
shall see that his guilt takes on a different form from
that of his predecessors. . . .

Protean man has a particular relationship to the
holding of ideas which has, I believe, great significance
for the politics, religion, and general intellectual life of
the future. For just as elements of the self can be
experimented with and readily altered, so can idea
systems and ideologies be embraced, modified, let go
of and reembraced, all with a new ease that stands in
sharp contrast to the inner struggle we have in the past
associated with these shifts. Until relatively recently, no
more than one major ideological shift was likely to
occur in a lifetime, and that one would be long
remembered as a significant individual turning-point
accompanied by profound soul-searching and conflict.
But today it is not unusual to encounter several such

shifts, accomplished relatively painlessly, within a year
or even a month; and among many groups, the rarity is
a man who has gone through life holding firmly to a
single ideological vision.

I am quoting from the original version of Lifton's essay, as
it appeared in *Partisan Review*, Winter 1968. In a revised
version of the essay, published in his book *Boundaries*
(Random House, 1970), Lifton adds to his list of historical
events causing this shift of consciousness the fact of
nuclear weapons. In his conclusion to the revised version,
Lifton notes that "protean man" is not only young, but that
he resides, in some sense, in us all. I am persuaded that he
is correct, and this is the reason I am taking seriously the
new consciousness movement, even though its media
phase is waning and the counterculture apparently dissolving before our eyes.

Nothing but masks; no face behind the mask. This
reminds us of the Doctor's words to Jacob Horner in John
Barth's *The End of the Road*:

> "It's extremely important that you learn to assume
> these masks wholeheartedly. Don't think there's any-
> thing behind them: *ego* means *I*, and *I* means *ego*, and
> the ego by definition is a mask. Where there's no
> ego—this is you on the bench—there's no *I*. If you
> sometimes have the feeling that your mask is *insin-
> cere*—impossible word!—it's only because one of your
> masks is incompatible with another. You mustn't put
> on two at a time. There's a source of conflict and
> conflict between masks, like absence of masks, is a
> source of immobility. The more sharply you can dra-
> matize your situation and define your own role and
> everybody's else's role, the safer you'll be." [Doubleday
> & Co., New York, 1958; quotation from Bantam Books
> edition, p. 90.]

But—we may be in trouble. Can Western man really
make the journey from the old world—Oedipus, Pro-

metheus, Orestes—to Proteus? Protean psychology, like polytheistic religion, may inevitably become pathological. Can we make this move without becoming mad?

At one point, Norman Brown thought that we could.

> The abstract antinomy of Self and Other in love can be overcome if we return to the concrete reality of pleasure and to the fundamental definition of sexuality as the pleasurable activity of the body, and think of loving as the relation of the ego to its sources of pleasure. Narcissistic love is fundamentally a desire for pleasurable activity of one's own body. Our problem then is: How does the desire for pleasurable activity of one's own body lead to other bodies? . . . Infantile sexuality affirms the union of the self with a whole world of love and pleasure. [*Life Against Death*, p. 45.]

> If we can imagine an unrepressed man—a man strong enough to live and therefore strong enough to die, and therefore what no man has ever been, an individual— such a man, having overcome guilt and anxiety, could have no money complex. But at the same time such a man would have a body freed from all the sexual organizations—a body freed from unconscious oral, anal, and genital fantasies of return to the maternal womb. Such a man would be rid of the nightmares which Freud showed to be haunting civilization; but freedom from those fantasies would also mean freedom from that disorder in the human body which Freud pitilessly exposed. In such a man would be fulfilled on earth the mystic hope of Christianity, the resurrection of the body, in a form, as Luther said, free from death and filth. [*Ibid.*, p. 291.]

More recently, Brown is not so sure that madness can or ought to be avoided. In "The White Negro" Mailer suggested that the psychopath "may be indeed the perverted or dangerous frontrunner of a new kind of personality." Freud and Dostoevsky, earlier, told us about the psychopath. But then he was the victim, at the mercy of the world. Today, the madman has become the victor, the model. Madness is one of the dominant themes of the new consciousness.

The alternative to mind is certainly madness. Our greatest blessings, says Socrates in the *Phaedrus*, come to us by way of madness—provided, he adds, that the madness comes from the god. Our real choice is between holy and unholy madness: open your eyes and look around you—madness is in the saddle anyhow, Freud is the measure of our unholy madness, as Nietzsche is the prophet of the holy madness, of Dionysus, the mad truth. ["Apocalypse: The Place of Mystery in the Life of the Mind." In *Interpretation: The Poetry of Meaning*, ed. Hopper and Miller, Harcourt, Brace and World, New York, 1967.]

The split of self from environment, and of self into both self and environment, is also the split of self or soul from body. The essence of dreaming is duplication, division; as in schizophrenia. [*Love's Body*, Random House, New York, 1966. I have made an analysis of Brown (along with Paul Goodman) in an article called "Two Gurus," *Soundings*, Spring 1968.]

Psychoanalysis is the rediscovery of the Orphic or Oriental vision of life as sleep disturbed by dreams, of life as disturbance in death. [*Ibid.*, p. 52.]

To make in ourselves a new consciousness, an erotic sense of reality, is to become conscious of symbolism. Symbolism is mind making connections (correspondences) rather than distinctions (separations). [*Ibid.*, p. 81.]

It is the erotic sense of reality that discovers the inadequacy of fraternity, of brotherhood. It is not adequate as a form for the reunification of the human race: we must be either far more deeply unified, or not at all. The true form of unification—which can be found either in psychoanalysis or in Christianity, in

Freud or Pope John, or Karl Marx—is: "we are all members of one body." [*Ibid.*, p. 82.]

The division of the one man into two sexes is part of the fall: sexes are sections. [*Ibid.*, p. 84.]

The goal of "individuation," or of replacing the ego by the "self", deceitfully conceals the drastic break between the *principium individuationis* and the Dionysian, or drunken, principle of union, or communion, between man and man and between man and nature. The integration of the psyche is the integration of the human race, and the integration of the world with which we are inseparably connected. [*Ibid.*, pp. 86–87.]

A person is never himself but always a mask; a person never owns his own person, but always represents another, by whom he is possessed. And the other that one is, is always ancestors; one's soul is not one's own, but daddy's. [*Ibid.*, p. 98.]

God does not go for personalities; nor does the Last Judgment consist in the award of prizes to personalities for the performance of their parts. The performance principle must go; the show must not go on. . . . Freud came to give the show away; the outcome of psychoanalysis is not "ego psychology" but the doctrine of "anatta" or no-self. . . . And with the doctrine of no-self goes the doctrine of non-action: action is proper only to an ignorant person, and doing nothing is, if rightly understood, the supreme action. [*Ibid.*, p. 105.]

Except in certain forms of neurosis and psychosis: the insane are closer to the truth. [*Ibid.*, p. 108.]

Contrary to what is taken for granted in the lunatic state called normalcy or common sense, the distinction between self and external world is not an immutable fact, but an artificial construction. [*Ibid.*, p. 142.]

The soul (self) we call our own is an illusion. The real

psychoanalytical contribution to "ego psychology" is the revelation that the ego is a bit of the outside world swallowed, introjected; or rather a bit of the outside world that we insist on pretending we have swallowed. The nucleus of one's own self is the incorporated other. [*Ibid.*, p. 144.]

The self being made by projection and introjection, to have a self is to have enemies, and to be a self is to be at war (the war of every man against every man). To abolish war, therefore, is to abolish the self; and the war to end war is total war; to have no more enemies, or self. [*Ibid.*, p. 149.]

It is not schizophrenia but normality that is split-minded; in schizophrenia the false boundaries are disintegrating. [*Ibid.*, p. 159.]

Dionysius, the mad god, breaks down the boundaries; releases the prisoners; abolishes repression; and abolishes the *principium individuationis*, substituting for it the unity of man with nature. . . . The soul that we can call our own is not a real one. The solution to the problem of identity is, get lost. [*Ibid.*, p. 161.]

Symbolic consciousness is between seeing and not seeing. It does not see self-evident truths of natural reason; or visible saints. It does not distinguish the wheat from the tares; and therefore must, as Roger Williams saw, practice toleration; or forgiveness, for we never know what we do. [*Ibid.*, p. 217.]

A void, an opening for us, to leave the place where we belong; a road, into the wilderness; for exodus, exile. The proletariat has no fatherland, and the son of man no place to lay his head. Be at home nowhere. [*Ibid.*, pp. 261–262.]

R. D. Laing has been making, in our time, the most startling and consistent inversion of our accepted understanding of sanity and madness, and the most influential.

There are forms of alienation that are relatively strange to statistically "normal" forms of alienation. The "normally" alienated person, by reason of the fact that he acts more or less like everyone else is taken to be sane. Other forms of alienation that are out of step with the prevailing state of alienation are those that are labeled by the "normal" majority as bad or mad.

The condition of alienation, of being asleep, of being unconscious, of being out of one's mind, is the condition of the normal man.

Society highly values its normal man. It educates children to lose themselves and to become absurd and thus to be normal.

Normal men have killed perhaps 100,000,000 of their fellow normal men in the last fifty years. [R. D. Laing, *The Politics of Experience*, Pantheon Books, New York, 1967, p. 12.]

Psychotherapists are specialists in human relations. But the Dreadful has already happened. It has happened to us all. The therapists, too, are in a world in which the inner is already split from the outer. The inner does not become outer, and the outer become inner, just by the rediscovery of the "inner" world. That is only the beginning. As a whole, we are a generation of men so estranged from the inner world that many are arguing that it does not exist; and that even if it does exist, it does not matter. Even if it has some significance, it is not the hard stuff of science, and if it is not, then let's make it hard. Let it be measured and counted. Quantify the heart's agony and ecstasy in a world in which, when the inner world is first discovered, we are liable to find ourselves bereft and derelict. For without the inner the outer loses its meaning, and without the outer the inner loses its substance. [*Ibid.*, pp. 32–33.]

In order to rationalize our industrial-military complex, we have to destroy our capacity to see clearly any more what is in front of, and to imagine what is beyond, our noses. Long before a thermonuclear war

can come about, we have had to lay waste our own
sanity. We begin with the children. It is imperative to
catch them in time. Without the most thorough and
rapid brainwashing their dirty minds would see
through our dirty tricks. Children are not yet fools, but
we shall turn them into imbeciles like ourselves with
high I.Q.s if possible. [*Ibid.*, p. 36.]

The family's function is to repress Eros; to induce a
false consciousness of security; to deny death by avoiding life; to cut off transcendence; to believe in God, not
to experience the Void; to create, in short, one-
dimensional man; to promote respect, conformity,
obedience; to con children out of play; to induce a fear
of failure; to promote a respect for work; to promote a
respect for "respectability." [*Ibid.*, p. 71.]

Some people wittingly, some people unwittingly,
enter or are thrown into more or less total inner space
and time. We are socially conditioned to regard total
immersion in outer space and time as normal and
healthy. Immersion in inner space and time tends to be
regarded as antisocial withdrawal, a deviation, invalid,
pathological per se, in some sense discreditable. [*Ibid.*,
pp. 86–87.]

This journey is experienced as going further "in," as
going back through one's personal life, in and back
and through and beyond into the experience of all
mankind, of the primal man, of Adam and perhaps
even further into the beings of animals, vegetables and
minerals.

In this journey there are many occasions to lose
one's way, for confusion, partial failure, even final
shipwreck; many terrors, spirits, demons to be en-
countered, that may or may not be overcome. [*Ibid.*,
pp. 87–88.]

What is entailed then is:
(I) a voyage from outer to inner,
(II) from life to a kind of death,

(III) from going forward to going back,
(IV) from temporal movement to temporal stand-
still,
 (V) from mundane time to eonic time,
(VI) from the ego to the self,
(VII) from outside (post-birth) back into the womb of
     all things (pre-birth),
and then subsequently a return voyage from
(1) inner to outer,
(2) from death to life,
(3) from the movement back to a movement once
    more forward,
(4) from immortality back to mortality,
(5) from eternity back to time,
(6) from self to a new ego,
(7) from a cosmic fetalization to an existential rebirth.
    [*Ibid.*, p. 89.]

The "ego" is the instrument for living in this world.
If the "ego" is broken up or destroyed (by the insurmountable contradictions of certain life situations,
by toxins, chemical changes, etc.), then the person may
be exposed to other worlds, "real" in different ways
from the more familiar territory of dreams, imagination, perception or fantasy. [*Ibid.*, p. 97.]

Sanity today appears to rest very largely on a capacity to adapt to the external world—the interpersonal
world, and the realm of human collectivities.
   As this external human world is almost completely
and totally estranged from the inner, any personal
direct awareness of the inner world already has grave
risks.
   But since society, without knowing it, is starving for
the inner, the demands on people who evoke its
presence in a "safe" way, in a way that need not be
taken seriously, etc., is tremendous—while the ambivalence is equally intense. Small wonder that the list of
artists, in say the last 150 years, who have become
shipwrecked on these reefs is so long—Hölderlin, John
Clare, Rimbaud, Van Gogh, Nietzsche, Antonin Ar-
taud. [*Ibid.*, pp. 98–99.]

There is no doubt, it seems to me, that there have been profound changes in the experience of man in the last thousand years. In some ways this is more evident than changes in the patterns of his behavior. There is everything to suggest that man experienced God. Faith was never a matter of believing He existed, but of trusting in the presence that was experienced and known to exist as a self-validating datum. It seems likely that far more people in our time experience neither the presence of God, nor the presence of his absence, but the absence of his presence. [*Ibid.*, p. 100.]

From the alienated starting point of our pseudo-sanity, everything is equivocal. Our sanity is not "true" sanity. Their madness is not "true" madness. The madness of our patients is an artifact of the destruction wreaked on them by us and by them on themselves. Let no one suppose that we meet "true" madness any more than that we are truly sane. The madness that we encounter in "patients" is a gross travesty, a mockery, a grotesque caricature of what the natural healing of that estranged integration we call sanity might be. True sanity entails in one way or another the dissolution of the normal ego, that false self competently adjusted to our alienated social reality; the emergence of the "inner" archetypal mediators of divine power, and through this death a rebirth, and the eventual reestablishment of a new kind of ego-functioning, the ego now being the servant of the divine, no longer its betrayer. [*Ibid.*, p. 101.]

There is the true compassion of a healer in these words, but there is something else. And it is that something else that was to create a community, not too many years later, which would elevate as its heroes Sirhan Sirhan, Charles Manson, Arthur Bremer.

As the new consciousness found itself extolling madness, it also found itself talking about the gods. For the madman has always been one who has seen something forbidden, something that only the gods are supposed to see. The demoniacs often perceived something in Jesus

that no disciple could. Let us observe the religious concerns of the consciousness revolutionaries.

E. NOTAE ECCLESIAE NOVAE

The new consciousness, as even Herman Kahn knows,
was appallingly religious. Christianity's secularizing theologies have not been wrong, just useful for a limited time
and for the limited constituency of seminary and church.
While theology still is often tempted to attack religion, the
world—or at least the portion of the young world we are
studying—can't get enough of it.

When, in the heart of the Eisenhower era, a confident
Christian theology was attacking religion and religious
revivals, Allen Ginsberg was setting the religious mood for
the consciousness revolution to come.

> I saw the best minds of my generation destroyed by
>   madness, starving hysterical naked,
> dragging themselves through the negro streets at dawn
>   looking for an angry fix,
> angelheaded hipsters burning for the ancient heavenly
>   connection to the starry dynamo in the machinery of
>   night,
> who poverty and tatters and hollow-eyed and high sat up
>   smoking in the supernatural darkness of cold-water
>   flats floating across the tops of cities contemplating
>   jazz,
> who bared their brains to Heaven under the El and saw
>   Mohammedan angels staggering on tenement roofs
>   illuminated,
> who passed through universities with radiant cool eyes
>   hallucinating Arkansas and Black-light tragedy among
>   the scholars of war,
> who were expelled from the academies for crazy & publish-
>   ing obscene odes on the windows of the skull. . . .
> who studied Plotinus Poe St. John of the Cross telepathy
>   and bop kaballa because the cosmos instinctively vi-
>   brated at their feet in Kansas,

who loned it through the streets of Idaho seeking visionary
  indian angels who were visionary indian angels,
who thought they were only mad when Baltimore gleamed
  in supernatural ecstasy. . . . ["Howl," in *Howl and
  Other Poems*, City Lights Books, San Francisco, 1956,
  pp. 9, 11.]

Holy! Holy! Holy! Holy! Holy! Holy! Holy! Holy! Holy!
  Holy! Holy! Holy! Holy! Holy! Holy!
The world is holy! The soul is holy! The skin is holy! The
  nose is holy! The tongue and cock and hand and
  asshole holy!
Everything is holy! everybody's holy! everywhere is holy!
  everyday is in eternity! Everyman's an angel!
The bum's as holy as the seraphim! the madman is holy as
  you my soul are holy!
The typewriter is holy the poem is holy the voice is holy the
  hearers are holy the ecstasy is holy!
              ["Footnote to Howl," *op. cit.*, p. 21.]

We're not our skin of grime, we're not our dread bleak
  dusty imageless locomotive, we're all beautiful golden
  sunflowers inside, we're blessed by our own seed &
  golden hairy naked accomplishment-bodies growing
  into mad black formal sunflowers in the sunset, spied
  on by our eyes under the shadow of the mad locomotive riverbank sunset Frisco hilly tincan evening sit-
  down vision.
              ["Sunflower Sutra," *op. cit.*, p. 30.]

It surely was inevitable. As soon as you decide to take on
the myth of objective consciousness, the idea of the
separate self, you are in the heart of the mystical tradition.

Indeed, we are a post-Christian era—despite the fact
that minds far more gifted than Ginsberg's, like that of
the late Thomas Merton, have mined the dominant
religious tradition for great treasures. But we may
have been decidedly wrong in what we long expected
to follow the death of the Christian God; namely, a
thoroughly secularized, thoroughly positivistic culture,

dismal and spiritless in its obsession with technological prowess. That was the world Aldous Huxley foresaw in the 1930s when he wrote *Brave New World*. But in the 1950s, as Huxley detected the rising spirit of a new generation, his utopian image brightened to the forecast he offers us in *Island,* where a non-violent culture elaborated out of Buddhism and psychedelic drugs prevails. It was as if he had suddenly seen the possibility emerge: what lay behond the Christian era and the "wasteland" that was its immediate successor might be a new, eclectic religious revival. Which is precisely what confronts us now as one of the massive facts of the counter culture. The dissenting young have indeed got religion. Not the brand of religion Billy Graham or William Buckley would like to see the young crusading for—but religion nonetheless. What began with Zen has now rapidly, perhaps too rapidly, proliferated into a phantasmagoria of exotic religiosity. . . .

At the level of our youth, we begin to resemble nothing so much as the cultic hothouse of the Hellenistic period, where every manner of mystery and fakery, ritual and rite, intermingled with marvelous indiscrimination. For the time being, the situation makes it next to impossible for many of us who teach to carry on much in the way of education among the dissenting young, given the fact that our conventional curriculum, even at its best, is grounded in the dominant Western tradition. Their interests, when not involved with the politics of revolution, are apt to be fathoming phenomena too exotic or too subterranean for normal academic handling. If one asks the hip young to identify (a) Milton and (b) Pope, their answers are likely to be: (a) Milton who? and (b) which Pope? But they may do no mean job of rehearsing their kabbala or *I Ching* (which the very hip get married to these days) or, of course, the *Kamasutra.* [Theodore Roszak, *The Making of a Counter Culture*, pp. 138–139, 141.]

Alan Watts, both as popularizer and scholar, contributed both a distinguished body of writing, and a challenging personal presence, to the new religious sensibility.

. . . Western cultures have bred a type of human being who feels strongly alienated from everything which is not his own consciousness. He is a stranger both to the external world and to his own body, and in this sense he has lost his connection with the surrounding universe. He does not know that the "ultimate inside" of himself is the same as the "ultimate inside" of the cosmos, or that, in other words, his sensation of being "I" is a glimmering intimation of what the universe itself feels like on the inside. He has been taught to regard everything outside human skins as so much witless mechanism which has nothing whatsoever in common with human feelings and values. This style of man must therefore see himself as the ghastly and tragic accident of sensitive and intelligent tissue caught up in the cosmic toils like a mouse in a cotton gin. [*Beyond Theology*, Pantheon Books, Random House, New York, 1964, p. 6.]

It is not yet entirely clear why Oriental mysticism, and especially Zen, came to take such a central position in the spirituality of the young. It is partly because it is a nontheological religious tradition; partly because it entails a doing and an action. It has a place for the body in practice, if not in theory or in history.

Harvey Cox, as Protestant and unmystical as any of us, comments on the new mysticism, and sees no reason why it should necessarily lead away from politics and militancy.

Today's new mystics represent a modern phase in a very old religious movement. They personify man's ancient thirst to taste both the holy and the human with unmediated directness. Like previous generations of mystics, the new ones suspect all secondhand reports. Also they wish to lose themselves, at least temporarily, in the reality they experience. Above all, like the mystics of old, when they try to tell us what they are up to, we have a hard time understanding them. Mystics speak a language of their own, and sometimes even their fellow mystics do not quite get the message.

The neomystics, unlike many of the old ones, lux-

uriate in loud music, bright costumes, and convulsive
dancing. Still, they are right when they use the word
"contemplative" to describe their way of life. . . .

So far for most of the neomystics the rediscovery of
celebration, though inventive and colorful, often remains nonhistorical and therefore nonpolitical. It can
even be an escape from politics. Man cannot celebrate
abstractions, so the celebration of "love" and "peace"
dissolves into frivolity unless it becomes more particular. People do not celebrate "love" but the love of John
for Mary. Nor do we celebrate "freedom," but the
liberation of the Israelites from Egypt or of black
people from modern bondage. Christianity and Judaism have a definite bias for persons and events rather
than for minds and ideas. This supplies the tension
point at which Christianity may most fruitfully interact
with the neomystics. It should welcome the verve and
brightness they incarnate. But it should help them
transform celebration into a way of being in the world,
not a way of getting out of it. [Harvey Cox, *The Feast of
Fools*, Harvard University Press, Cambridge, 1969, pp.
102–103, 111–112.]

Paul Goodman had credentials to interpret both the
religious and the political sides of the new sensibility; he
lived in both places for a long time, and he taught us all.
Toward the end of his life, it became increasingly clear
that his personal understanding of himself was primarily a
theological one.

Now this basic faith [in science and technology] is
threatened. Dissident young people are saying that
science is antilife, it is a Calvinist obsession, it has been
a weapon of white Europe to subjugate colored races,
and scientific technology has manifestly become di-
abolical. Along with science, the young discredit the
professions in general, and the whole notion of "disciplines" and academic learning. If these views take
hold, it adds up to a crisis of belief, and the effects are
incalculable. Every status and institution would be
affected. Present political troubles could become end-

less religious wars. Here again, as in politics and morals, the worldwide youth disturbance may indicate a turning point in history and we must listen to it carefully.

If we start from the premise that the young are in a religious crisis, that they doubt there is really a nature of things, and they are sure there is not a world for themselves, many details of their present behavior become clearer. Alienation is a powerful motivation, of unrest, fantasy and reckless action. It leads, as we shall see, to religious innovation, new sacraments to give life meaning. But it is a poor basis for politics, including revolutionary politics.

All the "political" activity makes sense, however, if it is understood that it is not aimed at social reconstruction at all, but is a way of desperately affirming that they are alive and want a place in the sun. "I am a revolutionary," said Cohn-Bendit, leader of the French students in 1968, "because it is the best way of living." And young Americans pathetically and truly say that there is no other way to be taken seriously. Then it is not necessary to have a program; the right method is to act, against any vulnerable point and wherever one can rally support. The purpose is not politics but to have a movement and form a community. This is exactly what Saul Alinsky prescribed to rally outcast blacks. . . . A major reason why the young don't trust people over 30 is that they don't understand them and are too conceited to try. Having grown up in a world too meaningless to learn anything, they know very little and are quick to resent it.

Religiously, the young have been inventive, much more than the God-is-dead theologians. They have hit on new sacraments, physical actions to get them out of their estrangement and (momentarily) break through into meaning. The terribly loud music is used sacramentally. The claim for the hallucinogenic drugs is almost never the paradisal pleasure of opium culture nor the escape from distress of heroin, but tuning in to the cosmos and then communing with one another. They seem to have had flashes of success in bringing ritual participation back into theater, which for a

hundred years playwrights and directors have tried to
do in vain. And whatever the political purposes and
results of activism, there is no doubt that shared
danger for the sake of righteousness is used sacramentally as baptism of fire. Fearful moments of provo-
cation and the poignant release of the bust bring
unconscious contents to the surface, create a bond of
solidarity, are "commitment."

But the most powerful magic, working in all these
sacraments, is the close presence of other human
beings, without competition or one-upping. The
original sin is to be on an ego trip that isolates. . . .

It is hard to describe this (or any) religiosity without
lapsing into condescending humor. Yet it is genuine
and it will, I am convinced, survive and develop—I
don't know into what. In the end it is religion that
constitutes the strength of this generation, and not, as I
used to think, their morality, political will, and common sense. Except for a few, like the young people of
the Resistance, I am not impressed by their moral
courage or even honesty. For all their eccentricity they
are singularly lacking in personality. They do not have
enough world to have much character. And they are
not especially attractive as animals. But they keep
pouring out a kind of metaphysical vitality.

Naturally, traditional churches are themselves in
transition. On college campuses and in bohemian
neighborhoods, existentialist Protestants and Jews and
updating Catholics have gone along with the political
and social activism and, what is probably more important, they have changed their own moral, esthetic,
and personal tone. On many campuses, the chaplains
provide the only official forum for discussions of sex,
drugs, and burning draft cards. Yet it seems to me
that, in their zeal for relevance, they are badly failing
in their chief duty to the religious young: to be
professors of theology. They cannot really perform
pastoral services, like giving consolation or advice,
since the young believe they have the sacraments to do
this for themselves. Chaplains say that the young are
uninterested in dogma and untractable on this level,
but I think this is simply a projection of their own

distaste for the conventional theology that has gone
dead for them. The young are hotly metaphysical—but
alas, boringly so, because they don't know much, have
no language to express their intuitions, and repeat
every old fallacy. If the chaplains would stop looking in
the conventional places where God is dead, and would
explore the actualities where perhaps He is alive, they
might learn something and have something to teach.
[Paul Goodman, "The New Reformation," *The New
York Times Magazine*, September 14, 1969. This material appears, in slightly altered form, in chapter 4 of
Goodman's *New Reformation*, Random House, 1970.]

We have not said quite enough when we have said
"mystical." When mysticism begins to worry about history
or time, and when it experiences political frustration and
impotence, it becomes apocalyptic. Alongside the gentle
mystic comes the demand for apocalypse. Sometimes men
await it; more frequently, they seek to bring it about. And
to bring an apocalypse to pass, if it can be done at all, can
be a most uncivil thing. An article by Earl Rovit had some
penetrating things to say about this period.

Recently I have been struck by the frequency, variety,
and intensity of such a question on our contemporary
scene. A deceptively simple, thoroughly loaded question: *Why not?* Once my mind became attuned to its
resonances, I seemed to be able to discern it at or near
the root of every radical dissension of which I was
aware. In art, in science, in politics. In the chatter of
public and private disputation. Over and over again in
the classroom, in dissident social discussions, in my
own introspective dialogues, in any situation where the
utility or justification of an action was under delibera-
tion. But *why not?* is not so much a question as it is an
answer, or, better still, a declaration of polymorphous
intent. It seems to be the instinctive response of a large
segment of our collective mind to any expression of
restriction, prohibition, formal limitation. . . .
　　Those of us with any pretensions to some formal
intellectual training may be particularly disturbed in

the face of this adamant *why not*. Part of our uneasiness
is doubtless caused by the threat posed to our tenuous
security; but, more important I think, we are made
uncomfortable in an almost philosophical way because
we have been brought up within the circumscriptions
of a very different question, the traditional *why*? Our
intelligences, such as they are, have geared to analyse
"givens", to search out the complexity of causes that
may lead to an isolated effect. The overwhelming
course of the Enlightment and the empirical tradition
has tended to enclose our worlds into comprehensible
capsules of why-and-because. For *why* is predicated on
the unassailable ontological certainty that what is—
simply *is*. The counterquestion, *why not*?, is the apocalyptic gesture of dismissal. It causally rejects all
becauses since it denies even the minimal certainty of a
bounded problem. *Why not* is the shrug that, at best,
cares enough not to care—and, at worst, doesn't care at
all. . . . And when anything goes, it means that everything flies apart. *Why not* is the apocalyptic shiver of the
stoop-shouldered earth just a moment before the
avalanche, just a moment before the mountains skip
like lambs and the great rock-faces crumble and crush
everything in their fall. . . .

The truth of the matter is, I personally find the very
notion of an apocalypse unsettling. It makes a mash of
my ordered world. It destroys my past and throws my
thoughts of a future into an ash heap. Its fashion of
assault is omnivorous, uncompromising, and treacher-
ously sophisticated in its capacities for instant adapta-
tion. It has fathered the movement for silence and
outrage in the arts; for anarchy and violence in social
and political affairs; for polymorphous perversity in
psychology, religion and metaphysics. Ultimately—and·
it is never less than ultimate—it will accept nothing
save spontaneity, immediacy of response, and the
obliteration of all stabilities. And while it offers the
lip-service promise of a restored innocence and puri-
ty—a miraculous rebirth of life—as a reward for its
services, these blandishments are the least beguiling
facets of its appeal. . . .

God is proclaimed to be dead in the world because we are not there. We ourselves are God in the processes of partial creation, dividing the firmament and bringing forth the waters and the dry lands from within ourselves, laboring to give birth to the new man who shall be first and last. Is it any wonder that modern thought is a consecration of the absurd? Is it any wonder that modern art is helplessly—as well as hopelessly—comic. . . .

Mimic it, expose it, caricature its most egregious extravagances, the metaphor of the Apocalypse is our best model for viewing our contemporary human condition. It alone gives us a large and flexible mythic form that is grand enough to allow a full expression of our agonies and aspirations. What other myth do we possess that is as responsive to the major cataclysms of twentieth-century life and death? . . .

The seeming anarchism of the New Left may be a more radical and lasting political alignment than is usually thought. A painting like Picasso's *Guernica*, Buckminster Fuller's geodesic dome, the wild certainties with which city planners contemplate exploding metropolises, the accelerating shift from psychoanalysis to group therapy, some—at least—of McLuhan's insights and strategies in making the global village, our current confusions on racial, sexual and generational stabilities—all of these may very well be symptomatic of the enormous and violent changes that life takes when the human imagination seizes upon a new metaphor through which to view and reshape its world. It is as though the old tried-and-true centers cannot hold the magnitude of energy release that our age has mustered, and the apocalyptic mode is emerging spontaneously in all fields of action and thought. We may very well be on the brink of a brand new epistemology—a new technique and concept of rationality, which may build on the advances of binary computation, field theory and games theory, and include the irrationalities of extrasensory perception, mental telepathy, hallucinogenic drugs, and other open-ended, nonteleological modes of understanding. . . .

The apocalyptic ethic utters a challenging command: "Distrust thyself!" it says. "Trust rather in thy congeries of selves. Look to the peripheries of thy being, for that is where life exists, not in some hollow center." This commandment scares me even as it excites me. I feel unjustly judged and evasive before it. I find myself casting about for some secure resting-place for my spirit. I am ready to enunciate a homily on the sanctity of compromise, of humility, of that acceptance of limitation that is the strategy of humor. The magic of man may, after all, lie in his capacity to enter into and exit from the metaphors that seek to capture him in rigid definitions. [Earl Rovit, "On the Contemporary Apocalyptic Imagination," *The American Scholar*, Summer 1968.]

If, in our collection of texts, we were seeking a fully rounded and complete portrait of the revolution in consciousness, attention would have to be paid to the drug experience in all its varieties, and to poor Timothy Leary. But we are doubtless overfamiliar with all this, and, besides, Theodore Roszak has devoted an excellent chapter (V) in *The Making of a Counter Culture* to drugs. I would rather include, at this point, some comments on the art, aesthetics, and especially the music associated with the revolution we are trying to figure out. Jimi Hendrix wrote, and it seems like ages ago:

Music is going to break the way. There'll be a day when houses will be made of diamonds and emeralds which won't have any value anymore and they'd last longer in a rainstorm than a wooden house. Bullets'll be fairy tales. There'll be a renaissance from bad to completely clear and pure and good—from lost to found.

Atmospheres are going to come through music because music is in a spiritual thing of its own. It's like the waves of the ocean. You can't just cut out the perfect wave and take it home with you. It's constantly moving all the time. It is the biggest thing electrifying the earth. Music and motion are all part of the race of man. . . .

But I can explain everything better through music. You hypnotize people to where they go right back to their natural state which is pure positive—like in childhood when you got natural highs. And when you get people at that weakest point, you can preach into the subconscious what we want to say. That's why the name "electric church" flashes in and out. [*Life*, October 3, 1969.]

In the late sixties other reflective statements on rock music began to appear. From the rock generation itself, this from Jonathan Eisen:

Rock is, or at least everyone has been ardently declaring that rock is where it's at. Yet in point of fact there is very little to hold the movement together, still no working definitions of what the whole thing is about, even less of a consensus as to where the whole thing is moving. . . .

What holds rock together, however, is not uniformity of sound or agreed on definitions or even a stable constituency. Rather it is a consciousness, an aesthetic and a framework of reference—a new reality principle if you will—that has set apart the rock people (rock fans is a bad term here because the whole movement has transcended the fan phenomenon and has embraced an audience that is as much participant as it is listener) from the rest of the culture in certain important and discernible ways. . . .

At the center of rock consciousness, at the very core of the rock community, is a new consciousness permeating the alternative culture that is founded on drugs, and behind drugs a new sexuality, and behind the new sexuality a new body and soul awareness that persists in flowing toward new forms of music and new life styles. . . .

I think that the chief explanation rests with drugs which do in fact tend to alter consciousness to the point where it is possible to achieve an ersatz alteration of the cultural or epistemological substratum. Hip people do in fact tend to think and moreover to see in new and radically different ways from other people: it is certainly not a matter merely of new styles.

The most interesting aspect of Woodstock, for example, was not the fact that it was the largest assemblage of people ever gathered at a musical performance (which it was) but the fact that everyone was stoned. And not only was everyone stoned but (surprise) they were all gentle and rather polite. . . .

One does not listen to rock as one listens to Prokofieff. One gets high and proceeds to get inside one's own head. Rock music is head music, and rock listeners are not merely passive appreciators; there is not nor will there ever be any rock appreciation courses. There is no intellectual content, no deciphering necessary; there is no one who can tell you how to listen to rock, or what to listen for. There is no guide.

You hear, really hear the music and go wherever you want to go, fully secure that there is no proper approach to rock. Without this knowledge there will never be an understanding of what rock is all about, or what the hip community is trying to convey with their music and their drugs and their whole tolerant approach to life and each other. . . .

Hip or stoned thinking is not really thinking at all, if thinking is the logical progression from one concept to another in ordered, synthetic ways. The stoned pattern is more along the lines of instantaneous understanding, a kind of awareness that proceeds as though unencumbered by the kinds of defenses that order thought in pre-ordained channels. . . .

There is only the need to share it with others in the community. Deeper than that resides the knowledge that ultimately both everything is shared and nothing is truly communicable. And that your thoughts are your own exclusively and what you can share is yourself. . . .

What rock has been saying implicitly is that there is a different way altogether of ordering or disordering one's mind and hence one's activity. ("I accept chaos . . ."—Bob Dylan) And it is through the process of disencumbering the self from the predominant forms that the only real revolution can emerge. As Kopkind says, however, in *Rolling Stone*, the kids are going to wake up one day to the realization that they are going to have to fight for their life styles, and when that day comes all hell is going to break loose. Meanwhile the revolution proceeds apace. . . .

Rock music is sexual music and there are important parallels to be made between the new radicalism that has approached social change through political channels and the rock radicalism which has been a Freudian revolution which links liberation together with sexuality at the center of the movement. . . .

Rock speaks pleasure and hedonism to a society that has always denied the present; it speaks of the senses and sexuality to a society built on plastic and colored with pastels. It is an involvement with the self and the community in a society that is still scared to sign petitions and talk to neighbors and cannot fathom the idea of the collective. And it denies the legitimacy of property in a country for which property is valued more highly than life. . . .

Rock is so popular it is becoming jaded, and glutted on its own greed. But it still speaks for the rebirth of awe, for the freedom to say "wow" and mean it, for the ability to feel and express surprise and for the right to free the self from the dead layers of an irrelevant sophistication that has alienated people from their own sensibility and their own capacity to understand what is really "going down."

Rock and Dylan and The Beatles have articulated an anarchism far deeper in content than anything dealing with program. They continue to speak to the metaphors of life in ways that propel the listener to abandon his social games. ("All you need is love.") For them, and for the movement generally, the oppressor of man is scarcely other men so much as it is the force of social conformity that pressures men into ego postures that in turn prohibit them from coming to terms with their own dishonesty. ["The Rock Rebellion: Anarchy as a Life Style," in *The National Catholic Reporter*, September 24, 1969.]

Equally instructive, but this time from outside looking in, are some remarks by Benjamin DeMott.

> But the chief need, perhaps, and there is no sense, incidentally, in pretending that only rock types share it, is relief from significant life quandaries and guilt. And first among the quandaries is one that comes down roughly to this: I, an educated man (or adolescent), thoughtful, concerned, liberal, informed, have a fair and rational grasp of the realities of my age—domestic and international problems, public injustices, inward strains that give birth to acts of human meanness. But although I know the problems and even perhaps the "correct" solutions, I also know that this knowledge of mine lacks potency. My stored head, this kingdom—my pride, my liberalism, my feeling for human complexity—none of this alters the world; it only exhausts me with constant naggings about powerlessness. What can I do? . . .
>
> That rock world includes, in addition, intricate human relationships in which people press themselves to define their feelings precisely (The Beatles: "She said She said"). And it blinks neither at sexual hypocrisies (The Rolling Stones: "Back Street Girl"), nor at depressing or disgusting visual details of urban scenes (John Hartford: "Shiny Rails of Steel"). Boosters of one or another rock lyric, true enough, often lose their cool.
>
> "'Learn to forget,'" a writer says in *Crawdaddy*, the rock magazine, quoting a snippet of a rock tune. ("What power that phrase has! It's possible to get stoned for days by listening to this song. For a while it will seem the one truth available to us . . . a catalyst with more potential for generating truth . . . than anything since middle Faulkner.") . . .
>
> "Bring along your views," says the rock invitation. "Your liberal opinions. Your knowledge of atrocities committed by numberless power structures of the past. Your analyst's ideas about today's oedipal hangup. Your own manipulative, categorizing, classifying, S.A.T. braininess. You can not only cross the rock

threshold bearing this paraphernalia, you can retreat to it, consult it, any time you want—by tuning back into the lyrics. No obligation, in this pop world, to mindlessness. . . .

"But now if you'd like something else—if you want your freedom, if you'd care to blow your mind, shed those opinions, plunge into selflessness, into a liberating perception of the uselessness, the unavailingness, the futility of the very notion of opinionated personhood, well, it so happens to happen there's something, dig, real helpful here. . . ."

Pounded by volume, riddled by light, the listener slides free from the restraining self and from the pretenses of a private, "unique" rationality. Preparation for the descent is of various sorts. One man may have given house room in his head for a desire for connection with the unconscious roots of life—D. H. Lawrence's blood being. Another, unbookish, has experienced frustration in the public world of objective laws, ethnic or money interests, learned his impatience with the procedural and the discrete outdoors, as it were. Another despises the tyranny of his "family self" or his student role. All are alike, though, in their relish for a thunderous, enveloping, self-shattering moment wherein the capacity for evaluating an otherness is itself rocked and shaken, and the mob of the senses cries out: "What we feel, we are!"

And, as indicated, the rock lyricist is himself hip to the phenomenon of the "mystical union." The truth "allowable only to the very great" which Professor Poirier heard in a Beatles song is an explicit assertion of the arbitrariness of ego separations and of the desirability of soaring free from the mind-ridden world of subjects and objects. "I am within you and without you," these sirens call. "I am he as you are he as you are me and we are all together. . . ."

The point is tricky, it isn't trivial. That rock is a mixed experience, appealing at once to my sense of my sophistication and my sense of the unavailingness of sophistication; that rock lifts from me the burden of knowing the good and yet believing my knowledge to

be useless; that rock permits me to be part of others,
not a mere resentful conscious self, not a perceiver
harried on every side by multitudes of other conscious
selves pressing their analyzable differences—their values, opinions, interests, greeds—forward into my
space and notice: All these truths matter considerably.
They establish that rock can possess quasireligious
force. It leads me past my self, beyond my separateness
and difference into a world of continuous blinding
sameness—and, for a bit, it stoneth me out of my
mind. . . .

And then you think: Sound judgment is quite
impossible anyway, for it must wait until we know
what's to come of us, what the next human beings will
be like, what qualities will be saved and lost, what "our"
future is to be. A long wait.

But if that is the best final word, a further word is
implicit in it—viz., people who like the tunes but reject
the salvation—moldy figs who play the music at the old
sound levels and hunt for the old musical pleasures
and go on making the traditional musical discrimina-
tions and persist in thinking that chaps are dotty who
claim they am I and I am they—these senior types,
never blowing their minds, may still preserve a civilized
value now beleaguered on many fronts.

What value, exactly?

Just conceivably, nothing less than that of the self
itself. [Benjamin DeMott, "Rock as Salvation," *The New
York Times Magazine*, August 25, 1969. Reprinted in his
collection of essays, *Supergrow*, E. P. Dutton and Co.]

The feeling of living at the "end" is one of the most
persistent feelings in the whole of the cultural revolution.
The end of the modern, the end of the Renaissance, the
end of the great humanizing liberal institutions of the
West—family, church, nation, and even, perhaps, the
university. Marshall McLuhan has often pointed to evidence that permits us to speak, as well, of the end of the
Reformation: of calling, having a real future, goals, guilt.

I had a friend visiting from Harvard the other day who said: "You see, my generation does not have goals." (He is a young architect.) "We are not goal-oriented, we just want to know what is going on." Now that means not a point of view but total ecological awareness. . . . The point this person was making was that it is absurd to ask us to pursue fragmentary goals in an electric world that is organized integrally and totally. The young today reject goals—they want roles. . . . ["Address at Vision 65," *The American Scholar*, Spring 1966.]

McLuhan is, of course, a dominant figure in the revolution we are sketching. His power is not that he tells us something we did not know, but that he tries to suggest some reasons lying behind what we do know, but never understood. At no point is he more acute than when he relates the new electronic technologies to the longing for new kinds of community.

In the electric age, when our central nervous system is technologically extended to involve us in the whole of mankind and to incorporate the whole of mankind in us, we necessarily participate, in depth, in the consequences of our every action. It is no longer possible to adopt the aloof and dissociated role of the literate Westerner. [*Understanding Media*, McGraw-Hill, New York, 1964, p. 4.]

The new electric structuring and configuring of life more and more encounters the old lineal and fragmentary procedures and tools of analysis from the mechanical age. . . . Concern with *effect* rather than *meaning* is a basic change of our electric time, for effect involves the total situation, and not a single level of information movement. [*Ibid.*, p. 26.]

The problem, therefore, is not that Johnny can't read, but that, in an age of depth involvement, Johnny can't visualize distant goals. [*Ibid.*, p. 168.]

Here is Roszak again, on community:

> What, then, do the disaffiliated young have to grow
> toward? What ideal of adulthood has the world to offer
> them that will take the place of the middle-class
> debauch they instinctively reject? . . .
>
> The answer is: you make up a community of those
> you love and respect, where there can be enduring
> friendships, children, and, by mutual aid, three meals
> a day scraped together by honorable and enjoyable
> labor. Nobody knows quite how it is to be done. There
> are not many reliable models. The old radicals are no
> help: they talked about socializing whole economies, or
> launching third parties, or strengthening the unions,
> but not about building communities.
>
> It will take a deal of improvisation, using whatever
> examples one can find at hand: the life-way of Indian
> tribes, utopian precedents, the seventeenth-century
> Diggers, the French communities of work, the Israeli
> Kibbutzim, the Hutterites. . . . Maybe none of them
> will work. But where else is there to turn? [Theodore
> Roszak, *The Making of a Counter Culture*, pp. 202–203.]

It is time to bring this assemblage to an end. I have tried
here to suggest some of the historical background and
early development of the demand for a new consciousness
which erupted, in late 1969 into an explosion, media and
literary and cultural. Today, Consciousness III is being
eroded by all sorts of solvents: despair, political lassitude,
the repressions of the new American conservatism, economic anxiety, as well as the classical threats to every form
of consciousness—greed, self-centeredness and fear. This
consciousness revolution has a reality to it, I am sure, and
the function of this eccentric chapter has been merely to
begin the task we all must take up, young and old alike, of
learning both our assent and dissent to it.

As I stated at the beginning of this long chapter, I
propose to make my response to this cultural and religious
revolution in the form of a short story. As a Christian, and
as one no longer young, my reaction cannot be anything

but ambivalent. I suppose I would summarize my reaction by citing those very elusive words reported to be spoken by Jesus: "He who finds his life will lose it, and he who loses his life for my sake will find it." Thus the title of the ensuing tale may be given: "Matthew 10:39." It ought not be taken as autobiographical.

It had been an eerily uneventful semester. "Professor Merrill." The voice came from behind me, as I was leaving the classroom building. I turned and saw two students from the seminar just over. I stopped, waited for them to catch up. Something odd in their manner. Respectful, almost somber. One gets used to the gay arrogance of the bright ones, but respect?

Tony and Chuck. Not used to seeing them together. Tony was probably my best student—cool, impudent, merry. Both radical and effective politically, somewhere between *One Dimensional Man* and guerrilla theater. Never did straight term papers. Last year he covered the steps of the chapel with a giant collage on the subject of pornography. Very effective. Made the CBS Evening News.

Chuck I knew less well. His hair was longer, his manner more languid. Less political, I guessed. *I Ching*, Zazen, sensitivity training. I remembered why I was surprised to see them together, coming up to me as if they shared some guilty secret. A week or so ago, Tony had published in the college paper an attack on encounter groups, calling the whole movement naïve, utopian, vulgarized psychoanalysis, and a counter-revolutionary strategy to beguile people into accepting the world as it is by withdrawing into dark corners. "Pot without Smoke" had been his title for the article.

They joined me, looking a little like Simon and Garfunkel, and we walked along together. "Do you have time to talk?" Tony asked. Teachers glow under such questions. I felt needed.

"Sure. Shall we get some coffee, or do you want to come over to my office?"

This wasn't what they meant. Chuck spoke. "No. It may take a little time, and we'd like to invite you to come to my room tonight."

I hesitated slightly at this. Though my field is religion, I am a very bad and very reluctant counselor. I saw their reaction to my hesitation, and caught myself. "I'll be glad to come."

Our directions separated, and Tony called over. "About eight. You may find it professionally instructive." There was a twinkle in his eye, and I decided to get ready for anything, even a put-on.

I entered Chuck's room a little after eight. It was dark, lit only by a few candles, and everything seemed very planned, very liturgical. Wine and glasses were laid out, music was quietly filling the darkness—Jefferson Airplane, I think—and a handful of other students, some women, were scattered around the room's edge, like dim stars in the early evening sky, on desk, bed, and floor. I was motioned to a place in the middle of the floor, opposite Tony and Chuck, the candles between us. The setting was not right for jokes or small talk or "putting them at their ease." I decided to wait, and we began the business by being quiet together for what seemed like a very long time.

"Perhaps you're wondering why we asked you here," Chuck finally said to me. The cliché relaxed the atmosphere, and a soft wave of chuckling came from the students sitting in the background darkness.

"Because I am a professor of religion and you are suffering from, say, the absence of God."

"No. It's not your field we want, it's your head," Tony corrected.

"I suspect my field is part of my head."

"Maybe. Our story may or may not be theological," Chuck said. "Let's find out. Tony, why don't you start?" And then to me. "I'm afraid you'll have to suffer a certain amount of narrative exposition."

He began, rather matter-of-factly. "Night before last, after dinner, I came back to my room—which is in this building on the floor below—to find my roommate hosting a large crowd, settled down for what looked like a long night of talk. I didn't feel like joining, and I had some reading I wanted to do. So I wished them well, grabbed my book, and found myself one floor up in the hall here in front of Chuck's door. I knew it was his room, though I had not known him well, and I don't really know why I was drawn here. I may have been feeling a little guilty about that article I'd written. I knew somebody was there because the record player was on, so I knocked."

Tony stopped as if to invite Chuck to pick it up, and Chuck took the cue. "I was reading alone, enjoying the music, and had taken a couple of dexadrines about an hour earlier. I was feeling very mellow, very smooth, and really into the book I was reading. I was surprised and glad to see Tony, who told me he was looking for a quiet place to read, and I invited him in. We didn't say much. He mentioned the article, and then we fell to our own reading. After a while, I said, 'I did some speed, and it is very nice. Like to do some?' He asked what it was, and I told him just dexadrine."

Tony broke in. "So I said, 'Sure, why not?' I have tried various things, from time to time, just to experiment, but I'm really not into drugs all that much. This seemed like the right time. But we didn't talk about drugs at all. It was all very matter-of-fact, and we spoke very little for the next hour or so. A very pleasant, low-key scene."

"Around nine or nine-thirty," Chuck went on, "I got up from my chair to boil some water for coffee and to change the record. This break somehow had the effect of changing the relationship, which up to now had been casual, and a little careful. We both seemed ready to put aside our own work, to give up our isolated enjoyment of the music-filled silence, and to become—how shall I put it—to become present to each other in a more straightforward way."

Tony started to speak again, and he was without his accustomed glibness, feeling for words. The other students in the darkened room were quiet and intent. "It was like we'd been walking separately on a nice level path and suddenly come to a barrier that we couldn't get around unless we worked together. You must remember"—Tony was directing his words partly to me, partly to himself— "we had never really been friends before this, and that in the hour or so I'd been in his room we'd really said very little to one another."

I knew very little about amphetamines or what people expected to get from them. "You were both on speed at the time of this break," I asked.

Chuck and Tony glanced at each other, as if to see whether either had a clear answer to my question. Chuck answered, and from Tony's manner it was clear he was answering for both. I must have become aware, at about this time, of the curious way in which the two of them seemed to be operating as a single consciousness. I was about to understand why this was. "I'm sure we were both still on it, but we just weren't focusing on it all that much. I'd taken two caps several hours before, and Tony had— what?"

"Just one, about an hour before," Tony said.

"Neither of us," Chuck continued, "were especially self-conscious about having a drug experience. I don't really know whether what was happening would have happened without speed or not."

I spoke again, mainly to clarify in my own mind what they were trying to say. "I understand what you're saying about the shift in the relationship between you. You came together in some way, and something new was added. What was so memorable about this? Was it the subject of your talk? Would it help me to know what you were talking about?"

Tony answered quickly. "No. I don't remember the subject of our conversation at all."

"It was more the way we talked," Chuck ventured. "The effect his words had on me. The medium, not the message."

"In the rather disjointed give and take I found that

Chuck was saying what I had always thought or felt myself."

"And when Tony would say something, I couldn't tell whether it was someone else speaking, or myself."

"I guess we were probably talking," Tony went on, "about authorities and fathers and freedom and the usual things. And I was beginning to see, more sharply than ever before, that I am really my own judge, my own master. No one, not even friends, can tell me what to do. Chuck, remember, you quoted a line from Hermann Hesse about 'dying for the things your father thinks are right.'"

"Yes. That seemed to sum up the enemy we were being freed from."

"We weren't arguing or analyzing," Tony continued. "We rarely spoke in complete sentences. We were really into each other, connecting, making new synapses, like those giant sparks that jump from one globe to another in old mad-scientist movies. It was like current, like flowing. Easy. Right."

"Remember," Chuck said, "when I went over to a pile of records on the floor and started going through them, kind of aimlessly? I came to *Sgt. Pepper*, looked at the back, and read out loud 'Where I belong I'm right.'"

"Then I joined him, reading over the lyrics on the back of the album cover," Tony continued, "and it was like we were all finished but still looking for confirmation. I had a feeling that there was something for us in Harrison's *Within You Without You*. I finally found it, and read it aloud, about how we're all one and life flowing on within you and without. And we said 'that's it' and it was over."

I waited a moment before I spoke. "The most striking thing about what you're telling me is the ambiguity of the experience. In one way it was apparently an affirmation of the radical isolation of man from man. No one can help, no one can judge. In another sense, it was an experience of identity, of solidarity. The two of you became one—one flesh, some kind of true community. Was anything sexual going on? I understand amphetamines are supposed to induce a pre-orgasmic sexual reaction, and that is why they can become addictive."

"Not sex as desiring or touching," Chuck responded. "I was not conscious of any latent homosexual impulses being released."

Tony nodded and went on. "Yet—there was something sexual there. Your phrase 'one flesh'—" And he turned to me.

"It isn't mine, you know."

"I know. That did ring a bell. Not sex as desiring or touching. Chuck is right. But certainly sex, or love, as caring, as valuing. We were valuing, or discovering, ourselves and each other, at the same time."

Chuck continued at once, as if to give evidence for the union or unity they were trying to describe. They were both much more sure of themselves now, and their words were coming more readily, more intensely. It was significant that no one in the room had felt the need to break into this serious mood with a semi-hostile joke or a piece of whimsy used as a putdown. "It was as though two planets were being born—out of nothing—him and me. We hadn't been before, and now we were."

If anything could bring a laugh to a group of undergraduates uncomfortable before too much seriousness or intensity, such a statement could. But it didn't. Chuck's simile served as a climax to their narrative. No one wanted, or needed, to say anything more, right away. So there was a short piece of silence, and, in a moment, it became clear that both Tony and Chuck wanted to de-intensify the mood, to find some secular way of saying "Amen," so they could move naturally on to whatever might follow. Chuck, as host, got up and poured some wine, passed it around, while othes lit up cigarettes and other things. The two of them clearly wanted to step back from this experience a little, and I began to understand why I was invited to the room.

Tony and Chuck seemed to be as unclear as their hearers in the room about just what this experience had been. They knew, or felt, what it might mean. But not what it was. Was it merely drugs? Was it religious? Was it something they had achieved, or was it given, and, if given, by what or whom? These were my questions, as we sat there in silence.

"In some ways," I ventured after a moment, "in the intensity of your language, in the indelible character you seem to grant this thing, it takes on some of the marks of a classical conversion experience. Certainly more like conversion than mysticism."

"I have a few old Protestant memories," Tony said, "and I wondered about that. There was a change, all right. But some of the things you expect to find in conversions were not present: movement from darkness to light, error to truth, sin to grace. There was nothing . . . from the outside. Nothing radically new."

"This experience lived," Chuck continued, "on the normal, natural level of our lives. No new space, no new character. Just the old, clarified."

"Yes. Seeing is the primary metaphor. What was dim, is now clear. What we partly suspected, we're now sure about."

"Yes," Chuck agreed. "There was something like joy, and there still is now in the retelling. But what we knew then, and know now, is not something about God, or even about anything as grandiose as the meaning of existence. It is simply something about ourselves."

"I've wondered about the role of the self," I said. "Was there a losing, or a finding?"

"I would say finding," Tony said, a bit tentatively. "Chuck?"

"It certainly wasn't losing anything. But it didn't really feel like finding either. You find something you had, but lost; or you find something you never had before. It wasn't either of those. Do I have to choose between losing and finding?"

"I may have been wrong to introduce the terms. The distinction between losing and finding is my traditional

Christian way for getting at the kind of thing that has happened to you, and it is pretty clear the distinction doesn't help."

Tony went on. "It was more like a giving, or a knowing. There are things you don't know; there are things you probably know, by convention or belief; and there are a few things you really know, from the inside, and these you'll never unknow."

"I can't conceal my surprise," I remarked, "that two such different life styles as yours could find a center in the same event. I would have guessed that what happened would be too unpolitical for you, Tony, and too unmystical for you, Chuck."

"It really was a political event for me," Tony reflected. "A certain human relationship took form, a certain way two people have of being with each other and in the world. I can get a radical politics out of that."

Chuck continued. "I am not a political person, and never will be, in Tony's sense. But I can draw ethical, even political conclusions from what happened. I have no right to force myself, or anything, on anyone else. I can only truly be with someone else when I let him be what he is."

"Or help him be what he can become," Tony added.

"That's where we may separate," Chuck said. "'Helping people be what they can become' sounds too earnest, too manipulative, too . . . Marxist."

"Too Protestant?" I asked.

"I guess so."

"Let me try to get back to the point before Chuck and I diverged," Tony said. "This is the content of our experience, I think: an overwhelming impression of the need for a radical tolerance of one another. The only person I have a right to push, persuade, or force into anything is myself."

Chuck seemed to accept this, so I decided to play the professor for a moment. "You both know the arguments against absolute tolerance. Tolerance of the radical right, or tyrants, or evil? Of a Spiro T. Agnew or worse, who does not tolerate you? And recall Marcuse's contention that tolerance is the ultimate weapon of a liberal society by which it embraces, permits, and finally defuses effective dissent or change."

Chuck answered, a bit impatiently. "That's all head-talk. Of course we'll have intellectual difficulties when we try to work this thing out. I don't want to get into these now. There is a moral absolutism in our experience that we'll have to take, the consequences of. But I'm not really interested in this academic stuff right now."

"All right," I said, "I hear your rebuke, though I hope you won't indefinitely postpone the intellectual work required of you. Let me ask another question that may or may not be head-talk. If every man is his own judge, and if the only authentic human relationship is one of radical tolerance and trust, what happens to education? Isn't the teacher tied to some kind of authoritative function that makes him inaccessible to you? He says do this, and, if you don't, you pay."

"I don't see any real problem with that," Tony replied. "Just a lot of little ones. There have to be some inauthentic relationships, and my relationship to a teacher may be one of them. Someone knows something I want to know, I go to him. No problems."

"A kind of friendly bibliography," I suggested.

Then Chuck: "I don't feel we've got to abolish, at once, all structures with functional differences or inauthentic relationships in them—families, universities, nations. Let them alone, they're dying fast enough by themselves. What our experiences does give me is a test for the right kind of teaching, and maybe a clue about how to respond to a teacher."

"Which is?" I asked.

"A teacher teaches well," Chuck was exploring, "when I am part of his data. When I feel he is receiving something from me as he gives something. This means irrelevance or stupidity or arrogance are not the worst vices of the academic. Only hypocrisy is truly evil."

"What did you mean about a clue for responding to a teacher?" Tony asked his friend.

"I mean this. Perhaps I mustn't allow even the wisest and most humane of my teachers to become a guru for me. I may, for a moment, take on gurus to compare them. But only to reject them, and the very idea of guru. We must become our own gurus, our own messiahs, our own gods."

"You're back to religious language, gentlemen," I noted.

"Well, does this sound like a religious experience to you, Professor Merrill?" Tony asked the question.

We were all a bit wrung out. I had a feeling that the question wasn't really very important to either Tony or Chuck, and that it was posed more out of a kind of politeness.

"I'm not sure how important it is to put any labels on it right away," I answered. "That may be part of what you call the head-stuff that comes later, after you've lived yourselves through this first stage. It is clear that there was no god lurking around. That doesn't by itself rule out the religious label. I suspect it would be religious in my sense. As some kind of Christian, I would take Jesus as the test case for experience or behavior that might be called religious. Jesus teaching, Jesus healing and casting out demons, Jesus on the cross, Jesus withdrawing, only to move back again into the ordinary world, Jesus refusing to define himself or give straightforward moral advice . . . Yes, I suspect there was something religious going on."

We were clearly at the point when little more could be said. The whole group in the room, Tony and Chuck included, had begun to loosen up and become more relaxed. Then Chuck spoke.

"I really think the drug may have been an important factor."

"I suspect you're right," I replied.

"That raises a nice point," Chuck continued. "If what happened was good, healing, beneficial, all the rest, shouldn't we want it to become available to everyone?"

"Through speed?" I asked.

"By any means necessary, as they say," Tony suggested.

"Speed kills, I'm told," I remarked.

Then Chuck: "So do revolutions and automobiles."

And then Tony, with his politics. "It was the farthest thing in the world from dropping out. It was more like dropping back in to the world, to love and justice and caring."

I was tired, but some answer was called for. "You are arguing at the very limits of my moral resistance. I thought I had purchased my ticket into today by achieving an unthreatened tolerance for marijuana, and now you are pushing me farther and faster than I am ready to go."

"It's not a question of inviting you to turn on," Chuck said.

"I know. That would have been easier to resist than what you are offering."

It was time for me to leave. I got up from the floor, stretched my legs, and moved to the door. Then a girl stepped out of the dark outskirts of the room and walked into the little patch of light spread by the candles. She was naked. Why, I wasn't sure. I looked at her gently. Then she put a hand on my shoulder. What was it? A pass, a put-on, a motherly pat from experience to innocence, a blessing? And this was what she said.

"Zap . . . you missed the point . . . who cares who's on the cross . . . richard nixon's on the cross . . . paul is there . . . jesus occasionally swings there . . . the point is, aside from the way we make our beds, there is an overthing . . . here comes the sun . . . rocked on momma's knee 'til the sun son sun smiles . . . then zapzap and sinatra makes us all grown up . . . out of college and no money no future nowhere to go but oh that magic feeling nowhere to go . . . I'm a loser nowhereman psst I'm the walrus . . . and boy there's nothing but that magic feeling but carry that weight tote that barge lift that cross . . . everyone is on the cross we've all moved next door . . . in the end the love you take is equal to the love you make all

you need is love . . . all you have is love? what else is there
to do . . . swing on the cross and watch yourself bleed . . .
that's somewhere . . . paul is death we all are . . . for years
he has been long before he died sitting on the coffin before
sgt. pepper yesterday today . . . I am he as you are he as
you are me and we are all together . . . sontag says it's the
word not the wordmaker . . . mick says it's the singer not
the song . . . the beatles enigma charisma run ahead and
are always on top . . . they end up selling those that sell
them . . . they are themselves they become the christ they
play all the games correctly . . . I say john knows where we
are going because he has it all thought out and we
listen—christ did that . . . christ you know it ain't easy
they're gonna crucify me . . . the beatles are the only ones
we can get into on this level . . . others sound better but no
one else is them . . . there you have the time-honored
tradition that is jesus god and paul . . . every little girl
would like to be with him like the women at that other
tomb . . . holy smoker don't you think the joker laughs at
you . . . john is laughing at us and he loves it john is
tripping out of his mind on to the cross weak and
powerless in the world only a suffering john can help . . .
while the whole world is lapping his blood or spilling
it . . . while on the other side of abbey road lies a beautiful
life with a free sample of salvation for every mailbox . . .
yinyang innocenceexperience . . . enough to feed my
blake . . . the beatles are blake as you are blake as you are
me and we are all the better for it . . . god is dead where is
the content no gods only crosses and prisons . . . they
know it . . . you know it . . . sitting on a cornflake waiting
for the man to come . . . hanging on the cross waiting for
the man to come . . . it's no secret there is no place to
go . . . I am john and john is you and how do we fill up all
this empty space . . . the silence terrifies me too watch out
for the blaise . . . as each day gropes toward the Day I am
sitting on the cornflake less mature less responsible less
acceptable less nice unless you become as a little child all

right I'm trying and society will see me cry at its appointed time and we'll all see each other in prison and send messages through the walls and we need to learn morse code and how to write on toilet paper and they'll take away our books so we'd better start remembering everything."

I managed to thank Tony and Chuck without words, there weren't any, and I plunged back out into the familiar night.

VIII

A.D. 2000

Surely some revelation is at hand;
Surely the Second Coming is at hand.
The Second Coming! Hardly are these words out
When a vast image out of *Spiritus Mundi*
Troubles my sight: somewhere in sands of the desert
A shape with lion body and the head of a man,
A gaze blank and pitiless as the sun,
Is moving its slow thighs, while all about it
Reel shadows of the indignant desert birds.
The darkness drops again; but now I know
That twenty centuries of stony sleep
Were vexed to nightmare by a rocking cradle,
And what rough beast, its hour come round at last,
Slouches towards Bethlehem to be born?
　　　—From W. B. Yeats, *The Second Coming*, 1921

I propose here to move from the recent past to the immediate future. Our reflections on the counterculture entailed a consideration of just what deposit the new consciousness movement may be leaving with us. This problem, in turn, led me to think about the year 2000. I first became intrigued by the year 2000 when recently, recalling that Yeats's second coming and great beast were expected in that year, I began to notice some parallels between my students and their gods with that rough beast being born in the desert. Beguiled by this vision, I began to ask myself: what will it be like to be religious and to teach religion in the year 2000? "No one knows," a wise man said. "But go to the futurologists." "To whom?" "To the wise men who have already written fat books and fashioned lush symposiums." It appears that the journey to the religion of 2000 and Yeats's vision entails a detour through—futurology. But what is it?

Futurology is only one of the eschatological styles making its appeal today. Apocalyptic we have already noted. Utopianism and science fiction are others . How do these differ?

Utopianism, in its purest form, is set in the future, and its function is either to set forth a desirable end that one might work toward now, or to offer some frightful portrait of the future that might have the function of dissuading us from present folly. Utopianism, in general, believes that man has a real, long-range future, and that he can be altered.

Science fiction, in its purest form, not only takes place in a future time, it takes place in some space other than this earth. It does not propose to be as predictive or as homiletic as the utopias; its realm is imagination rather than ethics, but it does derive its special character from its habit of extrapolating from present scientific or technological discoveries. Science fiction can exist in utopian or dystopian forms.

Futurology is like dull utopianism, or plodding science fiction, which is to say it is a social science. It does not usually posit anything like a long-range future: most futurology is talking about the year 2000, and some is concerned with even shorter intervals. But the special value of futurological thought is that it can be moralistic; it can say something about the desirable organization of society, since it is freed from an excessive concern about the details of the present or near-future.

My interest is limited. I want to know what is likely to be the ethical and religious climate of the university in the year 2000. What will the teaching of religion be like? This means a number of assumptions and restrictions. I am assuming there will be a university, a harder assumption than that there will be religion. And I am assuming that the Black American will have obtained a decisive and creative role in that university of the future. I will have, furthermore, nothing to say about overpopulation and the possibility of a world famine in the seventies or eighties. I am less sanguine that this problem will have achieved a solution than I am about the problem of the Black American, but the restriction must stand. And I am compelled to leave aside many of the issues that the specifically educational futurologists worry about: mass education, curriculum, the impact of educational technology (TV, teaching machines, computers and information storage).

It is likely that our teaching will in fact be altered by technology more than any other single factor, and the humanities in the future will need to develop far more sophisticated means of protest against some elements in this technological revolution. Let me simply record here some remarks by Hans Magnus Enzensberger, which I suspect are correct.

> Above all, however, we are not sufficiently aware of the fact that the full deployment of the mind industry still lies ahead. Up to now it has not managed to seize control of its most essential sphere, which is education. The industrialization of instruction, on all levels, has barely begun. While we still indulge in controversies over curricula, school systems, college and university reforms and shortages in the teaching professions, technological systems are being perfected which will make nonsense of all the adjustments we are now considering. The language laboratory and the short-circuit TV are only the forerunners of a fully industrialized educational system which will make use of increasingly centralized programming and of recent advances in the study of learning. In the process,

education will become a mass media, the most powerful of all, and a billion-dollar business. [The Industrialization of the Mind, *Partisan Review*, Winter 1969.]

There are three different patterns of thought and
feeling in the university today that especially pertain to
our concern with religion and the future.

1. The training and formation of the perceptions and the
   emotions will increasingly become a factor in the
   schools (see Peter Drucker, *The Age of Discontinuity*, p.
   319) and the university will inherit and have to face this
   movement. A vulgar way to put this problem is this: if
   the American young are increasingly becoming persuaded that the body–mind dualism is false, how long
   can an educational system still largely grounded on that
   dualism remain intact?
2. The student protest movement will be very much alive.
   It has recently been predicted that the number of
   students at college and university by the year 2000 will
   be nearly twice that of today. I assume, therefore, that
   economic anxiety and the other factors that slowed the
   flow of men and women into higher education in the
   early seventies will prove to be temporary and short-
   lived. By the end of the century, it will be taken for
   granted that a bachelor's degree in the twenty-first
   century is as necessary for survival as a coat of armor
   was in the thirteenth. I am assuming (perhaps I should
   say, hoping) that a protest movement will emerge
   again from the current inertia and quiet, and that it
   will make a series of theoretical demands. Students will
   come to see that the shape of the real world in which
   they will live their productive lives is hidden from us all,
   and that they need to be taught to live in a world no one
   can tell them about. The issues will not be merely: the
   relevance of the subject matter taught, Hesse instead of
   Beowulf, McLuhan rather than Marx, Cage for
   Stravinsky, Dylan Bob not Dylan Thomas. Not merely

curricular reform and protest against restrictive campus rules on housing, sex and drugs. But a common theoretical attack, backed by whatever is left of the political activists, the drug culture, dropouts, and mystics.

a. A systematic attack on the whole of Western intellectual history since the Renaissance, and not merely because this is largely a white history.

b. Our generation attacked limited targets like capitalism. They will be attacking all of the modern moralizing and socializing institutions of the West—family, church, nation—and wondering whether the university might not have to go as well.

c. An attack, common to political and consciousness revolutionaries, on the very idea of the separate self, and the elevation of the idea of expansion or loss of self as the proper end of man, whether by pharmacological experiences, or by new political communities of healing.

d. An attack on the very idea of history or tradition or past, as necessary to the experience of being freed from parochialism and limitation.

e. A protest against the idea of art as mastery or discipline—the very distinction between artist and subject matter is at stake, and all men will become, not prophets, but artists.

For some of the young, then, the issue is not the reform of the institution. It is a deeper question that threatens the foundation of the university itself: can anything like learning go on between older minds and younger? Or, given all the generational and authority hangups, is not the only possible higher education self-education?

3. The university will increasingly become, for the young, the last possible moral and spiritual community. The Freudian revolution provided us all a way to dissociate ourselves from the sick communities that bedevil us. Freud, however, never really saw that, after the death of God, since man cannot heal himself alone, only communities can heal. But what healing community did

he put in the place of the dying family? Only the doctor–patient relationship, the community of the couch. The young today have experienced the impotence of the family, the church, and the nation. These are not possible objects of loyalty. They are not communities that can effectively pass on the moral wisdom of the past. Are they indeed terminally ill? If they are, then can the university take over their functions of socialization, healing, providing therapeutic communities, critically passing on values? This is what the young are asking the university to do, to act not only *in loco parentis*, but *in loco ecclesiae* and *in loco patriae* as well. This is the reason the student is presenting himself to his teachers, not merely wanting to know what he knows, but as wondering whether he represents a possible model for adult existence. They doubt it, for the academic life appears to them as singularly joyless and somber. *Gaudeamus igitur, iuvenes dum sumus*, they sometimes sing. And they mean it. But what teacher is qualified to teach a student how to rejoice?

This is the piece of the contemporary university that I am in closest touch with—my blind hand on the elephant's tail. It is the place from which I venture into futurology.

It is time to see what the real futurologists have to say on our problem. And "real futurologist" means, inevitably, Herman Kahn—or, more exactly, futurology's first canonic book, *The Year 2000*, by Kahn and Anthony Wiener (Macmillan & Co., 1967). Where are we going, intellectually and spiritually, according to them? They have spotted what they call "a basic, long-term, multifold trend" toward an "increasingly sensate (empirical, this-worldly, secular, humanistic, pragmatic, utilitarian, contractual, epicurean or hedonistic, and the like) culture" (p. 7).

The presence of the term "sensate" reminds us that Kahn and Wiener apparently presuppose the interpretation of history of Sorokin, and with it his conviction that all cultures begin with an ideational, dogmatic, religious phase, and gradually degenerate into a sensate and then a late sensate period. Kahn and Wiener feel that today we are sensate becoming late sensate, and thus becoming nihilistic, weary, rebellious, alienated. As if this weren't enough, the coming society will be radically permissive, while work, obligation, and duty ride their downward curve. As affluence intersects with permissiveness, we will see more and more disbelief in the future of man, and a mood of privatistic withdrawal.

The basis in Kahn and Wiener for this prediction is primarily economic. As the Puritan ethic wanes, we have fewer and fewer conscience-dominated types, and the parent is no longer willing or able to inculcate the older virtues of thrift, diligence, postponement of gratification. Thus, our "now" generation, occupied with "instant every-thing," coffee as well as Nirvana.

Now this is pretty old stuff; indeed, it is old Marxist stuff (although ex-Vice President Agnew said it), assuming that culture is directly determined by the economic order and that as soon as the economic pressures that sustained the older work ethic are released, people will inevitably withdraw into cynicism and privatism. Kahn and Wiener's projection may be true enough for some people and some conditions. But quite another prediction would follow if we adopted some other model—one from the world of urbanization, for example. That would enable us to end up at quite another point. One could predict that, in the urbanized society of the future, as more and more affluent people bump into each other in more and more crowded spaces, with less and less food, air, and power, a concern for the public good will become a matter not of altruism but of survival.

We are probably going to see both things happening at the same time, and, if they do, we may see emerging two quite different religious–ethical styles based on the two directions. The first might be called an *ethic of celebration*, and I think this will take two forms, the withdrawn and the involved, the commune and Madison Avenue. The withdrawn ethic of celebration will have the privatistic style Kahn and Wiener foresee: communes, drugs, expansion of consciousness. But there will also be involved and hip celebrationists, and they will be found in the ad agencies, in publishing, and in broadcasting. They will groove on technology and whatever happens. The medium will be the ethical and religious message, and life will be full of color and balloons and laughter. Enjoy. Do whatever needs to be done to keep the circulation up, to keep the affluent kids buying, the ratings high, the audiences pleasantly shocked, the highrises steadily rising.

The second ethical style might be called an *ethic of refusal*. The work ethic will not be so firmly rejected, and older artistic and ethical habits will still persist: make something beautiful, dissent, protest, help. When something old fails, don't run away and don't pretend that the old really has a camp kind of charm, but make something new that won't fail. This ethic may live either in the commune or the city, and it is suggested not by the hippie drug scene today, but by the student activists, the draft resisters, and the consumer and ecology movements. It will say, with Ralph Abernathy, that a launching pad cannot really become holy ground until the naked are clothed, the poor fed.

Kahn and Wiener make one more obvious point. They seem to share the fascination of other popular philosophers of history with the fall of the Roman Empire as an instructive model for our current decadence. So, as with Rome, we too are to have a resurgence of new religiosity, and the authors cite all the current evidence you might expect them to. But they have nothing interesting to tell us about this new religion, and perhaps it is time to leave behind our futurological guides. It does not appear that a great deal can be learned from such ponderous exercises in the art of the obvious, and it might be noted in passing that Kahn and Wiener were able to write a very large book about the year 2000 without saying a thing about the problems of the environment.

Perhaps the lesson of futurology is that no one else can tell you much. You must become your own futurologist. Let us try it. And, since futurology seems to be strangely drawn to three-stage philosophies of history, let me propose one of my own. My stages do not move toward decay or toward the kingdom of God on earth. I hope that the scheme will function as descriptive, rather than evaluative.

I do not take my three-stage scheme very seriously. But it does take account of some observations, and it does make possible some enlightened guesses about religion on the campus in the year 2000. There is something like a religious revolution going on in the West, and we need to understand it. I am proposing that it can best be understood as existing in the overlap between the end of the modern and the beginning of the post-modern world, between stage two and stage three of the following structure.

Western religion can be discerned in three successive stages. The first stage, the classical era, extends roughly from Abraham to Martin Luther. Its main question is "Who art Thou?"; its central problem is the naming of the gods. It is the era in which the Jewish–Christian tradition as we know it is formed. The Roman Catholic Church is perhaps the greatest institutional achievement of this era; the canonic scripture the greatest document. It is the period of Gothic architecture, the Gregorian chant, the *Divine Comedy*, the ontological argument.

Men begin to feel a decisive alteration in their religious sensibilities with the intellectual revolutions of sixteenth-century Europe, and this permits us to discern the second stage. This is the modern era; it goes from Luther to Freud, and its main question is not that of the first era, but rather "Who am I?"—the naming, not of the gods, but of the self. The question of the first era is of course still passionately asked, but it is asked in terms of the question about the self. Faith, rather than arguments for the divine existence. Luther's question, "How can I achieve a gracious God?" was a revolutionary question of the second age, but his answer was in the conservative form of the first age: "You can't achieve God at all, but He can achieve you, if you let Him."

The marks of this stage, which most of us know from the inside because one way or another we are living at the end of it and we may never be able to leave it in any decisive sense, are easy to note. They are, in part, the Protestant era, the time in which America comes into being, and the key words are all self-words: pietism, experience, identity, work, goals and values, romanticism, psychoanalysis, existentialism, sin, alienation. Artistically, it is the time not of the Gothic arch which points upward, but of the novel which "points" within.

In Christian theology, nearly everything of interest that has been going on for the last fifty years has been an attempt to adjust the loyalties of religious man to both of these eras or stages. To be "authentic," Christians had to affirm their commitment to the first era, for there they "began." To be "relevant," they were obliged to affirm the second era, for there they lived and loved and did their work.

Something new has come upon us, and the problem is precisely that many of the clearest minds today are not at all certain that the second age *is* the one we are living in. The third stage I am calling the post-modern era, and it stretches from Freud or Sartre (or from whatever particular place you believe the problem of the self has been most effectively solved), and it goes, open-ended, into an unknown future. I assume that the revolution in consciousness or sensibility has something authentic in it, and that it is not wholly a fad. (Defenders of passing eras always describe signs of a new stage as fads, or relevance-mongering, or publicity-seeking.) The problem of the third stage is neither "Who art Thou?" nor "Who am I?", but "Who are you?" or "Who is my neighbor?" Or "how can I find a healing community?" Can I find this community through the answer of the first stage (God calls true community into being in His church), or through the answer of the second stage (psychoanalysis, the group movement)? Or are new forms and institutions required? The characteristics of the third age have often been listed:

> concern with style or life style; cool; not pursuit of goals, but getting with it, asking "What's happening?"; protest; drugs; the abandonment of the self–world distinction and even of the very idea of the separate self; the disappearance of the past, and thus the disappearance of rebellion against the father and the Oedipal problem; the disappearance of the future; true community must be achieved, and now.
>
> (I have chosen to stress here what the political and consciousness revolutions have in common, rather than the obvious things that separate them. What they hold in common, I think, is their demand for an immediate and authentic experience of community. This is least true of LSD (and its child, the Jesus movement), use of which might be impishly defined as an atavistic attempt by the children of the post-modern world to leap directly back to the concept of the holy in stage one. Marijuana, that social weed, is the primary drug sacrament for the post-modern world.)

Now we know that the stages of all proper philosophies of history don't neatly fit together. There is always overlapping. The problem of the self does not emerge in the sixteenth century. It is posed, of course, in a definitive way, deep in the midst of the first era, with Augustine's *Confessions*, and this is why we call him the first modern man, and his book the first autobiography. The problem of self is again raised, at the end of the first era, in the mystical tradition, and it might be suggested that mysticism is the primary ideological bridge between the first and the second eras.

Furthermore, the problem of the third era doesn't begin

with today; it is raised within the modern era or second stage, primarily by the political revolutions of the eighteenth century. There, somewhere, is where the post-modern era really begins: with regicide, and deicide, and the end of political and moral absolutes. Marx is likely to be as important for an understanding of the religion of the third age's beginning as Freud is important for an understanding of the religion of the second age's end.

Each succeeding era assumes that it has solved the problems of the previous age or ages in terms of its own main interest. The modern or second era solved the problem of God in terms of the self—this is the meaning of faith. And the post-modern age faces the problem of self by dissolving it in community, or at least by a radical anti-individualistic definition of selfhood. I suspect that the post-modern age may even come to define God, the problem of the first age, in terms of community or being in the world. This is a direction I find at least implicit in the recent words and deeds of Daniel Berrigan. This direction is permissible, I assume, but at that point the age becomes not only post-modern, but post-Christian, for, while God in general can be defined in any way you choose, the Christian God cannot be so loosely redefined. And as soon as we really believe that God *is* a mode of being in the world, that God *is* our future, that God *is* the moral coherence of our lives, that God *is* the sense of the unfinished and mysterious character of our lives, then the death of God will have done its limited work, and we are all post-Jewish and post-Christian indeed.

If mysticism is the ideological bridge between stage one and stage two, I would suggest that Norman Mailer, for whom the struggle for God and the struggle for America have become a single struggle, is a decisive representative of the bridge; that "revolution" is the bridge idea between the second and the third stages; and that we will really become clear on the nature of our revolutionary ferment today when we make up our minds just to what extent we can use the experience and the heroes of the second stage, and to what extent new theories and new models will become necessary.

Let me summarize my observations up to now. I think I see some things now going on in the university, and some things that are happening religiously, ethically, psychologically, and it is these observations that form the basis of my projections for the future.

1. A systematic attack on the whole Western intellectual enterprise, particularly the body–mind distinction and the conception of a separate self or the self–world distinction. Theodore Roszak's analysis of the myth of objective consciousness shows the direction that this attack will take.

2. This attack entails a desire to expand or extend the self in either mystical or political directions. I am guessing that the idea of community is the decisive one, and that the individualistic mysticism of the post-modern era will prove to be the faddish portion of it—that drugs will never effectively depoliticalize the young.

3. The past and the future are equally remote, the present alone is real. Why this has happened, if it has, and who or what is to blame, is by no means clear, though there are many explanatory models: technology, the electronic media, the war in Vietnam. (I have a half-serious hunch that the real answer may be the guitar—at the very least we need a definitive study of the electric guitar today—is it a cause or a symptom?)

4. Many things are called into question, when all this has happened to the sense of time:
   —liberal education is called into question, with its assumption that the past is there to be ransacked and raided so that man can

be freed, liberated, made rational, and independent.

—the distinction between artist and subject matter, the ideas of mastery, technique, discipline.

—there are no goals, because goals live in a real future, and clearly beckon to you from that future, inviting you to enter into your prepared place, to which you may have been "called." Vocation, work, calling, and the Reformation itself, seem to fade.

—sin and guilt would appear to have far less a role to play in the post-modern age, for these ideas assume that the past continues to live in the present even when one does not experience the past. It was Baudelaire who wrote that true civilization (what I am calling the post-modern world) "does not lie in gas, nor in steam, nor in turn-tables; it lies in the reduction of the traces of original sin." The Woodstock Festival in August 1969 impressed many observers as a massive experiment in the abolition of sin and guilt. (Can they do it? Has that experience already proved illusory? Are we sure of their failure? Perhaps at least we should be attentive enough to say: if they do succeed, if there is really something new coming into being, how would the rest of us have to change?)

5. The experience of the failure of most of the moralizing institutions of the "modern" era, second stage—family, church, nation. Can the university be rescued from the general deterioration of these other great achievements of modern man? Can it in its present form, or in any form we can imagine, become a healing community? Walter Lippmann and Daniel

Bell have argued that the university will become the dominant institution of political
America; it can be argued that it will also be
the central ethical and religious institution of
America, for at least that early portion of the
post-modern era during which we will see just
what can be rescued from the modern, Jewish–Christian stage of our history. Either the
university will in fact become the central ethical–religious institution, or many new smaller
groupings will emerge. Or, more likely, both
at once, with pitched battles, and even small
wars between the university, reformed and
unreformed, and the post-university communities—communes, healing groups, and
the like. Harvard versus Woodstock.

This is what I see as a teacher today. It may well be that I
am wrong, that this is not everything, or that this isn't even
very important. I don't want to get too defensive about it,
but one analysis has been of considerable help in persuad-
ing me that the line I am taking is worth taking. I am
referring to Robert Jay Lifton's article "Protean Man" first
published in the Winter 1968 issue of *Partisan Review*.
Lifton, as we have already observed, sees a new kind of
psychological pattern emerging at many points in contemporary life. He sees the older ideas of self, and perhaps
even the very idea of personal identity, as no longer
adequate, since they presuppose too optimistically that
man's relations to his nurturing institutions and symbols
are still intact. He prefers to speak of a new kind of
self-process being at work. The protean style is characterized by "an interminable series of experiments and explorations" each of which may be abandoned in favor of a
new psychological quest. This includes all areas of human
experience, politics and sex, the holding of ideas and
ideals, the way life should be organized and lived.
If these "proteans" *are* our children and students, then

what follows for the teaching of religion as the post-modern era gathers steam, makes old fogies at thirty, creates mod, with-it intellectuals who should know better, renders our familiar world of Christian and Jew, integration, psychoanalysis and Scotch, Mozart, jazz, and dinner parties, obsolete?

So far, I have made two separate approaches into our problem: the first moved from some observations on what is happening at the university. The second, from what is happening to individuals, particularly the young, at the level of psychology and value.

It may be useful now to make a final approach to the same issues, beginning not with the university nor the student, but with the world. Here my decision not to consider the impact of technology on education proves to be a weakness. For both our experience and the writings of the futurologists suggest that the primary problem from which our ethical and religious concerns will emerge in the next several decades is likely to be the problem of technology. Western ethics, religious and otherwise, has often taken its character from the type of problem it considered normative and central: for the sixteenth-century Protestant, work and vocation were the dominant categories; in the late nineteenth century, the nature of capitalism served as a model; more recently, in our century, human sexuality was the model that determined the debates on the new morality and situation ethics. Technology will have its chance, I suspect, for a good part of the rest of this century, to set the main ethical and religious problems with which we have to deal.

It will be useful to recall the announcement of the arrival of the "technetronic age" made several years ago by Zbigniew Brzezinski. He believes that the next few decades will bring about a human mutation as decisive as that from animal to human experience. Computers will reason as well or better than man, and will begin to approach man's creative capacities. Human behavior will become more determined, more programed. We will be determining the sex of our children, and their intelligence and character as well. Mechanized surveillance over every citizen will be achieved, and a ruling class of the technological elite will emerge. The university will lose its old character as humanistically oriented repository of respected wisdom, critic and dissenter, and become a collection of experts serving the new sources of technological power. The university will become, in effect, the center of what we now call the military–industrial complex.

Brzezinski has a few qualms about the implications of all of this, but not many, and he is certain at any rate that so efficient will be our control of environment and information that no real reversal of this movement can be or should be attempted. He has little but contempt for what he calls the "sullen withdrawals" from this new world: Black revolutionaries, the New Left, student revolt. Change must be affirmed; we cannot return to a more simple life or age. This new age apparently demands an ethic of celebration and joy, while we wistfully hope that not too many Blacks or kids or poets are stepped on in the process.

What Brzezinski foresees will almost certainly come, and he has recruited many distinguished co-visionaries, B. F. Skinner, for example. It is virtually here. And the new mandarins may even be correct in their assumption that protest against this movement will ultimately become impossible—but it is not yet impossible. Protest exists, and in spite of the current calm and careerism and economic anxiety in the university, it is likely to grow. If fascism does finally make it in America, it is likely to come from the liberal technologists in government and the university, and resistance to it may gain converts from unexpected sources. Mailer's attempt, in the summer of 1969, to fashion a coalition of the hip right and the hip left was unsuccessful in New York City, but it may well have been prophetic politics.

Arthur Mendel, in responding to Brzezinski's vision, has described the direction an ethic of refusal might take (*New Republic*, January 11, 1969):

The Great Refusal may be either active or passive. It is
active when the rebels insist on action that has clearly
human, moral or creative value: they may be activists
in the more publicized civil rights movement, Peace
Corps, community action committees, or anti-war
demonstrations, or in the more private ways in which
they choose careers of social service or aesthetic crea-
tivity rather than those associated with traditional
success and the pursuit of power. There is a drop in
engineering school enrollment. Law firms raise beginning salaries sharply to counter the decline in appli-
cants. Scientists forgo the lush military and commercial
contracts. And should they willy-nilly find themselves
caught in the commercial-industrial world, the rebels
undermine its essential ethos, make it more mellow
and humane. The Great Refusal is passive when the
rebels just let go, step down from the treadmill of time
and achievement into a timeless present, the residence
of sensual and contemplative delight. Here, too, there
are the dramatic and the more covert expressions, both
the spectacular hippies and the more reticent but more
important millions who are finding the time that was
supposedly never there to enjoy the books, music,
sports, arts and crafts, travel, open companionships
and all the other joys that economic man could only
skimpily, grudgingly and guiltily allow himself.

Kahn and Wiener share Brzezinski's doubts that protest
is possible in the face of the inevitable technologizing of
our lives, for they consider the disappearance of work and
the work ethic as a calamity. They argue that work is the
primary contact with reality for human nature. And with
the disappearance of work they fear that any humanistic
element in the ethic of protest or refusal is likely to
degenerate into irrational behavior, self-indulgence,
"bumming around." And, one may add, with the attrac-
tions of the occult, astrology, and witchcraft lurking just
beyond.

Who can tell? What is going on in this debate about the
possibility of an ethic of refusal is a debate about the
nature of man. And debates about the nature of man have

a curious way of never being settled or finished, of never being "correct." The language of this emerging debate on man is being shaped, not by the theologians or the psychoanalysts, but by the social scientists. On the one hand, contemporary society is providing greater opportunity for the individual, with new mobility, new vistas, new ideas. On the other hand, men are more and more fragmented and alienated, more harassed, despondent, trapped.

Our religion and ethics will be occupied with this debate about man, and concerned to extend to all men experiences of liberation and health that are becoming available to some in the technological society. What we will be demanding is the same kind of power and control over our lives that our technological managers themselves enjoy and praise their machines for making possible for the few. When their mastery and control infringes or ignores someone else's liberation and choice, then the ethic of refusal will need to find some techniques for limiting or denying the managers their freedom and power. For we already have seen in the antiwar movement, and especially in the anarchistic moralism of people like Noam Chomsky and Paul Goodman, successful examples of how this refusal can be carried on. It already appears that these techniques of protest, developed largely in the antiwar movement, are being put to use on the problems of the environment.

Our religion and ethics will need to keep on center stage, in full illumination, what the technocrats are doing and saying. Several years ago, during the television coverage of the first moon landing, CBS assembled a good many technological apologists: house theologians, science fiction writers like Arthur C. Clarke, and we watched Walter Cronkite and Eric Sevareid join them in saying "Wow" to what was happening. But in another corner of the studio, Harry Reasoner was allowed to bring to the camera, for a moment or two, some gifted nay-sayers like Kurt Vonnegut, Gloria Steinem, and a nutty professor and radical student or two.

Celebration and refusal in face of the new technetronic age. This will be a dominant theme. What appears to be happening is that religion is being invited to play a real role, but a far more modest one than it has generally found itself playing. The Western theologies of the last 100 years have been seeking to escape from the realm of the personal and private, and to become everything, or at least to become related to and relevant to everything. Now, something different is being called for, something beyond what the liberal and modernizing and secular theologies provided. Religion is having to do with the spaces in our lives that the technocrats leave out or ignore. Religion is becoming related to our leisure, to our play. Religion, with its theologies, may not turn out to be everything, sovereign, queen, lord, but more like an expert in limits, a watchdog. Guarding the boundary between the public and the private realms, noting what properly belongs to each. This does not necessarily mean that the pietists are taking over, and that religion becomes merely private. Whitehead's definition did not say that, when he called religion what a man does with his solitariness. Pietism claims that religion is what a man does *in* his solitariness. What we do *with* our solitariness is to make sure that every man has it, that no man or class makes off with it, and that true communities and thus a real political existence remains possible and lively. For one of the things that man must do *with* his solitariness is to resist self-righteousness and irresponsible power, and to fashion communities in which all people, and not just the white male technocrats, may be liberated and healed.

Finally, I wish to append a few theological reflections on the religious situation that I am imagining for A.D. 2000. It might be noted that the phrase "theological reflections" is itself a reflection of the modern, rather than the post-modern, world, a phrase out of the world of Promethean man, or Oedipal man, or Orestean man, but not protean man. For "theology" must emerge from a distinct and living religious tradition that makes something like absolute or radical claims on a man of faith; and it is precisely this idea of a religious community with power to make absolute claims that is disappearing. There is as yet, on the horizon, no theology for the religion of post-modern man as we have sketched him, but there is no reason it cannot emerge. In the meantime, some theological reflection out of one of the older "modern" traditions may still be appropriate.

1. There will, of course, be what we call Protestantism, Catholicism, and Judaism—churches, synagogues, and temples of your choice. These institutions will die very slowly, even after their tax-exempt status is removed. Attempts will continue to be made to develop relevant post-modern versions of each of the major religious traditions. This will serve to deepen the splits within the traditions between the progressives and the traditionalists, and to increase the solidarities between the progressives across sectarian lines. In Protestantism, evangelicalism will grow and move more and more to the center, become dominant, and virtually take over the centers of interdenominational and denominational power. And, as racial integration continues to collapse in the mainline Protestant churches, the holiness and Pentecostal movement will advance.

2. Progressive Protestantism, developing a postmodern style, will continue to do theological reflection, and it will largely be related to the task of preserving the church, renewal, relevance. There will still be radical and secular theologies asking how one can be Christian in the post-modern world. The theology of the future will become firmly fixed as Protestantism's received theology, and Roman Catholicism may well come along, on its progressive side. This will provide a solid theological jus-

tification for the Protestant entrepreneurial class, for it is a theology that can go with change and technological innovation. Theologians of the future will continue to be summoned to microphones, and called by religion desks of magazines and newspapers, to help develop an ideology of praise for the unfolding developments of space, medical, and industrial technology.

3. The imaginative young will not be found among the ranks of those attempting to develop relevant or post-modern versions of the Western religious traditions. A theology of the future is perfectly designed to turn the genuine post-modern off, precisely because it is the future that he neither has nor cares about, and postponing God and grace to the future sounds to him like just another trick of the older generation: "just wait—for God—and you'll see that I'm right."

4. The new consciousness, already deeply religious, will prove to be a durable part of our experience and will continue to function as one center of a religious revolution in the West. This revolution will exist largely outside the traditional Western religious institutions, and they, in turn will be unable to co-opt it. This religion will become increasingly polytheistic; the gods will become metaphors; we will believe in none and use all.

Now any child of Moses or Calvin will know why he cannot greet polytheism with unambiguous applause: when everything is divinized, nothing can be shaped or altered. Jews and Christians are likely to be further persuaded that there may be something inherently pathological about the polytheistic psyche. But perhaps, as we retire to the gun room for the coming battle, we would do well to remember David Hume's cooling comments in *The Natural History of Religion.* Monotheism, he grants, has advantages. It makes rational understanding possible and thus permits the question of truth to be raised. And polytheism has some disadvantages. It must permit any practice or opinion and can thus become debased, or at least morally ambiguous. Without any principle of coherence, it has affinities with absurdity and inconsistency. But (unlike monotheism) it is naturally open and tolerant; it leads to courage rather than to self-abasement, doubt rather than to willful certainty.

In any case, polytheism, and the whole futuristic picture herein sketched, cannot but elicit in us reactions of bewilderment, horror, and excitement. We shall all (or, better, some of us) be changed, as the man said. That problem of the dictionary may become more complicated than we first imagined.

IX

Revolution

The perfectability of man is really all we have to
sustain us, however illusory it may prove to be.
—John Leonard, *The New York Times*, January 11,
1971

Melville understood the idea of the new; he understood that the discovery of the final New World
ended, rather than began, man's eternal dream of a
happy land where sorrow and pain would be no
more. He knew that the New World, because it was
the last, would necessarily be the place where men
would have to face themselves without the comfort of
that ancient faith that elsewhere life could be better.
America meant that there was no place left to go, no
more escapes, no more freedom growing in virgin
lands. The gift of new space was finished, and hence-
forth men would have to make instead of receive
their felicity. Melville knew that they would fail.
American comfort had been genuine so long as
Americans received it, so long as the land had been
fertile and unoccupied. With the end of land came
the beginning of true civilization, came men's need to
fashion ways to live together. Melville's own life
overlapped the lives of both John Adams and Frank-
lin Roosevelt. He had witnessed the growth of America from a primitive to an industrial order. He had
seen the passing of the land and the development of
civilization. With civilization in America came the
ultimate tragedy: the eternal passing of the Typee
valley from mankind's sober hope. America now took
her place among the nations as a land like any other.

> Americans now were merely men. The land had
> come of age, and age was time and tragedy and the
> end.
>
> —Loren Baritz, *City on a Hill*, pp. 330–331

Is the phrase "religious revolution" in any sense a useful
one to describe the patterns of change experienced today
by Western religious man, Christian, Jew, devout unbe-
liever? Surfeited readers of the "theology and revolution"
material over the last ten years may have become suspicious of some Christian uses of "revolution." It has
become a good thing, something to get with, to come to
terms with, develop a theology for. Something to co-opt, to
put it another way. Some use revolution as a synonym for
rapid social change; some wish to hold it to its Marxist
meaning; many question whether America is now in a
revolutionary situation; many distinguish several "revolutionary" strands lying about, more or less developed:
political, consciousness, educational. Daniel Berrigan
writes of an explosion of the biology of the spirit—
whatever that means—while Jean-François Revel an-
nounces in Paris a new American revolution in *Without
Marx or Jesus*, one attacking the normative character of the
whole of our traditional Christian civilization. Yes, the
word revolution may be allowed, so long as it can be
delivered from the bondages of rhetoric, journalism, or
cliché.

I find myself drawn to "revolution" in the sense that
Raymond Williams has used it:

> It seems to me that we are living through a long
> revolution, which our best descriptions only in part
> interpret. It is a genuine revolution, transforming men
> and institutions; continually extended and deepened
> by the actions of millions, continually and variously
> opposed by explicit reaction and by the pressure of

habitual forms and ideas. Yet it is a difficult revolution to define, and its uneven action is taking place over so long a period that it is almost impossible not to get lost in its exceptionally complicated process. . . .

In naming the great process of change the long revolution, I am trying to learn assent to it, an adequate assent of mind and spirit. I find increasingly that the values and meanings I need are all in this process of change. [Raymond Williams, *The Long Revolution*, Columbia University Press, 1961, pp. x, xiii.]

But even if "revolution" is acceptable, do we still need to defend a definition of the cultural crisis as a religious one? It hardly seems so. Today, in fact, those who have discovered the religious element in the revolutionary ferment are voices somewhat outside the traditional religious world. Yesterday, Christian theology tried to say that everything was theological, while secularists demurred. Today, theologians are afraid to say that anything is religious, so the nonreligious or extrareligious come along to remind us. Northrup Frye has made the point as well as anyone.

The earlier closed mythology of the Western world was a religion, and the emergence of an open mythology has brought about a cultural crisis which is at bottom a religious crisis. Traditionally, there are two elements in religion, considered as such apart from a definite faith. One is the primitive element of *religio*, the collection of duties, rituals, and observances which are binding on all members of a community. In this sense Marxism and the American way of life are religions. The other is the sense of a transcendence of the ordinary categories of human experience, a transcendence normally expressed by the words infinite and eternal. As a structure of belief, religion is greatly weakened; it has no secular power to back it up, and its mandates affect far fewer people, and those far less completely, than a century ago. What is significant is not so much the losing of faith as the losing of guilt feelings about

losing it. Religion tends increasingly to make its primary impact, not as a system of taught and learned
belief, but as an imaginative consistency and imaginative informing power. In other words, it makes its
essential appeal as myth or possible truth, and whatever belief it attracts follows from that. . . .

And perhaps, if we think of the reality of religion as
mythical rather than doctrinal, religion would turn out
to be what is really open about an open mythology: the
sense that there are no limits to what the human
imagination may conceive or be concerned with. [*The
Modern Century*, pp.118–119, 120, Oxford University
Press, Toronto.]

David Bazelon, without apparently checking with Frye,
has an interesting variant on the same theme. We are now
engaged, he writes, in a major religious crisis, which
means that

more and more deeper emotion is dissociated from
everyday life forms, emotion which finally demands
expression. With this meaning assigned, I am guessing
that there is more religion today without God than
there has been for some centuries with Him. ["Notes
on the New Youth," *Change*, May–June 1971, pp. 44,
45.]

Two other definitions of the religious revolution have
come from highly visible religious outsiders. In his Phi
Beta Kappa oration at Harvard in 1967, just before his
immersion into the world of power, Daniel P. Moynihan
put down the new youth as the first heretics of liberalism,
and finds parallels for them all over the world of Christian
and Jewish history. Today's young are like the primitive
Christians in second century Rome, outrageous, impudent, intolerant. They are the seventeenth-century Jewish mystical heretics, the Sabbatians, proclaiming the holiness of sin. They are Brethren of the Free Spirit. Today,

like the heretics of old, they want immediacy, Nirvana
now; they are unwilling to wait for the end, as a good Jew
or Christian should.

Paul Goodman, as we have already noted, used other
strands of religious history to describe the young revolutionaries. He spoke of our cultural crisis as a "new
Reformation" (Cf. *New Reformation: Notes of a Neolithic
Conservative*, especially chapter 4), and he made a fairly
systematic attempt to connect the Protestant Reformation
to the cultural revolution among the young. Yesterday,
tradition in the form of the Catholic church was attacked;
today, science and technology are attacked as the new
church. Then and now, the university was in the vanguard
of the movement. Goodman saw some other interesting
parallels: Luther's 1510 visit to Rome, with his attendant
disgust, is paralleled to current moral repudiations of
the establishment. Luther's protest against works-
righteousness is related to today's rejection of liberal or
moralistic tests of human achievement, such as alleviation
of suffering, maximizing justice or freedom through pru-
dential, political or legal channels. No apology is needed
for speaking of some kind of religious revolution as a part
of our contemporary experience in America.

The striking thing about this revolution is that it is going
on almost entirely outside the traditional institutions and
theologies of America. Its relation to the mainstream is
much like that of ancient Gnosticism. This leads us to
expect that the responses of the church and theology will
vary, in our time, as widely as did those of the ancient
church to the earlier heresy. We can expect outright
resistance, uncritical acceptance, and nearly everything in
between.

There is a pathos in the forthcoming encounter between
the Christian and the post-Christian religious revolutionaries. The theological and institutional self-confidence of
Christianity and Judaism has never been at a lower ebb.
Theologically, we are at a time of paradigm-change, to

adopt Thomas Kuhn's influential and suggestive language. It may be useful, for a moment, to remind ourselves of what Kuhn means by this. (I am referring, of
course, to his book, *The Structure of Scientific Revolutions*.) A
scientific revolution takes place, Kuhn argues, when
anomalies emerge in scientific work, when new investigation leads to new sets of commitments, and older traditions
are jettisoned. There is a move from one paradigm to
another. A paradigm is a theory that is better than its
competitors, but it need not explain all the relevant facts.
A new paradigm attracts most of the younger generation
of practitioners, but some will still cling to the old paradigm.

Theologically, we are not yet at a revolutionary point in
Kuhn's sense, because—while the old paradigm is being
deserted, a single new one has by no means emerged.
What we have is an external religious revolution moving
on some sort of course, collision or otherwise, toward the
Christian and Jewish (and old-secular) world.

Let me suggest, very unsystematically, what I mean by
the desertion of the old religious paradigm. I will list a
series of statements attached to the old paradigm, some of
which are being rejected by some or many of the religious
leaders in this country, and (perhaps to a lesser degree at
the moment) in the Western world in general.

> One's religious identity can be adequately af-
> firmed through the distinction between Catholic,
> Protestant and Jew.
> New Testament, Old Testament, church histo-
> ry, systematic theology, are disciplines with their
> own interior justifications and integrity.
> The church is the body of Christ, or the pilgrim
> people of God.
> The ecumenical movement is the great new
> fact of our time.
> Man is a sinner, in need of grace and redemp-
> tion. He is radically dependent, anxious, caught

in a trap of meaninglessness. He is, in fact, *homo religiosus*, restless until he rests in God.

The church can be renewed and restored by: a recovery of the Gospel, a recapturing of celebration and wonder, a new worldly spirituality.

The basic apologetic issue is the struggle between belief and unbelief.

If there is desertion from the old religious paradigm of the West, there is also what can be called a loosening of the paradigm. This, it appears, is a reformist venture, a struggle for survival by slightly redefining the old paradigm so that the revolutionary situation may be averted. In one sense, these loosened paradigms are offered as new paradigms. Among these are:

a plea for a Christian–Marxist dialogue
a theology of revolution, of hope, or play: God the revolutionary, God the Future, God the Dancer
an encounter between East and West
God and Jesus are Black
salvation through body-awareness
participation in the death of God
the de-masculinization of Christianity

Assent of the relevant community, Kuhn states, is the only standard for paradigm choice, but theologically no single new paradigm has anything like this assent and may never have it. So we are in crisis, without being ready for revolution as Kuhn defines it. Wandering between two paradigms, one might say. One dead, the other powerless to be born. A real religious revolution is outside us, and the question of a revolutionary renewal of the Christian and Jewish worlds remains tantalizingly unsettled and unclear. The following diagram may render the confusion somewhat more clear, or at least more visual.

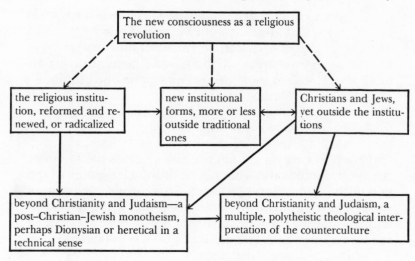

The experience of the death of God *is* not the religious revolution, but the experience has made it both possible and necessary. As Dustin Hoffman remarked on a talk show a while back: "Since God died, we have all had to find some way to make it by ourselves. Some are into the occult, some into Buddhism, some drugs; I find psychoanalysis works best for me."

Furthermore, if the problem of religious revolution must be separated from the death of God, it must also be distinguished from other movements today that are called revolutionary, and which are indeed so in the sense I am using the term: for example, the Black revolution, the Women's Movement, and the revolutionary movements in consciousness and politics.

It is not easy, at this early date, to evaluate the religious implications of the Black revolution in America. Malcolm X was a radical critic of both his own and of white Christianity and began to raise, at the end of his life, the problem of the color of God. The Christian

God, even in Black Protestantism, was white for James Baldwin as well. But in general it appears that Black consciousness, as applied to religion, has had a conservative impact. Jesus, church, God all remain; just recolor them Black.

The relation of theology to the Women's Movement is beginning to be explored. Mary Daly, in her book *Beyond God the Father* (Beacon), connects the death of God the Father to the rise of woman's consciousness, and there is work to be done on this interconnection. There is some evidence of a bond between the male chauvinist and Protestant man, some evidence that the idea of womanhood from which the movement seeks liberation is partly, perhaps even largely, shaped by sixteenth-century Protestant–capitalist man. The new middle-class European male of the sixteenth century created the woman he felt he needed: a nonsexual ambiance to relieve himself from the pressures of work, and a sexual ambiance to assure him of the integrity of his newly won powers to order and shape. He thus created the virgin–whore; today, the old enemy of the new woman remains Luther's Katie. It is likely, therefore, that the woman's revolution will be influential in shaping a critique of Protestant–capitalist man, as well as giving some clues on the problem of the desexualization (or demasculinization) of our language, theological and otherwise. The relation between the death of God and the end of dominant masculinity remains to be spelled out. William Blake may prove to be here, as at so many other points, our most useful (male) guide.

The historical connection between the political revolutions of the late eighteenth century and the experience of the death of God has long since been noted, and negative evidence for this connection can be amply collected from the anxiety of the current theologians of hope and revolution to redefine God himself as the prime revolutionary. If Jesus cannot be made into a zealot, perhaps God can be. Just now, however, the relation of Western religious thought to the political left remains unclear; in any case, it is a matter of ethics and church renewal, and it is not yet clear what deeper theological changes will need to be made in response to the practice and theory of political radicalism.

When observers like Goodman, Moynihan, and Frye speak of a religious revolution, they are referring mainly to what has been called the new consciousness. This is my primary focus. It is within this general frame that some real religious alternatives to the Christian and Jewish worlds are emerging.

POLYTHEISM

If we begin by looking at the problem of God, it might appear that the religious ferment I am trying to grasp can be clarified by reading it merely as a struggle for a new god. This is the argument presented by Harvey Wheeler in his article "The Phenomenon of God" (*The Center Magazine*, March–April 1971). Such a new god might turn out to be a better definition of the old one, or it might turn out to be an unrecognized "neo-god," to use Wheeler's phrase. If this model were acceptable, we could still be monotheists: either Christian or post-Christian, depending on what the new god looked like. But I do not believe that post-Christian monotheism is a wide enough model for purposes of interpretation or description. It may be a proper response to the religious revolution, a critical or counter-revolutionary response. But the revolution does not look like monotheism, Christian or post-Christian. What it looks like is polytheism.

When God dies he comes back as a metaphor, and he brings back with him all the other gods. The death of God has appeared to mean, in the twentieth century (as it meant the end of moral and political absolutisms in the nineteenth), the end of the monotheistic principle.

The God of the Jews and the Christians, as careful readers of the *Genesis* myth of creation have always noted, willed the de-divinization of everything except himself. Now that the principle of a de-divinization has been broken, everything can be partly or potentially re-divinized: man, space, matter (drugs), and all older and newer divinities. The principle is Gilbertian: "When everyone is somebodee, then no one's anybody!"

Richard Rubenstein has been studying the process of the re-divinization of the ancient pagan gods of the Mediterranean world. He has been confident that the Jew, after the death of God, could actually participate in this re-divinization. He has become less certain of late, and I am inclined to share his latter skepticism about the capacity of Judaism or Christianity fully to affirm any new polytheism. It seems clear that the death of God theology may be, after all, a kind of monotheistic faith. No more than one, it affirms, and preferably less. It is simply that man must do for himself what before he has asked God to do—in this case, to de-divinize or de-sacralize his world. In any case, the new religiosity can be read as the beginning of a major polytheistic revival. Students coming to the university used to define their religious situation by locating first their inherited tradition, and then asking the university to clarify that tradition for them, so they might better affirm or deny it. Today it appears that fewer and fewer accept a religious self-definition in terms of personal biographies. What they are asking of their teachers of religion is no longer that they serve as a sophisticated or upper-division Sunday school, but that they offer them a massive and total access to all of the gods of men: Eastern and Western, primitive and modern, heretical and orthodox, mad and sane. The gods are there, not to be believed in or trusted, but to be used to give shape to an increasingly complex and variegated experience of life. We will not *be* any one thing religiously, but use any or all of the isms that may be needed to get through the day.

Polytheism versus monotheism will be the basic religious problem for our immediate future. This means setting aside the dominant model of "belief versus unbelief" that we have been living with for perhaps 150 years of European and American history, and we are brought closer to more ancient periods: to the encounter between the prophet and the Canaanite fertility cults, and to the struggles between Christianity and late classicism and Gnosticism in the first four centuries of our era. Tomorrow, theologians of the West may be reading the great unbelievers less—Nietzsche, Freud, and the rest—and returning more and more to Elijah against the prophets of Baal, to Origen against Celsus, to Athanasius against the Arians. The death of God theologies will continue to be skeptical of any possible mergers with the new polytheism, as their Biblical and orthodox forebearers were skeptical about alliances with the old ones, and the problem of Christianity without God will merge into the problem of monotheism without God. The new theological debates will raise such questions as this: can any new polytheism give an adequate rendering of the lives we have to live today? Is polytheism a psychological possibility? Was not early Christianity's victory over classicism based on the fact that it faced, more thoroughly than classicism itself, the problems of anxiety and security? Isn't there a connection between polytheism and madness? Can an impotent and effete madness survive the technological wizards of the seventies and eighties? What do we need to survive?

INSTITUTIONS OF THE RELIGIOUS REVOLUTION

As Mao has written, if there is to be a revolution, there must be a revolutionary party. What is the party of the new revolution; what are its institutional possibilities? We don't know very much yet about the answers to these questions.

I am clearly drawing my material from what people have come to call the counterculture. And this culture has (had?) a very slender interest in institutions. We can guess that the substance of this revolution will not be located in the church, though churchmen and ministers, in discerning the sources of their frustrations and failures, are often resourceful analysts of the new situation. Is our revolution to be carried on, then, in the university? That would be an obvious answer to offer, but one cannot be so sure. The new religiousness is all life and little doctrine, and it appears that the professor of religion is not being asked to help. He is not being asked to be guru to the new movements (though we should note the role of the charismatic pentecostal minister in the Jesus movement): indeed, it is doubtful if this revolution really wants leaders or gurus at all. It is even doubtful if it wants theology or curricular changes or study in any sense. So, while the revolution will be active at and around the university, it will not be active in the classroom, so that the problem of the revolutionary party remains obscure and unsolved.

OTHER MARKS OF THE RELIGIOUS REVOLUTION

At the risk of taking the religious revolution more seriously than do the revolutionaries themselves; at the risk of imposing more form and permanence upon it than it wants or merits, I wish to continue describing some of its qualities. I am assuming, it should be clear, that what we call the revolution in consciousness (and which I am claiming should be read as a religious revolution) will be with us for some time. The revolutionaries, when they come around to the task of clarifying and understanding themselves; when they make the move from life to doctrine (as all revolutions must if they are to last—Luther knew that well), will find that they are in fact mounting a massive, radical, and systematic attack—not only on the

Jewish–Christian tradition—but on the whole religious–
intellectual tradition of the modern West. To justify this, I
wish to make three points.

Work. The revolution proposes an attack on the presupposition of the modern Western world that work is the
primary, indispensible way by which man is related to his
world. The world of sixteenth-century man—Protestant–
capitalist–masculine—is being denied. This attack is still
amorphous and unsystematic. It entails a defense of
passive modes of being in the world, of suffering, of
receiving, of what is called the feminine. It entails a
defense of play and celebration, for play is purposeless,
futureless, now; work entails purpose and goals and belief
that there will be a real future.

Christian theologies have of course been discovering
and rediscovering *Homo ludens* for many years, and it is
probable that they would not be doing it again today had
they not been in part instructed by the young revolutionaries. But theology does this to redress a balance; the
revolutionaries are experimenting with an all-out rejection
of work, of money, of jobs and professions alike.

The revolution in woman's consciousness provides an
interesting context to look at this attack on work and
masculinity. In its more conservative forms, the woman's
movement is a defense of work as possible for the woman,
an insistence that "we, too, should be allowed to practice
the professions and to receive equal reward for that
practice." In the more radical forms of the woman's
movement, there is a deep rejection of man himself and all
that he symbolizes—work, aggressiveness, action—and an
attempt to redefine woman's sexuality in such a way that
man and the orgasm he can offer are excluded. This
reminds us that a consistent repudiation of work entails a
massive psychological project of rejecting the father and
of recovering the pre–sexually-differentiated child latent
in everyone. Economics, politics, technology, and sexuality
are all involved in this attack on work. At its depth, this
attack is quite simply an attack on modern man, from
Erasmus to Freud, in all his varieties and forms.

Self. The religious revolution is also an attack on the idea of the self: the separate self, the ego and its trips, the self–world distinction, even self-consciousness and identity as necessary roads to maturity and humanization. This form of the revolution has been observed by both its adherents and reporters; none has clarified it so well as Robert Jay Lifton in "Protean Man." Lifton began to observe protean man among his patients, with weakened identities and lack of ego strength. He came later to see it outside the clinic and the hospital as a phenomenon of what might be called normal consciousness. (Sartre's discovery, recorded in his autobiography, that he was without a classical super-ego, is an important event in this story.)

We can distinguish two types of the attack on the self, a mystical and a political; but there is an inner affinity between the activist and the drug mystic for just this reason: both, though in different ways, are engaged in the repudiation of self. The activist radical would give the self to the group, to the brothers and sisters, to the comrades; the mystic, oriental, drug, or Jesus in form would give the self to the cosmos, to nature, to God. LSD is holy matter, an audiovisual aid guiding you to the second kind of loss of self; marijuana, done together, passed around, is a sacrament for the political form of self-loss.

Both the child and the madman are models for the enterprise in which the self is annulled, and so we should not be surprised to find defenses of both the child and the madman in writers like Norman Brown, Allen Ginsberg, and Ronald Laing, who are leaders in the war against the self.

Something of the pathos of this attack on the self can be discerned in this passage from Walker Percy's *The Movie-goer*:

> What is the malaise? you ask. The malaise is the pain of loss. The world is lost to you, and the world and the people in it, and there remains only you and the world and you are no more able to be in the world than Banquo's ghost.

When you undertake the project of the annihilation of the self, you not only lose the world, but you lose language as well. The mystics, in their usage, have always known this. For language is the very substance of the self's presentation of itself to the world. So we are not surprised to find that the selflessness of the new revolutionaries has begun to show up in their speech. Paul Goodman called attention to the "speech-embarrassment" of the young, who, feeling that they have no self, feel also

> that they have no world to assert, and therefore they pepper every sentence with "like" or "you know?" meaning that, though they are speaking, they do not mean to be saying precisely what they are saying, and the world is not theirs to say. [*The New York Review of Books*, May 20, 1971, p. 41.]

If no self, then no world and no language and "the world is not theirs to say." In such a linguistic world, you do not "believe in" something; you are not "committed" to a value or an ideology; you are "into" it. And what you are "into" you can be quickly "out of."

As with the rejection of work and the defense of play, Western theologies have their characteristic ways of responding to this rejection of the self. Rediscover your mystical roots; and there is already evidence that Jewish, Protestant, and Catholic theologies are beginning to do just that.

But difficulties lurk along the way should any of us try too eagerly to theologize, from our older religious traditions, the consciousness revolution I am describing. In the West, certainly in the Protestant tradition, the self is always both enemy and friend. It must be lost, for it is in sin; but, when it is given in humility and trust, it will be returned—redeemed and renewed, not obliterated and destroyed. To seek anxiously to withhold it from the other, or to seek too anxiously to give it to the other—both are equally suspect, and the Christian mystical tradition has usually lived most comfortably in the dialectic of Jesus's words in *Matthew* 10:39: "He who finds his life will lose it, and he who loses his life for my sake will find it." This is to say that the encounter between the older theo ogies and the new attack on the self will continue to be wary, fascinating, and perilous. It is my impression that the two worlds are ultimately irreconcilable; our conceptions of the real world differ radically; Western religions have always held onto a dialectical relationship between the self and its loss. In the new revolution, this dialectical balance is lost. Christian trips are always designed to make the return possible; highs must always come down. One suspects that the trips and the highs are valued, in the more recent tradition, for their own sake. The end of the political trip is often undifferentiated violence and death; at the end of the drug mysticism trip is the experience of being strung out and radically dependent. From neither of these revolutionary trips is a ready return or descent conceivable.

Time. Underlying the attack of the religious revolutionaries on work and on self is, I think, a more fundamental challenge. What they are really proposing is a new conception of time, a new model of how one senses the actuality of time itself. Let me try to say what I mean. Both secular man and religious man in the West have shared, for several centuries, a kind of consensus on the experience of time. Man stands in a real present, and he faces two ways from it. He is first encouraged, in his process of maturation and education, to look backward into his past—his biographical and national past and indeed the past of the whole humane tradition of which he is an heir—and to take from it. In psychoanalysis he is helped to discern the points at which the past has dealt him blows, and he is helped to undo that damage by recollection and introspection. Then, he is further encouraged to look ahead to a real future awaiting him, prepared to receive his life and his shaping. He relates to this real future by making plans, setting goals, postponing gratification, developing understanding and mastery in order to shape or alter that future most productively. Standing between memory and hope, both the journeys he undertakes are credible and possible. This is a rough and untechnical portrait of the modern time sense. I do not claim it is specifically biblical or Christian, but it has been shaped by the Jewish and Christian time schemes and most of us no longer find it a plausible model to exist in.

But the young religious revolutionaries, whether as a weakness or a strength, do not seem to live on our time line any more. The past is oppression, symbolized by lying or weak fathers, by lying or weak presidents and leaders. All of the past-words come to them clouded and suspect: history, tradition, authority. Past for them is not there to be learned from, or—in Brecht's words—to be raided from time to time, but to be fled from, escaped. The past is Watergate.

And the future is just as unreal. We don't really know why, and we don't know how indelible this sense of time-mistrust might prove to be. And we don't know the connection between rejection of the past and rejection of the future, whether one is a cause of the other, or whether both are caused by something else. When we ask "why this futurelessness?" we can not do much better than to mouth the cultural platitudes of the moment: the experience of the Vietnam war, the flooding of imagery in the new media, economic anxiety, and breakdown of the nurturing symbols and institutions that have ordinarily borne the past into the present and which—whether nation, family, or church—no longer appear to do it. All we really know is that they—our students and children—really feel a terrible futurelessness.

With the disappearance of the past goes the disappearance of guilt; and with the loss of the future goes the loss of goals, of vocation, of the whole modern sense of being called—whether by God or super-ego or vocational testing—into a real future. Without past or future, there is only the terrible present in which to disbelieve.

The rest of us still seem to believe in the prophetic idea

of time. Israel still can be called to repentence, for there is a real future in which she can choose to affirm or deny her identity. The revolutionaries are often apocalypticists, prophets in despair, and time future is beyond control, unreal, not to be counted upon. The last days are either already here, in which case there is only waiting; or the end will come upon us from beyond our control, and there is still only waiting. The most radical and the most recalcitrant form of the consciousness revolution we are calling religious may well be its adherence to the apocalyptic model. The "end" may be imagined, or not; when it is, it is imagined under a variety of models: nuclear holocaust and swift destruction; biological poisoning and slow death; political tyranny controlling, supervising, and incarcerating all resistance and rebellion. Powerless before the future, in any case. And all of my generation's success stories of how we have mastered and controlled our futures fall upon incredulous ears. We cannot disbelieve in our futures, for we are living well into them already. They cannot believe in theirs, for they do not expect it will come. Instead of goals and purposes: get with it, what's happening, discern the signs of the times.

This is in part pop McLuhanism (the adjective may be otiose), and it is, from my point of view, bad news. But I am sure it is there, and growing. The point is this: this combination of work-rejection, self-rejection, and apocalypticism describes a specific, very real, revolutionary situation in the religious consciousness of the West. We are not permitted, I think, to deny its presence and power, to label it faddish and ignore it with some mutterings about the dangers of relevance-mongering or of how silly it is to do one's work by discerning the *Zeitgeist.*

It is, as I have said, a movement going on largely outside of the structures and ideologies of Judaism and Christianity today, though both the theologies and the institutions of the religious world are already making some provisional attempts at interpretation and accommodation. It is part, though not all, of the data we have to master, if we are

serious about the theological vocation of the Jewish–
Christian tradition today. If we assume that neither we nor
they will go away, and if we assume that neither will
capitulate to the other, a number of problems remain. Is
there a possibility of a Christian or theological interpretation of this revolution? Can it be taken into the Christian
world, or affixed to the other revolutionary currents at
work? Is it heresy or schism? How are we to move? Are we
really like Elijah on Mount Carmel? Melville trying to find
his religious way? Tillich theologizing the postwar intellectual world?

I have tried to offer a brief description of the religious
substance of what Raymond Williams has called our long
revolution. Like Williams, I too am "trying to learn to
assent to it." But comprehension and assent are not
enough. We curmudgeons—Christians, Jews, theologians,
old consciousness types at least in (indelible?) part—must
learn to dissent as well. For our other religious revolution—the one we are seeking to constitute within our own
religious traditions—does not entail giving a simple assent
to this newer revolution. Even if the death of God has been
the midwife for the new gods, it was not their mother, and
thus it has no maternal obligation to love either the new
gods or the new consciousness demanded by them. These
gods may turn out to be idols, or demons. But, it should be
added, God does not automatically return at the moment
we perceive idols to be bad.

Let me state how a reasonable adversary relationship to
the religious revolution might be constituted. We will want
to reject the new polytheism, for reasons already suggested. There will be a future, and it may well be worse
than the present. But I do not take this as wholly desperate
news. We will have to give up the illusion that our future
will be just like the futures other ages have dreamed of: a
nice balance between work and leisure, for example. Ours
may well have shadows in it, and behind those shadows
may lurk: civil disobedience, exile, the continued presence
of absurd death, contemplation of violence, jail, loneliness,

mistrust of all language, even our own. But it may also include a few familiar presences from today: human love, holding fast to one's friends and the few things one knows.

Now, if the revolutionaries are right and the future is not to be, then we are all free to dance on the edge of the abyss, free from morality and love, from freedom and compassion. But if they are wrong and we are right, then we will both have to decide how to say "yes" or "no" to the future, and to our power to shape it. If we can come to say "yes" to the future, then we will be asked to do even harder things. To say "yes" to the past, for instance. For to say "yes" to the past is also to say "yes" to all the words for the past that have become synonymous with repression, ugliness and evil: fathers, tradition, authority, history, wisdom. Thus, for the anti-apocalypticists, the fundamental problem of our future may prove to be survival: physical, psychic, intellectual, spiritual, and theological survival.

Survival. Will it be possible, tomorrow, to live as an American without going mad, or leaving? Some, of course, are already beckoning us to madness. To choose survival is to reject the apocalypse. For if the last days are here, or are shortly to be here without our power to control, then there is no real time left to any of us. We have but to decide how to take care of the unreal time remaining, or as Lennon and McCartney said of Mother Mary's words of wisdom, to "let it be." And it is a tempting invitation, particularly if you have been disappointed or hurt by personal or political failure. Those who yesterday declared "never trust anyone over thirty" are today turning thirty, and saying, "I don't expect to be around after thirty." Consciousness III is no sooner defined than it falls into despair. The deaths of Joplin and Hendrix are added to the list of symbolic deaths defining our lives.

It is the function of the adversaries to point to the inauthentic ways out of the impasse. One would be to look for something holy to save you or cleanse you: some holy person, the ultimate guru, a new hero or messiah or redeemer, or an old one, set to new music. Or to seek out, by a mythic or actual journey, a new holy space: an altar, perhaps, restored or redecorated; or a bed or a needle, or an abandoned farmhouse or an unpolluted stream. But the adversaries are not persuaded by any of these. Even Richard Rubenstein has begun to notice oil slicks and submarine periscopes in the Mediterranean, abode of the old gods.

To choose survival to avoid madness is to go another way, and it is not to be without a modest kind of hope. Not because one is persuaded by Woodstock, nor because one disbelieves in Freud or in sin. But because the enemies can be located and defined (they will turn out to be both men and machines), and they can be outwitted, out-thought, out-performed. It is a task that will take us all together, young and old, Black and white, male and female. It will require both humor and intelligence.

The American tradition knows a little about the connection of theology, survival, and madness. For Captain Ahab, our most distinguished American madman, was mad because he was a believer. In God, in myths and metaphors and the symbolic consciousness. In whales that weren't really whales, but signs of something "deeper." Our modern Ahab, John Lennon, became mad because he was a believer. Today he is struggling for sanity and survival by attacking the myths that tried to do him in. "I don't believe in Beatles; I just believe in me." My life, he has stated in an interview, "is dedicated to living, just surviving is what it's about, really, from day to day."

There is something here for us all. Demystify yourself and your world, reduce all myths and symbols to metaphors. To clarify, I will follow Sam Keen's admirable advice and tell a story. As a birthday present in 1971 my son took me to the closed-circuit television version of the Ali–Frazier fight. I had a few days before watched Norman Mailer, on one of the talk shows, endow the fight with a full Maileresque load of symbolism. It was to be an encounter between grace and power, a struggle for the secret to America's future. I was sure, in some ways, that I was suppoed to be for grace and against power, but I was still confused about who I was supposed to be for. This mythic bewilderment lasted through the seventh or eighth round. I was not enjoying the fight at all: I was busy looking at myself and at America. Suddenly, I called a halt to my confusion by getting at its root; by excising, by an act of sheer will, the heavy symbol-system that was depriving me of a direct relation to the fight. I decided that the fight was not an American myth, but a chapter in the history of professional boxing, and from there on in I thoroughly enjoyed the fight. And then, of course, the right man did win. Ali was symbolic consciousness, and he lost. Frazier was just a fighter, an anti-symbol, and he had to win. Even that great confuser of our inner lives, Freud, admitted that a cigar could sometimes be just a good cigar. The same is true of jet planes and everything else. The death of God is everywhere.

Therefore, the radical theologian is not automatically enamored of every radical and revolutionary game going on in his yard. The new religious revolution I have been describing is abiding and important, and it is a genuine post-Jewish, post-Christian, post-historical, and post-modern alternative. Our task, I am claiming, is the same task that Gnosticism offered Christian theology, to discern the revolution's true shape, to give some assent or other, to crack open its shell, and to resist and repudiate where we must. This revolution gives us the wrong direction but the right paradigm for our work. Of all the paradigms or models for our work now clamoring for our assent— renewal of the church, the Christian–Marxist dialogue, the encounter between East and West, a theology of revolution or hope or play, the one closest to reality is the one which sets us all in a time of transition or overlap between the world of the Jewish–Christian tradition and the post-Christian future.

My point, up to now, has been not merely to describe a religious revolution, but to propose a direction for fresh theological research for a theologically dispirited and enervated generation of epigones. This might be called a project for a new theology of crisis or theology of revolution, were not those shibboleths already spoken for elsewhere. Let this remain a proposal for a direction without a name.

I have only a few indications of what we are looking for. It will not, I take it, be a Biblical or a church theology in any primary sense. It will, insofar as it is Christian, exact a fresh study of Jesus, of mysticism, and of the massive ethical and political problems surrounding the issues of technology and survival.

I am particularly interested in the historical tasks now opening up, tasks I am particularly ill-fitted to tackle. Have there been similar challenges in the past, and how have they been faced? If one rejects the orthodoxy–heresy model, does there remain any way of distinguishing fruitful from unfruitful responses to external challenges?

It would appear that the Reformation is not likely to be a primary source of guidance. The Reformation did not emerge from an external challenge, but from an internal dissolution. Old questions continued to be asked, but with new answers—answers that turned out to be older answers than the ones currently given.

The Reformation was both a return and a reduction; it was an archaizing return, if you take justification as its clue; it was a revolutionary return, if you take the doctrine of vocation as its center. It was, furthermore, a compromise formula, seeking the best of both the Biblical and the sixteenth-century worlds, and Luther achieved this, as Erik Erikson observes, by limiting "our knowledge of God to our individual experience of temptation and our identification in prayer with the passion of God's son" (*Young Man Luther*, p. 253).

The Renaissance, as a model for religious revolution, can be studied in the light of our contemporary problem. Will it prove to be more suggestive than the Reformation? In some ways, the Renaissance too is a response to an

interior need, not an external threat. The Italian humanists found themselves returning to a remoter past, when
medieval traditions and culture proved inadequate to the
task of shaping an explanation for the new urban experience in Italy. It was carried out, initially, not by philosophers, but by scholars of grammar and history. The
literature and art of Greek, and even more, Roman
antiquity, was the creation of an aristocratic, secular, and
nonfeudal culture that reflected an urban experience in
which the intellectuals of the new Italian cities could feel
themselves at home. These ancient historians and poets
were concerned about worldly, civil, moral, and artistic
matters that struck a responsive note in the mercantile and
professional men of northern Italy.

Of course, Renaissance humanism was a Christian movement, though more of an educational regime than a total
philosophy of life. Nearly all the Italian humanists were
Christian; they accepted the authority of the church, but
their attacks on theology, Papacy, or Vulgate were in the
interests of a more simple, more ethical Christianity. But,
if they did not sketch out a view of life contrary to
Christianity, they did open up the possibility of developing
a culture independent of Christian ideas. This was the
significant ambivalence of the Renaissance. Man in the
Renaissance was not on the edge of the world theater, in
the eleventh heaven; he was in the center, in spite of the
fact that, after Copernicus, he knew that he was not in
the cosmic center. His role at the center placed his body in
the center of things, as a human and disciplined tool. This
is why medieval asceticism had to be rejected. Self and
body at the center made it inevitable that Renaissance
humanism was, as Erikson has stated, "the ego revolution
par excellence" (*Young Man Luther*, p. 193).

Our problem today is thus both like and unlike that of
the Renaissance. They would wish, as do we, to be both
Christian and modern; they would affirm the body, as do
we; they would affirm the self, as we have seen our
revolutionaries do not. William Blake has, not surprising-

ly, called Bacon's writings "good advice for Satan's kingdom," saying that his philosophy ruined England. For
Blake, as perhaps for our revolutionaries today, the Renaissance, for all its perfunctory Christian piety, was a
glorification of man and nature, a second fall, a new pride
and hubris. The Renaissance humanists can and cannot
help us. Can we then turn to their spiritual heirs, to the
philosophes of the Enlightenment?

As we have noted, the problem of the Renaissance was
to find a compromise formula "that would enable men to
live comfortably with classical forms and Christian convictions, trust in man and trust in God. . . . (Peter Gay, *The
Enlightenment*, p. 270). The Enlightenment was also a
search for a compromise formula, but not between Christianity and classicism, but between modernity and classicism. If the real significance of the Renaissance was to
attack the allegorical interpretation of classicism that
Christianity had featured, the Enlightenment turned to
the classical world as a means of freeing man altogether
from his Christian heritage. Feeling himself come of age,
the Enlightenment *philosophe* turned to the past so that he
could turn even more fervently to the future. The *philosophe* was an urban, universal, and pan-European, and he
saw the world divided between enemies of the flesh and
myth-makers—on the one hand—and generous, open,
life-affirmers on the other, realists, destroyers of myth.

But, if we can speak of the secularization of life in the
eighteenth century, and if we must recall Voltaire's brutal
remark that "every sensible man, every honorable man,
must hold the Christian sect in horror," it is still the case
that the Enlightenment was a religious age, less Christian
but religious still. What we have is a subtle shift of
attention; religious institutions and religious explanations
are being displaced, in their Christian forms. The Deist's
God, withdrawn and irrelevant, made this new focus of
attention possible. Divinity must now be relocated in the
midst of human life, and this eighteenth century proposal
for a relocation of divinity led—through the next cen-

tury—to the twin project of finding God in nature (romanticism and the rise of landscape art) and in history (the scientific socialists and Marx). Both the Renaissance and the Enlightenment begin with a kind of euphoria, and end with a kind of lonely and courageous despair. Montaigne and Machiavelli are examples of the first, David Hume of the second.

It appears as if the Enlightenment will indeed repay careful scrutiny. It is concerned with many of our problems today: Christianity and religion; the old God and new gods being born; the possibility of living without myths, symbols, and dependence; how to choose your ancestors; how to look backward effectively in order to look forward; and how to become liberated from old bondages without falling into new ones.

If David Hume reminds us of how important it has been for some men to protect themselves from disorder by liberating themselves from Christianity, Christians should not be so full of self-hatred to forget that they themselves were born, historically, in precisely the same experience of liberation and freedom, freedom from the tyrannies of classical culture. It will be necessary, in our time, to rehearse and relearn what is perhaps the classical revolutionary situation in the Christian tradition—the victory over classicism.

It has become a truism for Christians to remind themselves how their tradition developed an adversary relationship to the classical tradition. Greek wisdom aimed at the perfection of human nature through cultivation of that rational principle that distinguished man from the animals, and it taught that man, focusing on the intellect and restraining the passions, might come through contemplation to share the very life of the gods themselves. Theologians came to define the classical error as lurking in the supposition that history could be understood in terms derived from the study of nature. Christianity argued quite differently, pointing to an historical revelation, conviction of sin, and a technique of redemption in history.

One has only to contrast the famous description of the magnanimous man in Book IV of Aristotle's *Ethics* with some of Paul's confessional outbursts, as in *Romans* 7 or *Philippians* 3, to see that Aristotle's ideal has become Paul's foe. Thomas à Kempis was later to put the difference aphoristically: *relicti mergimur et perimus; visitati vero erigimur et vivimus* ("left to ourselves, we sink and perish; visited, we arise and live"). A passage from Justin's *Apology* describes this tremendous sense of newness that Christianity brought in contrast to the folly of living in the *saeculum* alone.

> Before we became Christians we took pleasure in debauchery, now we rejoice in purity of life; we used to practise magic and sorcery, now we are dedicated to the good, unbegotten God; we used to value above all else money and possessions, now we bring together all that we have and share it with those who are in need. Formerly, we hated and killed one another and, because of a difference in nationality or custom, we refused to admit strangers within our gates. Now since the coming of Christ we all live in peace. We pray for our enemies and seek to win over those who hate us unjustly in order that, by living according to the noble precepts of Christ, they may partake with us in the same joyful hope of obtaining our reward from God, the Lord of all.
>
> [*Apology* 1.14. In our time, C. G. Jung has made the same point. Christianity, he writes, "was accepted as a means of escape from the brutality and unconsciousness of the ancient world. As soon as we discard it, the old brutality returns in force, as has been made overwhelmingly clear by contemporary events." *Psychological Reflections*, p. 344.]

The new Christian sense of living in what Erikson has called "the kind of clean and clear atmosphere which exists only after a catastrophic storm" (*Young Man Luther*, p. 178) was based on the simple fact that it offered man a release from his anxious strivings for perfection. It gave him a God who came to him, where he stood. Augustine remarked in Book VII of the *Confessions* that in his study of certain books of the Platonists he found some hints of the Christologies of John and Paul, but "that the word was made flesh, and dwelt among us, I read not there."

The primitive rule of faith declared that Christ was the only Son of God, the last God, the God to end all other gods, and thus the decisive rejection of both the divinization of man and of the emperor. Eternal life was promised on the basis of the flesh's redemption, not repudiation, while Nicaea and Chalcedon added the clarification that the fully divine Son genuinely assumed human flesh, assuring that the appearance of Jesus in history was no pagan theophany, but a real event overcoming the classical split between being and becoming, spirit and matter. The Christian overcoming of classicism reached its climax, perhaps, with Augustine's *City of God*, an assault on the philosophical foundations of *Romanitas*, historical cycles, and the body as a source of sin. It may indeed be suggested, Charles Norris Cochrane has written,

> that the function of fourth-century Christianity was to heal the wounds inflicted by man on himself in classical times and, by transcending while still doing justice to the elements of truth contained in philosophic paganism, to revive and give direction to the expiring spiritual ideals of classical antiquity. [*Christianity and Classical Culture*, p. 360.]

The point of these historical notes is a modest one. Those of us that continue to be serious both about our theological vocation and about discerning the signs of the times have some historical work cut out for us. Confronted by what we have been calling a post-Christian religious revolution, learning carefully what shall be our assent to and dissent from it, holding blithely, without anxiety, to the Christian possibility, we must re-enter much of our past for the new clues it may have for us. I would like to raise just one more historical signpost before I am finished.

I have been, over the past several years, considerably helped by a fairly careful re-study of the religious pilgrimage of Herman Melville. Everyone has his own Melville, and Melville scholars are a notoriously suspicious lot, tolerating interlopers very grumpily indeed. But an interloper I have been compelled to be, and I wish briefly to state what my Melville looks like and why I think that a theological return to him can be fruitful.

1. *The protest against Christianity.*

"I'll try a pagan friend," Ishmael remarks at the beginning of *Moby Dick*, "since Christian kindness has proved but a hollow courtesy." And Starbuck shortly emerges as an example of that hollow Christian kindness, a man made soft and pliable by Christianity, no match for the transcendental madness of his captain.

2. *The end of transcendentalism.*

Clarel, in one of his reveries, speaks of "False pantheism, false though fair" (I.5). Emerson had given classical expression to the transcendental mood:

> Standing on the bare ground—my head bathed by the blithe air and uplifted into infinite space—all mean egotism vanishes. I become a transparent eyeball; I am nothing; I see all; the currents of the Universal Being circulate through me; I am part or parcel of God. ["Nature," *Collected Works*, I.10.]

Ahab, with his belief that "all visible objects, man, are but as pasteboard masks" (*Moby Dick*, Modern Library edition, p. 162), is a character partly designed to work out the psychological implications of transcendental consciousness. In June 1851 in a letter to Hawthorne, Melville had delivered his most succinct death-blow to transcendentalism as a way to the divine.

This "all" feeling, though, there is some truth in. You
must often have felt it, lying on the grass on a warm
summer's day. Your legs seem to send out shoots into
the earth. Your hair feels like leaves upon your head.
This is the all feeling. But what plays the mischief with
the truth is that men will insist upon the universal
application of a temporary feeling or opinion.

After his early flirtation with primitivism, Melville here
gives expression to a new view of nature, not made for
man, a brute fact without transcendence.

3. *The dark teaching of the wicked book: the relationship of
the symbolic consciousness to madness.*

The dark teaching of *Moby Dick*, Leon Howard has
written, "is that a man invites destruction if he accepts the
transcendental theory of knowledge which makes physical
objects emblematic of some spiritual reality" (introduction,
pp. xii–xiii, to Modern Library edition). This connection
between Ahab's madness and his transcendental view of
nature is unmistakable in the novel. Ahab says that he is
madness maddened (p. 166), unable to endure without
being mad (p. 482); he is mad the way Pip was mad, who
"saw God's foot upon the treadle of the loom, and spoke
it" (p. 413.) Ahab was mad because he had fallen into what
Ishmael called "Plato's honey head, and sweetly perished
there" (p. 343.) "O Nature, and O soul of man!" Ahab
cried, "how far beyond all utterance are your linked
analogies; not the smallest atom stirs or lives on matter,
but has its duplicate in mind" (p. 311.) Melville's greatness,
I think, was to focus on this connection between what we
would call today the symbolic consciousness and madness.
Whales are merely whales. This Melvillean connection
permits us to see beyond the sometimes chic defenders of
madness today into the horrors of it, horrors expressed so
memorably by Sylvia Plath. Ahab was mad because he
could not disbelieve; only the death of God could have
made him a survivor, but perhaps the death of God would

have taken away his heroism as well. Loren Baritz has written: "If it were not for God, Ahab could worship Christ, and might, perhaps, when God was dead" (*City on a Hill*, p. 306).

4. *Clarel and the search for Jesus after the death of God.*

In *Typee*, Melville concluded that civilization was repression; after *Moby Dick* it appears that he has concluded that America itself is repression. Is this not the meaning of the haunting phrase from *Moby Dick*: "in landlessness alone resides highest truth" (p. 105). *Billy Budd* can then be read not as a defense of submission or acquiescence, but as the final condemnation of a civilization that could, with justice, make war on innocence.

Between *Moby Dick* (1851) and *Clarel* (1876) America had gone through a period of war, reconstruction, and economic exploitation, in which an unregulated capitalism used self-justifying language about a Christian democracy. During this period, Melville himself went through a period of exhaustion and depression. His romantic or transcendental view of the world collapsed around him. Against this background, Melville drew on his notes from an earlier journey to the Holy Land for his extended poem, *Clarel*. Is there not, the poem asks, still one sacred space remaining, Palestine? Is there not some Jesus, or some love, amid the ruins of gods and creeds, primitivism, and transcendentalism? The answer to this final form of his religious question is a not quite firm "no." In the poem, again and again, it is asserted that the Christian God, like the classical gods earlier, has disappeared. Perhaps He may return. Rolfe (the Melville figure in the poem) appears to hope so:

> Yea, long as children feel affright
> In darkness, men shall fear a God;
> And long as daisies yield delight
> Shall see His footprints in the sod.
> [I.31.]

Yet it appears that Rolfe's deeper convictions lead him away from even such a forlorn hope.

"Whither hast fled, thou deity
So genial? In thy last and best
Best avatar—so ripe in form—
Pure as the sleet—as roses warm—
Our earth's unmerited fair guest—
A god with peasants went abreast:
Man clasped a deity's offered hand;
And woman, ministrant, was then
How true, even in a Magdalen.
Him following through the wilding flowers
By lake and hill, or glad detained
In Cana—ever out of doors—
Ere yet the disenchantment gained
What dreams they knew, that primal band
Of gipsy Christians! But it died;
Back rolled the world's effacing tide:
The 'world'—by Him denounced, defined—
Him first—set off and countersigned,
Once and for all, as opposite
To honest children of the light.
But worse came—creeds, wars, stakes. Oh, men
Made earth inhuman; yes, a den
Worse for Christ's coming, since his love
(Perverted) did but venom prove.
In part that's passed. But what remains
After fierce seethings? golden grains?
Nay, dubious dregs: be frank, and own.
Opinion eats; all crumbles down:
Where stretched an isthmus, rolls a strait:
Cut off, cut off! Canst feel elate
While all the depths of Being moan,
Though luminous on every hand,
The breadths of shallow knowledge more expand?
Much as a light-ship keeper pines
Mid shoals immense, where dreary shines
His lamp, we toss beneath the ray
Of Science' beacon. This to trim

Is now man's barren office.—Nay,"
Starting abrupt, "this earnest way
I hate. Let doubt alone; best skim,
Not dive."
                    [II.21.]

But if God is gone, not to return, surely Christ may be
found in the land of his birth. Clarel, the poem's protago-
nist, wonders:

Christ lived a Jew; and in Judaea
May linger any breath of him?
If nay, yet surely it is here
One best may learn if all be dim.
                    [I.7.]

And again,

. . . But of the reign
Of Christ did no memento live
Save soil and ruin?
                    [I.10.]

In one of the most striking theological passages from
Melville's entire work, Celio meditates on the Jesus that is
to be found in the Holy Land. Here we see not merely the
conventional gulf between the unknown God and the real
Jesus, but we also see that Jesus himself has become a
menace and a torturer to seeking man.

No raptures which with saints prevail,
Nor trouble of compunction born
He felt, as there he seemed to scan
Aloft in spectral guise, the pale
Still face, the purple robe, and thorn;
And inly cried—*Behold the Man!*
Yon Man it is this burden lays:
Even He who in the pastoral hours,
Abroad in fields, and cheered by flowers,

Announced a heaven's unclouded days;
And, ah, with such persuasive lips—
Those lips now sealed while doom delays—
Won men to look for solace there;
But, crying out in death's eclipse,
When rainbow none His eyes might see,
Enlarged the margin for despair—
My God, My God, forsakest Me?
   Upbraider! we upbraid again;
Thee we upbraid; our pangs constrain
Pathos itself to cruelty.
Ere yet Thy day no pledge was given
Of homes and mansions in the heaven—
Paternal homes reserved for us;
Heart hoped it not, but lived content—
Content with life's own discontent,
Nor deemed that fate ere swerved for us:
The natural law men let prevail;
Then reason disallowed the state
Of instinct's variance with fate.
But Thou—ah, see, in rack how pale
Who did the world with throes convulse;
Behold Him—yea—behold the Man
Who warranted if not began
The dream that drags out its repulse. . . .

   'Tis eighteen cycles now—
Enigma and evasion grow;
And shall we never find Thee out?
What isolation lones Thy state
That all we else know cannot mate
With what Thou teachest? Nearing Thee
All footing fails us; history
Shows there a gulf where bridge is none!
In lapse of unrecorded time,
Just after the apostles' prime,
What chance or craft might break it down?
Served this a purpose? By what art
Of conjuration might the heart
Of heavenly love, so sweet, so good,
Corrupt into the creeds malign,

Begetting strife's pernicious brood,
Which claimed for patron Thee divine?
  Anew, anew,
For this Thou bleedest, Anguished Face;
Yea, Thou through ages to accrue,
Shalt the Medusa shield replace:
In beauty and in terror too
Shalt paralyse the nobler race—
Smite or suspend, perplex, deter—
Tortured, shalt prove a torturer,
Whatever ribald Future be,
Thee shall these heed, amaze their hearts with Thee—
Thy white, Thy red, Thy fairness and Thy tragedy.
                    [I., pp. 52–54.]

Melville wonders, as Christ continues to elude him in *Clarel,* if there cannot be saved something of the love of Jesus, separated from what he calls the "lore" or the doctrine.

Thy love so locked is with thy lore,
They may not rend them and go free:
The head rejects; so much the more
The heart embraces—what? the love?
If true what priests avouch of thee,
The shark thou mad'st, yet claim'st the dove.
                    [I.13.]

It appears that human love alone is left, and that this will somehow overcome Christ.

And youth and nature's fond accord
Wins Eden back, that tales abstruse
Of Christ, the Crucified, Pain's Lord,
Seem foreign—forged—incongruous.
                    [I.28.]

But the girl Clarel came to love died, and so, after all, there may be neither sacred space nor lore nor love left.

But in her Protestant repose
Snores faith toward her mortal close?
[III.5.]

One need not draw the obvious parallels between our contemporary religious revolution and transcendentalism, between Consciousness III and Emerson's proposal to become a transparent eyeball, to suggest the possibility of a contemporary rehearsal of the Melvillean journey. He has been most of the places we have been and, like most of us, was happy neither in his belief nor unbelief. If our pressing problem in this decade is survival, perhaps we should take the survivor, Ishmael, as our modest model, eschewing both the splendid Ahab on his mythic journey and the admirable American innocent, Billy Budd. Can Ishmael become a model for the Christian theological enterprise? Survival may be asking too little of our times; if it is, then Ishmael will appear too tame, too liberal. But it may be a valuable beginning for those still committed to theological work after the death of God and in the presence of the religious revolution.

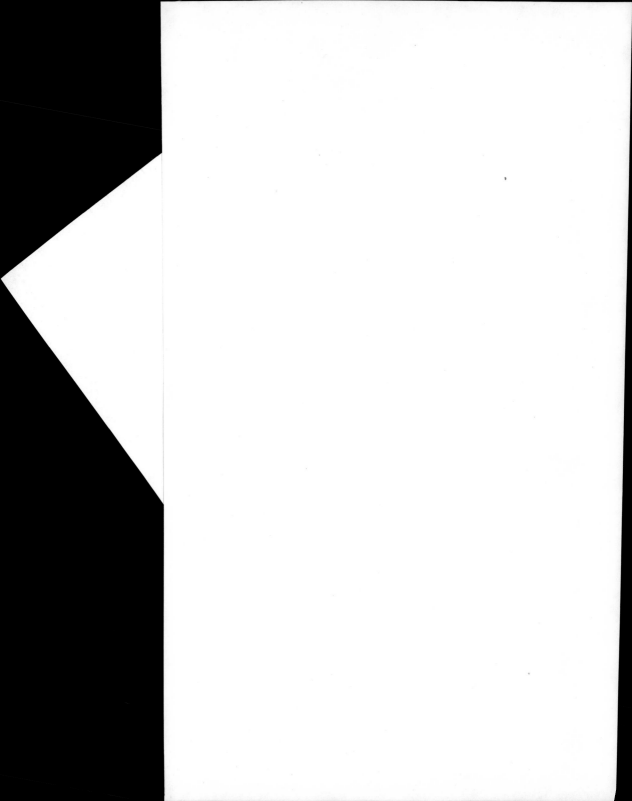

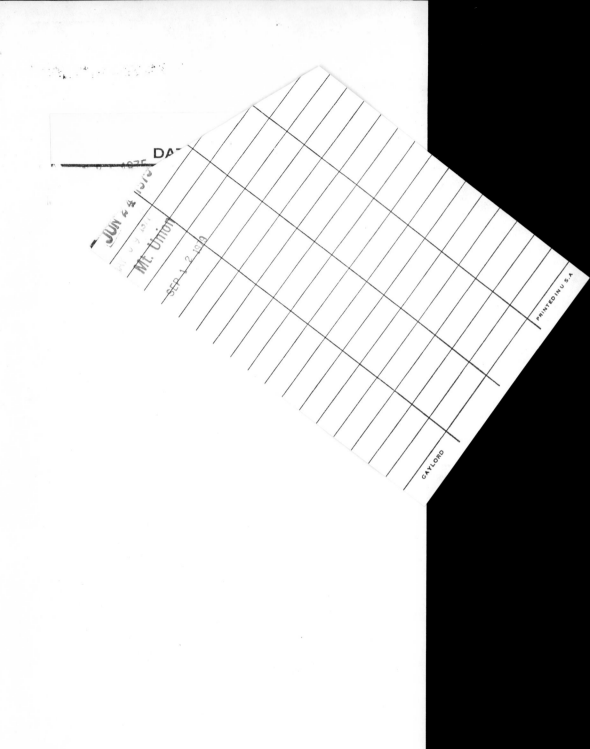